In The Dread of Night

Ralph D. Nybakken

Visit www.booksurge.com to order additional copies.

CHAPTER ONE

The throaty rumble of the engine attested to its power. Burton Alexander Helmsley sat smugly in his recently renovated '57 Chevy convertible, painted a canary yellow. It was cold in the dark early morning hours, so Burt had put the top up and locked it into place.

He pulled away from the curb. He received a little extra squeal from the tires as he popped the clutch between gears. Finally he settled down for the long haul in his dream car, his fantasies partially realized.

His shoulder length, blond ringlets framed his youthfully handsome face. Pleased with himself, he smiled. A thin blond mustache followed his upper lip. He was incredibly satisfied with the way things had worked out. A few months ago in September, he had been working in the automotive garage of a large department store in Chicago, installing tires and batteries. Now he had all the money he would ever need.

He had recognized the opportunity the first day on the job...

*　　*　　*

"Burton Alexander Helmsley?" the foreman stared at the hiring notice. After a slight pause, he looked up and continued. "I'll call you Burt. Okay?"

"Yes, sir," Burt answered politely for effect, but his facial expression indicated otherwise.

This ol' man's got to be fifty if he's a day, he thought. *I can tell I could be in big trouble, if I don't watch out.*

"Okay, Burt," said Mr. Bender. His thin body looked fragile, but there was strength reflected in his craggy face, topped by thick, gray hair. "I'll have you start in tires. Come on, I'll introduce you to the guy who'll teach you the ropes."

Burt followed Bender into the shop area. The noise was deafening; air hoses hissing, hammers clanking, tire irons banging, air jacks grinding and men shouting above the pandemonium.

"Mitch," Bender hollered to a youth in his early twenties. He had thick black hair pulled into a pony tail. His round cherubic face turned into a "happy face." His large stocky frame stretched his overalls to the limit, especially around the midsection. "This is Burt. I want you to show him what to do. Okay?"

"Sure thing, Mr. Bender."

As Bender left, Mitch stuck out a grimy hand. "Welcome, Burt," he shouted over the noise.

Burt started to shake hands until he saw the dirt, then pulled his hand back.

Mitch extended it a little further and laughed. "Yours'll be just as dirty in a few minutes!"

With a slight smile, Burt shook hands.

"You ever do this type of work before?" Mitch asked.

"No, but I've changed flat tires."

"This is what we do." Mitch easily picked up the wheel and placed it on the pneumatic tire changer. Grabbing a round, cone shaped tool, Mitch slammed it over the center stem and spun it around. It quickly settled into the center of the wheel. "This is the way we secure the wheel on the changer," he continued as he tightened the cone.

Then he grabbed a long iron tool that had a cup attached to one end, which he fit over the center stem with the leverage handle sticking in the air. In the middle of the handle was a hinged arm with a crescent end that he placed just outside the rim of the wheel. "Now," Mitch grunted as he pulled down on the leverage handle, "this is how we break the bead on the tire, to separate it from the rim.

"Next," he said, as he removed the tool and replaced it with what looked like a tire iron, "we do this." He put one end into a slot at the top of the center stem, the other between the tire and rim, and stomped on a peddle underneath the changer that slowly turned, removing the tire from the rim.

"It's as easy as that." He turned and looked at Burt. "And it's basically the same to put the tire on, except in reverse. C'mon. I'll get you some coveralls."

After a few tries under the supervision of Mitch, Burt felt like an old hand at it. Out of the corner of his eye Burt could see Bender checking on him. He knew if he could impress him enough that first day the man would probably not look over his shoulder as much in the future. He worked hard all morning, until Mitch tapped him on the shoulder.

"Lunch time. Or are you going to work through it?"

"Naw. I just want to make sure I get the old guy off my back, man. Old eagle eye's been watching."

"He's okay. I never have a problem with him. I do my work, and he leaves me alone. C'mon, let's eat."

The main entrance of the department store sat on a three-corner crossing. Behind the big store was the automotive sales and installation building. A long sidewalk from the rear exit of the store separated the automotive work area from the receiving and loading dock with a three-foot high cement block wall.

After eating fast food across the street, Mitch and Burt returned to the rear of the garage area and sat on one of the walls, sipping their milk shakes. Customer cars in for tires, batteries, oil changes or tune ups were backed up against that wall, waiting for service.

During lunch Mitch and Burt talked a little about their job, but mostly about girls. Neither had a steady girlfriend.

"I love 'em all," Burt said with a chuckle.

"Me, too. I was out with this gal the other night. She was a real looker. All the guys that saw us from the neighborhood were jealous. She had the longest..."

"What 's that armored truck doing here?" Burt interrupted, pointing.

The truck had gone down the ramp into the loading area, ten feet below the sidewalk behind them.

"They're gonna make their weekly pickup. They always come on Mondays and walk right past us on this very sidewalk. This joint brings in a lot of dough in a week's time. I've heard it's in the millions during the Christmas rush."

"In the millions?"

"Yep."

"I sure could use some of those millions."

"Me, too!" Mitch laughed.

Burt watched as two guards pulled out a large canvas cart on wheels. The cart was three feet by four and three feet deep. They wheeled the cart up the ramp, onto the sidewalk, past Burt and Mitch, and into the store.

"That's it?" Burt mumbled, his eyes still fixed on the door they had entered.

"Yeah. In a little while they come out with it loaded with dough and leave the same way." Mitch looked at his watch and stood up. "We better get back."

Burt slowly followed. "In the millions during the Christmas rush?"

"That's what I said."

Burt smiled, "Maybe we could give each other a nice little Christmas present."

"Yeah, sure." Mitch laughed again as they returned to work.

*   *   *

Back at work, Burt's mind kept thinking about the money. Before the day was over he had a plan, simple, but well thought out.

Burt made sure that he and Mitch sat on that wall every Monday, eating their lunch. They laughed and talked normally, but his mind raced as the plan came into focus.

It's like we're invisible, he thought. *With these work clothes on, we just blend in. They don't pay any attention to us. And they follow the same pattern every week. I like it. It could be incredibly easy.*

The only worry or question I have is: Will Mitch go along with me? What do I do if he won't cooperate?

The answer came to Burt a few days later, shortly after closing time. He changed into his street clothes and went back inside the shop to get a drink of water. The lights were off, except for a dim night-light. The water fountain faced the auto parts retail store that was dimly lit, and inside

Burt saw Mitch looking around furtively. Evidently feeling confident that no one was looking, Mitch picked up a car radio from a shelf and slipped it into his coveralls that were rolled up under his arm.

Stepping behind a rack of tires, Burt kept watching as Mitch came out of the store and relocked the door with his lock pick.

"Hi, Mitch," Burt said with a slight grin.

Mitch jumped back in surprise, protectively grasping his coveralls, staring at the silhouetted figure until he finally recognized Burt. "Don't ever do that to me again!" he almost shouted. "What're you doing here?"

"I just came back to get a drink of water and saw you, but I wish I'd known ahead of time what you were going to do, because I would've asked you to get me one, too."

"You saw?"

"Yeah, but don't worry. I'm not gonna tell anyone. I'm not a snitch. In fact, I almost got busted myself a couple nights ago. I was in the electronics store over on the corner, and I spotted a packet of CD's I wanted. I slipped them inside my jacket, and as I turned around, I spotted this guy in a mirror watching me. I walked around to the next aisle and dropped the disks into another bin while I played like I was looking at another item. Then I walked out.

"The guy in the mirror and a store manager followed me out. They did the usual frisk, up against the wall and all that, then the manager says, 'What did you do with it?'

"'What're you talking about?' I asked him.

"They just told me to get lost." Burt laughed.

Mitch laughed, too. "We'd better get outta here."

As they walked out, Burt said, "Did you ever get busted, Mitch?"

"Yeah, twice. Let's go across the street and get a beer and I'll tell you all about it."

"Okay. I've got a little time. Gotta date later, though."

Mitch waited until they were seated and had ordered a pitcher of beer. "It happened to me twice," he began. "The first time, I was just a kid. About twelve, I guess. My buddy, Ron, and I were in a Buck or Two store. He was on one side of the double counter, and I was on the other. In the middle is where the clerks worked, but there was no one in the middle slot between us.

"I held up a nice new yo-yo, looked around, and slipped it into my pocket. What I didn't know was that a clerk who had been bending down, working in the slot of the double counter behind me had just stood up. She saw me put the yo-yo in my pocket. Like a dummy, I hold up another yo-yo and motioned to Ron like, do you want one, too? Then I pocket that one, too.

"As Ron comes around to my side of the counter, the clerk calls out, 'Mr. Bracket, would you come here, please?'

"In a moment, she's out from behind her counter, holding my arm and saying to Ron, 'You come here, too, young man.'"

Mitch was interrupted by the buxom barmaid with straw-colored hair. Her bright red lips were pulled back in a smile over crooked teeth. "Here you are, boys." She set the pitcher and two mugs down and left.

"Anyway," Mitch continued, "the manager comes up and the clerk tells him what happened. So he says to us, 'Two yo-yos at five dollars each, means you boys will have to work two hours to pay for them, or else I'll have to call the police and your parents.'

"I didn't care if he called the cops, but if he called my dad, I'd be dead. He didn't spank; he used his fists on me."

"That's rough."

"Yeah, on me. The funny thing was that we did the work, but we never got the yoyos."

"Why? You worked for them."

"We were just glad to get out of there. I never even thought about them again until now."

Mitch sipped his beer and continued. "The second time I got busted was when I was just sixteen, but I looked a lot older than that. I started shaving when I was fifteen."

"Really? I didn't start until I was twenty," Burt said in amazement.

"You're just a slow starter." Mitch laughed. "Anyway, I used to live in Janesville, Wisconsin, a little town northwest of Chicago, right over the state line.

"One Friday night on a Memorial Day weekend, I was on my way home from a movie. I spotted a friend of mine by the name of Wes Collins. He was about to go into the Big Pitcher, a dumpy bar, and I hollered at him. We talked for a few minutes, and he invited me to go in for a few beers. I went inside, and he introduced me to his friends. The gal was kind of a spindly thing. Not much meat on her. Had stringy, colorless hair. Two of the boys, I found out later, were only sixteen. Still in high school, too, although I didn't recognize them. Maybe they went to another school. And the other two had just graduated from high school. None of them were old enough to be drinking, but all of them were drunk. Those sleazy bar owners would sell to anyone. Gotta make a buck.

"Anyway we slopped it up for awhile and, in fact, I was already feeling pretty mellow when one of the other guys says, 'Hey, Wes, we're going over to Emerald Grove, to a little bar that has shuffleboard. And we feel like shuffling. You wanna come along? And bring your friend, if you want to.'

"'Sounds good,' Wes said. Then to me he said, 'Come along, Mitch. Have a little fun.'

"And that's where I made my second mistake. I said, 'Yes.' The first mistake was when I went in to have a couple of beers that turned into too many beers.

"The seven of us piled into an old clunker. Three guys in front and three guys in the back with this little broad sitting on two laps; the guy in the middle, who I thought was her boyfriend, and her legs stretched across me. Her head was on his shoulder, but she was looking at me. I swear she had a thing for me, not that idiot whose lap she was sitting on.

"We were really jammed in the back. Fortunately, it wasn't too far to where we were going. Only five or six miles. On the way, one of the guys in the front turned around and said to the guy in the middle, 'You're gonna share her with the rest of us, aren't you?'

"Sure," he answered. 'One for all, and all for one.' Then he looked right at her and added, 'Isn't that right, Sweetheart?'

"Most of the others snickered."

"When I looked at the girl, I could see the fear in her eyes. She looked at me like she wanted my help. But there was nothing I could do.

"On the outskirts of Emerald Grove we pulled off the highway in front of the 'Three Star Bar,' the effects of those beers I guzzled really hit me.

"When we piled out of the car, the guy who sat next to me in the middle, I never did find out his name, said, 'I really need a drink,' and walked on ahead of the girl and me.

"One of the others hollered, 'Let's find us a blanket. We're going to need it. Look around.'

"That spindly little gal pulled Wes to one side and asked him, 'Would you help me get out of here?'

"I saw him nod his head, and then I spotted a blanket in the back seat of a parked car. The front door was locked. The one in the back was locked, too, but on the other side the back door was unlocked. When I pulled the blanket out of the car, I heard someone yell, 'Hey, What're you doing? That's my car.'

"I turned in time to see a deputy sheriff run up to me, and I panicked. He had his hand on his gun, so I slugged him defensively, at least that's what I thought. But I only hit him once, and he went down hard, hitting his head on the bumper of his car. I grabbed his gun to make sure he didn't get up and use it. What I didn't know was that he had a fractured skull and wouldn't be getting up for quite awhile.

"When I was arrested the next day, I was charged with assault, assault with intent to commit murder, robbery for taking his gun, resisting arrest, theft for the blanket and unlawful flight."

"Wow. That's heavy!" Burt exclaimed as he raised his hand to order another pitcher of beer. When the bar maid nodded, Burt said, "Go On."

"Well, we ran out, jumped in the car and split. All of us, especially me, were shaking in our boots. I wound up spending only two years at a youth camp for bad boys, because the deputy sheriff didn't die, and also it was my first offense. But since

I was underage, that record has been removed. I have no record now."

"That's really interesting. But listen, I'm gonna have to hurry, or I'll be late for my date. Maybe we could finish this conversation during lunch tomorrow, and then I'll tell you about my escapades." Burt stood up. "I'll see you tomorrow, Mitch."

As Burt was leaving, he thought, *I think I've found my man.*

*　　*　　*

Burt did not mention his idea to Mitch until the middle of November. They were sitting on the wall again.

"You're out o' your mind, Burt. Those guys have guns."

"So what? We'll have guns, too. Look, we'll be sitting here just like we are right now. They never pay us any attention, 'cause we work here. The Monday before Christmas, three weeks from now, we do it just as they pass us with the loaded cart. We pull our guns and tell them to drop theirs over the wall into the loading zone. Then we open the trunk of a customer's car that is backed up against this wall." Burt patted the wall. "We'll tell the guards to throw the loot in. We jump in and drive off. It's simple."

"Yeah? And where do we go? The cops'll be all over us in no time. I don't want to spend most of my life in the joint."

"Don't worry. I've got it all figured out. I've already rented a furnished house two blocks from here. Three, four minutes after we leave here, we'll have the getaway car parked in the attached garage. No one will know where we are. The owners live out of town. I rented it by phone, under an assumed name. I even bought my '57 Chevy fixer upper under my new name, Anthony William Garber. I have all the papers to go with the new name, like driver's license, Social Security number, credit cards and so on. And you know, I even look a little like this guy. I'm sure I can fix myself up enough so when I get a new driver's license in our new state, I won't have any trouble."

"Where did you get the papers? Are they phony?"

"Naw. They're the real thing. I got 'em from my aunt's new husband. I think he's connected. Gonna cost twenty G's."

"Twenty thousand bucks?" he asked. "You gotta be kidding!"

"Yeah, but we'll have plenty of dough," Burt bragged with a grin. "Anyway, this guy died. I don't know how, and I don't want to know. You don't ask questions. But his body disappeared, and I'll buy his identity. I'll keep his checking account and so on. If anyone looks into my background, there won't be any problem. Of course I'll never go near his hometown where people could identify him, but I do understand that he was somewhat of a loner."

"You're really serious about this."

"You bet. This is probably the only chance I'll ever get to be rich, and I'm not going to miss it, even if I have to do it myself. Now, are you in or out?"

"I don't know. I kind of like the idea, but I don't know if I could do it. It's not the robbery part, but getting caught afterwards. You seem to have everything planned and worked out. You even have a new name and everything."

"Don't worry. You'll have a new identity, too. And we'll be partners."

"But I think we'd have to split up, 'cause the cops'll be looking for two guys.

"They will. But only for a few months. Then we'll leave here separately and meet in another town far from here."

Burt's face lit up with an after thought. "In fact," he continued, "We'll meet supposedly for the first time in that town. We'll both do business with a certain person. Later, when he and I are having lunch in a designated restaurant, you'll come by to say hello to him, and he'll introduce us. From that time on, if anyone asks us how we met, we'll just say he introduced us. And after that, we'll become friends in front of everyone and form a partnership in some kind of business."

"You just got that idea, didn't you Burt?" Mitch cried out in surprise.

"Yeah. It just hit me."

Ralph D. Nybakken

"I think if we were partners, I could do it. But I'll need to be with you."

"We get along real well, Mitch."

"Yeah, we do."

"Then you'll do it?"

"Well...." Mitch hesitated, then finally agreed. "Yeah. Okay. I'll do it," he said with a big grin. "As long as I'm with you."

"Great!" Burt exclaimed. Then noticing the Brink's truck, he added, "Okay. Here they come. Watch how they ignore us, but don't look directly at them."

*   *   *

That night Mitch went to see Burt's new rental. It was a one story, two bedroom home with an attached double car garage. The clapboard siding, painted an off-white, had emerald green shutters and trim. "This is really nice," Mitch admitted while looking around.

Burt flourished his arms in an expansive gesture. "All we have to do between now and then is to stock up with food, reading materials, movies for my VCR, and everything else we need to hole up for about a month or so. We can also finish working on my car for my final getaway."

"Sure, I'll help you. But if you drive the Chevy, how will I go?"

"My aunt's husband, I guess,. He will come over when I'm about to leave, give you your new I.D.,

16

take you to Gary, Indiana, fifty miles from here, and drop you off at the bus depot."

"We meet like you said before," Mitch said thoughtfully, and then with curiosity asked, "Can I see your driver's license picture? I mean this Tony guy's license?"

"Sure."

Burt picked up a large brown envelope from the desk and dumped the contents on the table. He pulled out the driver's license and handed it to Mitch. "Here."

Studying it for a moment, Mitch said, "Yeah, he does look a little like you...longer hair, but real curly. How you gonna do it?"

"I'll let my hair grow, lighten it with Just For Men and presto, in five minutes it's done. Then you can give me a permanent."

"What? Not me. I don't know how to do that."

"All you have to do is follow directions."

"Well, as long as you don't tell anyone," his voice was surly, then added. "Ever!"

Burt chuckled. "Don't worry. I won't, if you won't tell anyone that I've had a perm."

Mitch laughed, too. "It's a deal." He shook Burt's hand. "And then what? With your looks, I mean."

"Well, next I'll have to gain about twenty pounds. On the other hand," Burt mused, "I think I'll just tell everyone I lost the weight. That would account for any change in the picture. And I won't have to gain any weight."

"That's real smart, Burt. You always know how to figure things out real good. What else you gonna do?"

"You remember when I started wearing glasses?"

"No. I thought you always wore them."

"Good. That's what I hope everybody thinks. My first day on the job was a Monday, and I saw the Brinks truck and what they did. All I could think about that afternoon was how to pull the job. I knew one thing. I would have to change my appearance. That's when I thought about getting glasses. Most fugitives would put glasses on for a disguise. I decided I would take them off. So after work I went to one of those One Hour places and got new glasses. I probably really didn't need glasses, but they said I needed just a little, maybe a little magnification, but that's all."

"That's great, but what about me?"

"Don't worry. You'll be even better off. First, you'll have to lose about twenty pounds, which will make a lot of difference. Then we get rid of your crew cut; let your hair grow and color it, too. For you we put glasses on, not take 'em off. And last we get you a new I.D. It will probably be a fake one, but a good one, professionally done."

"I feel a lot less nervous, now."

"Speaking of now, we now need to get down to specifics...to go over our stickup plans in detail."

*   *   *

Four days later on a dark and dreary, overcast Monday before Christmas, it had snowed heavily, but all the snow now lay in dirty piles along the curb, not pristine white as it had been when it first fell.

What's wrong with me. I'm not worried about the job. I can't put my finger on it. I just don't know what it is, and I don't like it, Mitch wondered as he put on his coveralls over a heavy sweater. He looked at his watch. Still early. Looking up he spotted Mr. Bender doing paper work at his desk in a small office behind the automotive display room.

Mitch moved over to the coffee machine, next to the restrooms, and poured himself a cup. He warmed his hands around his coffee mug.

"Good morning, Mitch. And a great day it is," Burt called out cheerfully in an Irish brogue. "And how is my best friend?"

"Fine," he answered automatically. "Well, not fine. Just a little jumpy, I guess."

"It's just pre-success jitters." Burt grinned. "I can understand that. But not to worry. Everything's working out perfectly."

"I hope so."

"I know so." Burt looked around to make sure no one was within earshot, and lowered his voice. "It won't be long. In just a little over four hours we'll be in the house with the you know what."

*   *   *

The four hours seemed like forever, though, especially to Mitch. He continually looked at his watch to find that only five to ten minutes had passed each time. With each minute, he grew a little more uncomfortable. If it hadn't been for Burt, he would have backed out. Burt kept him going with encouragement. He constantly joked, laughed and made comments like, "We're going to be partners. It's going to be a piece of cake. Think of the fun we're going to have. Just stick with me, pal. We're gonna be rich."

Shortly after the Brinks guards passed to make their pick-up, Burt grabbed Mitch by the arm, beaming with confidence. "Show time. Let's get our lunches."

Within minutes they were sitting on the wall eating. Burt glanced around. Seeing that the coast was clear, he took the keys out of the customer's car next to them and unlocked the trunk, but left the lid down, unlatched. He put the keys back into the ignition.

"I don't know if I can go through with it, Burt," Mitch whispered. "I just feel too shook up. I don't know why. I just can't shake it."

"You'll be okay. Everyone gets a little nervous before a big performance. I feel a little jittery myself. But we'll both settle down once it starts." Burt looked up suddenly. "Oh, oh. Here they come. Just keep eating and don't look at them. I'll start

telling you a story. You keep looking at me."
Slowly one of the guards pushed the cart while the other followed with his gun in the ready position, looking around circumspectly.

Before the guards were within earshot, Burt started his story. "I'm trying to maneuver the conversation so I can ask her for a date. And just as I'm about to ask her, this bozo hollers at me to tell me he needs to talk to me. And..."

As both guards passed, Burt pulled his Walther PPK pistol out and jumped off the wall. "Hold it, chumps. Drop the weapons over the wall," He said firmly.

Mitch finally brought his Ruger .357 magnum to bear on the guards, too.

One of the guards glanced over his shoulder. Seeing the weapons, he said to his partner, "Do it, John."

They dropped their guns into the loading area.

Burt waved his gun at the guard. "Now open that trunk and throw all the loot in it. Be fast about it."

The guards quickly wheeled the cart over to the west wall and opened the trunk of the car, throwing all the money into it..

Burt stepped over the wall next to the customer's car, one hand on the trunk. "Now back off," he told the guards. Turning to Mitch, he said with a mischievous grin, "Let's go, buddy," and slammed the trunk lid shut.

Mitch grinned back.

This time there was a third guard, the driver, who had remained in the truck, hidden by the glare of the windshield. When he glanced up and saw the holdup taking place, he retrieved his rifle, slipped out of the armored vehicle quietly, and nervously took a position across the hood of the truck. His hands shook. Beads of perspiration broke out on his forehead, in spite of the cold. He took aim at the robber on his left, but that man had already disappeared behind the wall.

Adjusting his rifle to the right a little, he brought the other man into his sights. Only the man's head was visible. His vision blurred when a drop of perspiration dripped into one eye. Quickly he wiped it away with the back of his hand. Taking up his position again and adjusting his aim, he squeezed the trigger.

Burt was grinning at his partner, when a loud crack shattered the air. Mitch's face disappeared. The bullet, a soft-nosed wadcutter, designed to spread as it hit flesh and bone, expanded while it exploded through Mitch's head.

Burt was stunned. He knew Mitch was dead the moment it happened. The two guards had already taken off in a run down the sidewalk. Quickly he jumped into the customer's car, started the engine and slammed the accelerator down.

Mr. Bender ran out of the garage screaming, "Burt! What are you doing? Stop!"

Burt almost hit him, but swerved away in time.

With tires squealing, all Burt could see as he frantically drove was Mitch's faceless head. His heart pounded. His eyes filled with tears. Tiny drops of perspiration broke out on his forehead. When he turned a corner, he spotted a police cruiser. Pulling in behind the car in front of him he slowed down..

With his heart beating fast, he held his breath until they had passed.

Whew, Burt thought as he let out his pent-up breath. *That was close. I'd better slow down.*

Minutes later, he pulled into his garage, parking beside his '57 Chevy. Burt jumped out and yanked on the garage door. It closed behind him with a thud. He leaned against the car, dazed, almost in shock. His best friend was dead. The tableau kept playing back and forth in his mind.

My God what have I done? I killed him, just as sure as I'm standing here. He didn't want to do it, but I talked him into it. And now he's dead.

"Mitch, I'm sorry," he whispered. "I didn't mean for this to happen." His eyes clouded. Tears coursed down his cheeks. He thought of what his father had said to him years before when he had cried over a broken toy.

"Crying won't bring your toy back, Burt," his father had snapped. "Put it behind you and move on to bigger and better things in life."

Burt didn't understand at that time, but his father kept telling him, "Failures are stepping stones to success, nothing more. Don't let problems manipulate your emotions. Put it behind you once and for all."

Yeah, I can't change what happened. I shouldn't blame myself. We took our chances and he lost. It could have been me. But it wasn't. I've got to go on. I'm sure Mitch would have wanted it that way.

Burt walked into the house, ignoring the money in the trunk of the car. He flopped down on the couch. He didn't want to dwell on what had happened. He decided he would just block it out of his mind. He had practiced the technique successfully before. Now when he tried, he couldn't do it. His mental image of Mitch being blown away overwhelmed him. He stared vacantly at the fireplace. Tears rolled down his face.

CHAPTER TWO

The Empire Crown hotel located just outside Champaign, Illinois stood tall against the night sky. The prestigious "Empire Suite" ballroom, filled with more than two hundred people, teemed with excitement. A colorful banner on the wall above the head table displayed "Man of the Year" in large block letters. Beneath it was printed, "Champaign Chamber of Commerce."

The people on the platform had finished eating. They sipped coffee and talked animatedly.

On the main floor, dishes and eating utensils clanked, coupled with laughter and conversation. Out on the perimeters, people had just received their meals.

While many still ate, the master of ceremonies, Johnny Matthew, a lanky man in his early forties with a high forehead and thin brown hair, bent over awkwardly at the waist and spoke into the microphone. "Good afternoon, ladies and gentlemen. Could we have it quiet, please? We need to get started. If you haven't finished eating, go ahead and finish. But we'd appreciate it if you kept it down a bit."

The talking quieted. Matthew straightened, bowed again, and continued speaking into the microphone. "Thank you. And thank you for coming to our annual Man of the Year Award luncheon.

This afternoon I have the distinct honor and pleasure of presenting the award to a friend and associate of mine who has been instrumental in the furthering of many causes in our illustrious city of Champaign.

"He is accompanied tonight by his lovely daughter, Sandra Lee, seated next to him." He gestured toward her. "Stand up, Sandy, so everyone can see you."

The applause started, and slowly she stood in embarrassment, exposing a slender figure topped with long blond hair, feathered and curled on the sides and ends. Her face was not "Hollywood" beautiful, but smooth, tanned and attractive in its own way. Her eyes, however, were her most striking feature, a deep violet blue that sparkled when she smiled.

As she took her seat, Johnny looked back at the audience and continued. "Our honored guest tonight is the CEO and chairman of the board of the Republic Bank of Champaign. He has been a past president of the local Rotary and Lion's Club. He has also helped and given his valuable time and contributions to the United Way, the Muscular Dystrophy Foundation and other organizations too numerous to mention.

"And now it gives me great pleasure to award this trophy to a man, who is an outstanding leader and model in our community, to a man you all know as Mr. Samuel G. Forrest!" With a smile he clapped as he looked down at the man who sat next to the podium.

Samuel G. Forrest quickly stood to his six-foot-one-inch height. The people came to their feet. Their applause swelled to a thunderous roar.

"Mr. G," as he is known to his friends and associates, wore a double-breasted, dark blue, pinstriped suit that emphasized his narrow waist and broad shoulders. He had dark curly hair that waved across the top of his head. Touches of gray at his temples lent a distinguished aura of maturity and intelligence.

Only business associates in Chicago knew why he was referred to as Mr. G.

Mr. G displayed a broad smile that showed even white teeth. Accepting the trophy from Johnny, he turned to the audience, set his trophy down on the table and held up his hands to stop the applause. "Thank you for your generosity and kindness," he stated with pride and dignity. "Please be seated."

Mr. G waited until there was absolute silence in the room, then began to speak softly, his voice rising only to make a point. "I don't want to overdo the word, 'honor,' but I have to say it is a distinct honor to receive this, and I appreciate it very much." He placed his hand on the trophy.

"To be a recipient of this award, Man of the Year, implies that success has to be achieved. Success is something that has to be earned, not something that is given to you. Now I have worked hard, and so maybe I do deserve this prize to some degree. But in a way, it was given to me by so many wonderful associates and employees who have dedicated themselves to excellence which ultimately makes me look successful. So I have to thank them, also.

"If I were to leave you with a word of advice, it would be from Shakespeare. He said, 'Unto thine own self be true, and it must follow as the night, the day, thou canst not then be false to any man.' In other words, don't be self-centered, but always think of others, give to them and love them, not for who they are or what they are, but as they are. When you are true to yourself, you'll be happy and successful. The selfish man is the most miserable man on earth. The self-centered man is the loser, a big-time loser."

Mr. G sipped his water, then finished with, "That is my suggestion to you. 'Give, and it shall be given unto you,' it says in the good book.

"Again I want to say thank you for the honor you have bestowed upon me." He picked up his trophy and held it high. The audience came to their feet again, cameras flashing, and wildly applauded. Then he took his seat.

Sandra Lee proudly looked at her father, her eyes brimmed to overflowing. She leaned over and kissed him on the cheek. "That was beautiful," she whispered in his ear. "I love you, Daddy."

Again he waved his hand and nodded thank you. The clapping slowed, then finally ceased.

*　　　*　　　*

Forty-five minutes later, as Sandra and Mr. G drove home, Sandra Lee was still bubbling over. "I'm so proud of you. But I didn't know you knew anything from the Bible."

He glanced at her with a grin. "That's one of the few scriptures I know."

"Even so, it fit perfectly."

"That's true, but I'm not as good as I made myself out to be."

"Well, I think you are," she admonished. Her eyes sparkled as she smiled up at him.

Mr. G chuckled. "I'm glad you think so."

"I just wish Mother could have been here to see you receive that trophy."

"I do, too."

His faced glazed in memory. *Those were good years*, he thought. *At least those years before the cancer started to eat her up. Then it turned into hell.*

"Daddy! Are you all right?"

He snapped out of his melancholy and looked at her. "Yes, Sweetheart, I'm okay."

He looked at her tenderly, then continued, "By the way, I have to go up to Chicago in the morning. Early. I'll probably be gone by the time you get up. I'll be away several days."

"No problem. Later this week I'll be driving up to my friend Greta's house. It's her birthday Saturday, so I'll be gone a few days myself."

"I'll leave a number where I can be reached."

* * *

The eighteen-story Regency Plaza Hotel did not change the Chicago skyline, but its magnificence revealed itself in grand style. Marble decorated the exterior walls of the first floor, and polished granite dominated the upper floors. Parking attendants scurried about parking late model cars. A plush lobby filled with busy bellhops, clerks and a scattering of women in Givenchy dresses and men in their Armanis suits, moved about with purpose. The price of a room for the night was not for the faint at heart.

Samuel G. Forrest stood in line at the check-in counter. He didn't mind waiting. Directly in front of him was the most gorgeous creature he'd ever seen. Her tall slender body displayed the kind of curves he liked. Her extraordinary figure was squeezed into a tight, charcoal black dress. A single strand of pearls hung eloquently around her neck. Her shining raven black hair hung loosely around her shoulders. Her graceful arms and legs were nicely tanned.

She has to have the ugliest face in the world, he thought. *No one this ravishing from behind could have a beautiful face, too.*

But when she turned quickly, bumping into him, he got his first glance. She was completely beautiful, even sensational. "Excuse me," she said batting long eyelashes. Her almond- colored eyes looked directly into his.

"That's quite all right," he answered as she backed away. "I actually enjoyed it."

At last he got the full effect. Her tanned face had flawless features, but something about her expression, especially her eyes, showed a hint of naivete, that struck him. She was someone he had to see again. Before he could say anything, though, she was gone.

With his eyes following her, he asked the clerk at the check-in counter, "Who was that lovely lady who just left here?"

The clerk's eyes were on her, too. "Her name is Karla Zambini."

"What room is she in?"

"I'm sorry, Sir. I can't give that information out."

Mr. G pulled out a one-hundred-dollar bill, placed it on the counter, and slid it toward the clerk, and looked at him in anticipation.

"As much as I'd like to help you, Sir, I can't accept that or tell you what room she is in. But if you'd like, I could connect you to her room through the house phone."

"No, never mind," Mr. G said retrieving the bill and slipping it into his pocket. With a touch of disappointment, he checked in.

After tipping the bellhop generously, Mr. G looked around his suite. The coffered ceiling and walls of the main living room were an off-white.

Pale blue brocade material with silver floral design covered the overstuffed couch and chairs that surrounded the ornately designed coffee table. On the couch, decorator pillows in various shades of blue provided a striking color accent. The floors displayed a deep piled, berber carpeting.

Stepping out onto the balcony, he looked down ten floors to a large, kidney shaped pool, housed in glass walls and ceiling with a Jacuzzi at one end. That's when the thought struck him. With that tan, I'll bet that good looker will be down at the pool soon to keep up her tan.

Thirty minutes later he was sitting in a lounge chair, pool side, reading the morning edition of the Chicago Tribune. At first he didn't spot her. When he did he noticed that she was wearing a cherry red swimsuit. It was a very conservative cut, but it could not cover her sexuality. It was obvious to everyone. Most every eye followed her as she walked into the pool area and took a lounge chair on the opposite side of the pool from Mr. G.

Picking up his towel and slipping his loafers on, he skirted the pool to the other side. "Is this chair occupied?" he asked pointing to the lounge next to her.

"Not that I know of," she replied with a slight smile.

"Have you been staying here long?"

"No. I just arrived a couple of hours ago."

"I did, too. You from these parts?"

"Not now," she answered. "But I used to live just a few miles from here when I was a kid."

"Where?"

"Around a hundred and third and Cicero."

"No kidding. I wasn't far away, near a hundred and tenth and Cicero. What street did you live on?"

"South Knox."

Mr. G showed his delight. "I lived on South Kenton, just a block east of you and then a few more blocks south.

"Really?" For a moment her eyes were lost in memory. "I'll bet you hung out at Benny's Convenience Store on Cicero."

"Sometimes, when he didn't chase us away. He used to yell at us, "You boys gotta get outta here. You spoila my beezness."

Karla Zambini laughed heartily. "I heard him holler like that a few times myself."

"Not when I was there. I'd a remembered a good looking chick like you. Excuse me, but that's what we called women then. Anyway, I would have remembered a good looking dame like you." Mr. G winked playfully with a broad grin on his face, expecting a reaction.

At first she looked a little surprised, then realizing it was all in jest, she got into the act, too. "Well you punks, as we used to call you, never knew how to treat a real lady."

Mr. G chuckled, and she joined in.

"I'm Samuel G. Forrest," he said, still chuckling, offering his hand.

Her hand was dwarfed in his. "And I'm Karla Zambini."

"And what does Karla do for a living?"

"I'm a dress designer from New York. But I'm moving my business here to Chicago. How about you?"

"I own and manage a small bank down in Champaign, Illinois."

"Impressive."

"I was hoping you'd say that. You see, I'm supposed to attend a semiformal dinner tonight in honor of an associate of mine, and I was hoping that maybe, just maybe, you would honor me by accepting my invitation to accompany me to the dinner. You see, I really do need a partner, and if you accept, every man in the place would be totally green with envy. I'd love that."

Karla smiled broadly, exposing her perfect teeth. "The dinner is right here in this hotel?"

"Yes."

"And we could meet in the lobby before, and say goodnight there, too?"

Mr. G felt a little disappointed, but replied, "Yes, of course. If that is your desire."

"Those are my terms, Mr. Forrest."

"Okay, agreed. Seven sharp, in the lobby."

*   *   *

Mr. G stepped off the elevator two minutes after seven. He had been delayed with a phone call at the moment he prepared to leave his suite. He was dressed in a freshly pressed, gray pinstriped suit. When he spotted her, near the cocktail lounge, he was extremely pleased. She was wearing a form fitting, black dress that revealed every curve. A plunging neckline exposed deep cleavage.

Not seeing him, Karla turned away from him, disclosing the smooth tightness of the dress and a bare back down to her waist. The exposure of her back and no lines around the buttocks, made him wonder if she were wearing any undergarments.

This thought excited him.

She turned back and spotted him. A smile spread across her face as she walked toward him. His eyes followed her every move.

She stopped in front of him. "Careful, big guy," she admonished. "Don't let your eyes pop out."

From the expression on her face, Mr. G knew she was not really scolding him, but was enjoying his attention. "The only way I can do that is to tear my eyes from you and just watch the other guys' eyes pop out. But let me say, you do look stunning."

"Thank you, kind sir. A woman never gets enough compliments. And let me say that you look very handsome right now, better than you did in a bathing suit this afternoon. But all you need is to put a little color on that fine-honed muscular white skin of yours, and you'll be gorgeous in a swimsuit, too."

"Why thank you, kind lady. Now may I," he said jocularly as he extended his arm.

She took his arm. "Shall we go?"

*   *   *

The Emperor Room at the Regency Plaza Hotel was a spacious ballroom. Its walls covered with a light-blue wallpaper with gold reliefs of stately crowned kings showed obedient subjects kneeling at their feet. The ceiling was sky blue with thousands of tiny lights that illuminated the room. Nearly one hundred people in small groupings were sipping glasses of champagne. Some were already seated at round tables. Waiters in black pants, white shirts and dark ties were carrying trays of drinks.

Mr. G, with Karla on his arm, stopped for a few moments at the entrance and surveyed the crowd. Many heads turned toward them.

"You certainly know how to make an entrance," Karla remarked as she looked up at him with admiration. *He must be an important man as well as being ruggedly handsome*, she thought.

"I really was trying to find someone. And I did. If there was a little grandstanding, that's okay, too. Come. I want to introduce you to someone."

Mr. G guided Karla through the crowd. He was sure there were many eyes following them; mostly on her, he suspected.

"Ah, here we are. Happy birthday, Sal."

Sal was short and rotund with black eyes. His black hair was combed straight back. "Thank you, Sam. And who do we have here?"

"I want you to meet Karla Zambini. Karla, this is Sal Fratenello, a business associate of mine."

There was a slight grin on Sal's face as if he thought of something that Sam and Karla were not privy to. "It's nice to meet 'cha." His eyes lingered on Karla. "You sure know how to pick 'em, Sam."

"I agree wholeheartedly. I just wanted to make all you guys jealous."

"Well, you certainly did that. There are a lot of eyes looking this way, and I know that they're not looking at us."

"Thank you, gentlemen. You are most kind. And I, Mr. Fratenello, want to wish you a happy birthday, too."

"I appreciate it. And Sam, when we have our meeting in a couple a days at my place, why don't you bring Karla along? We'll have lunch first, and she can enjoy the pool area while we talk." Sal's eyes were still on her. "In fact, I think my beautiful daughter and my beautiful granddaughter would join you.. You're three of a kind, all gorgeous."

"That really would be nice if you could, Karla," Mr. G said, his eyes questioning.

"How can I refuse such an elegant invitation? I'll be happy to. I'm sure I may be able to rearrange my appointments ."

"Great!" Mr. G exclaimed.

"Now, Sam," Sal explained, "you, of course, are sitting at the head table with me tonight. And Karla will sit next to you. I'll have my son moved to the end."

"It would be an honor," Karla said.

"It's settled, then. And now I'd better mill around with my guests." Sal moved away.

Karla looked up at Mr. G and said, "I guess we have our orders."

"You'll have to excuse Sal, he's just that way. He's a very powerful man and without thinking about it, he expects people to do whatever he suggests."

"That's very interesting."

"Well, it is interesting, but not enough to poke around in his affairs. He doesn't like snoops."

"Understood."

Mr. G was about to suggest they meet some other people, when a middle-aged man, tall and slender, stepped in front of them. His straight hair had a razor sharp part . His bushy eyebrows shaded pale green eyes. His mouth was thin and hard. "What hole did you crawl out of?" he said between nearly clenched teeth.

"The hole three steps above yours, Arthur. This is Karla. And this, Karla, is Arthur Bocha."

Arthur, with his eyes turning to Karla, gave a slight bow. "It's my pleasure, Karla. And when you're ready to dump this fellow, I certainly would be available."

Irritated, Karla remarked, "I absolutely have no plans of 'dumping' him as you say. I think he's perfect in every way."

"Thank you, Arthur. You just cemented my relationship with her."

With his eyes still on Karla, Arthur said, "I'm sure he'll do something to turn you off. And then I'll be waiting to make my move."

"Don't bother, I wouldn't be interested."

Mr. G turned Karla away and shouldered past Arthur. "Why don't you crawl back into your hole," he said as they left.

Mr. G guided Karla toward the head table.

"Who is that nasty man," Karla asked, "and why does he hate you so?" "It goes back a long way. He's an accountant for Sal. Years ago, Mr. Fratenello gave me an opportunity to purchase the bank in Champaign and to manage it. It was an extremely good deal for me and one that Arthur believed he should have been offered."

"In other words, he's extremely jealous."

"Yes. He has hated me ever since."

"Nice guy." Sarcasm edged her voice.

"Oh, yes. In fact, he would like me dead, I'm sure."

"Do you think he might try something?"

"I seriously doubt it. He's too stupid to come up with any viable plan. Besides, hate causes a person to lose logic. And of course, he'd have to answer to Mr. Fratenello."

"Why?"

"Because I'm a business associate of Mr. Fratenello, and wasting me would disrupt business."

A young waiter approached them as they arrived at the head table. The waiter said, "Mr. Fratenello pointed you out to me, Mr. Forrest. You're to sit here with Miss Karla next to you."

Mr. G held Karla's chair for her, then sat down himself.

After dinner, one of the waiters carried in a large cake with a profusion of candles and set it down in front of Mr. Fratenello. Mr. G began singing happy birthday to Sal and everyone joined in, building the volume to the final note.

CHAPTER THREE

Burt, who had adopted his new name, Tony, was glad to get away from the house. *I almost went stir crazy, as they call it in the movies.* He smiled. He had been cooped up for almost three months. Every day he had watched the news on television about the robbery. The police were after him and had even broadcast his photo. *I wonder where they got that picture,* he thought. *At least I have completely changed my appearance.*

He had been driving his yellow convertible, leaving just before dawn. He wanted to get out of Chicago while it was still dark. He stayed on back roads, for the most part. By eight a.m. rain came down in sheets, causing driving conditions to deteriorate. Visibility was poor. Reducing his speed, he followed highway 394 to highway 14. He mentally went down his check list. *First, I left the customer's car hidden in the garage. Second the money, a little over two point five million, is safely locked in my trunk. That's about as safe as I can make it, I think.* He had been ecstatic when he had finally counted it the first time. Then he had counted it again, down to the last five-dollar bill.

"Sorry you can't be here to share this, Mitch," Burt whispered. "It went exactly as I had planned, except for what happened to you. If you'd kept your head down, you'd be more than one point two five mil richer. And going into business with me."

Burt shook his head. Now I'm talking to myself, he thought. *I've got to get rid of that kind of thinking. I can't keep worrying about what happened to Mitch, or maybe I feel guilty. I don't know.*

"Arrh," he groaned, trying to shake free of those thoughts.

Now back to my list. I changed my appearance, hair much lighter, longer and curly. And it looks like I've lost about thirty pounds, from what my Tony's driver's license shows. At least that's the excuse I'll use, if anyone asks why I look different. And last I've got a new name, Tony, with all his background, including Tony's diploma from Indiana University with a major in business among other things. This guy must have been smart, real smart. Now I'm smart. The new Tony chuckled.

Suddenly, he spotted a little red sports car racing toward him. The car swerved sideways, hydroplaning on the wet pavement. The car shot across the road, hitting the angled stanchion of a small bridge. The car became airborne, rising up and sailing over the guardrail before plunging into the Kankakee river below.

Tony hit his brakes and skidded to a stop. He flung open his door, slipped and slid down the wet embankment to the edge of the river, kicking his shoes off. He dove into the river.

The water was icy cold, but he was barely aware of it. Keeping his eyes on the bubbles rising from the sunken vehicle, he descended deeper. He reached the car and grabbed the door handle on the driver's side. Frantically, he struggled, but the door would not budge. He peered inside at what appeared to be an unconscious young woman. The water was rapidly filling the car, but he needed air. Pushing himself off the car, he rose quickly.

He gulped air as his face broke the surface. Someone was shouting. He spotted two men on the shoreline, silhouetted by a big rig. He couldn't understand what they were shouting, so he hollered, "Telephone for help!" The men waved and turned toward their truck. Tony doubled up and dove down again. He knew he couldn't get the door open until the car had filled with water. Upon reaching the car, he found the water had risen to the headliner, and when he pulled on the door, it opened slowly.

When he reached in to grab the girl, he painfully cut his forearm on a piece of broken glass. Instinctively, he pulled back. Then lowering his hand under the broken glass, he pushed it out of the way. Tony unlatched the girl's seat belt and pulled her out of the car. He swam with his left arm across her chest, gripping her belt at the waist, and reached upward for the surface. He struggled against the current. His lungs were about to burst. The cold water was taking its toll, along with the effort of swimming fully clothed and dragging a dead-weight body. Finally reaching the surface, he gulped air desperately, trying to catch his breath as he treaded water, being sure to keep her face above water. He looked for the shoreline. A small wave caught him. His mouth filled with water, causing him to gag and cough.

Tony headed for shore. He scissor kicked with his legs, and stroked strongly with his right arm. After swimming for what seemed like an eternity, he looked up again to check his position. He couldn't believe he had only traveled a short distance. He was already fatigued and he still had a long way to go. But it's only thirty feet. Wait a minute, it's not the distance, but the current that I'm fighting.

Tony lowered his head, trying to flow with the river, while heading for shore at an angle. Getting a better grip on her belt, he shifted his load and stroked again.

Tony's mind screamed, I'm not going to make it. He tried not to think about it, but that was impossible. I have to keep going, he told himself, or we'll both die.

With each stroke, his right arm weakened. He kept telling himself, Just one more stroke, just one more. But more and more his tired mind was screaming, You're not going to make it. You can't. You're too exhausted. And slowly he was beginning to believe it.

It was at the moment of exhaustion that his hand brushed against a tree root, which had grown into the river. Grabbing it, Tony tugged with all the strength he could muster, trying to get to safety. He frantically gulped air. Coughing and gasping, he pulled the girl closer to shore. He laid in the shallows until two strong truckers grabbed Tony and the girl and dragged them to shore.

Tony could hear sirens approaching. Momentarily, paramedics arrived and scrambled down the embankment. One of the paramedics began mouth to mouth on the girl while the other knelt by Tony's side, but Tony waved him off.

Within moments, the girl coughed. By this time Tony was kneeling by her feet. His left arm was hanging down at his side, blood dripping from his fingers, but he was not conscious of it.

He saw that she was a young attractive girl, even though she was wet and disheveled. When she opened her eyes, Tony was mesmerized. He moved in a little closer. He had never seen such exquisite eyes in his life. They radiated a deep violet blue.

As her eyes focused on him, seeing his wet straggly hair and clothes clinging to his body, she mumbled through a weak smile, "You're the one who saved my life, aren't you?"

"I guess," he answered shyly, not knowing why he was acting this way. *I'm not a shy person,* he thought. *Never have been.*

One of the medics noticed the cut on Tony's arm. "You'd better come along. Looks like you'll need stitches."

Tony's first thought was that he'd better just disappear. He didn't want to be caught, just when he had everything going for him. "Just tape it up, and I'll follow you to the hospital."

Tony shivered.

The medic wrapped a blanket around him. "You feel dizzy or lightheaded?"

"No, not at all."

"Well, that arm still needs stitches. Come up to the ambulance, and I'll wrap it for you, then follow us to the hospital," he ordered.

As he followed the medic up the embankment, he thought of that beautiful girl he'd saved. *I do want to see her some more. Maybe I can stay in this area,* he reasoned. *I've changed my looks enough so that no one would connect me to the robbery. Maybe I will stay. At least until I find out more about her.*

*   *   *

The Riverside Medical Center, located not far from the accident site, was a large, modern, three story structure. Tony followed the ambulance around to the back emergency entrance. His arm ached. He found a parking place and locked the car carefully. He didn't want to lose his valuable possessions.

The medics pulled the young lady from the back of the ambulance and called to Tony as they pushed her into the hospital. "Follow us in," one said. He was the stocky one with rolls of fat above and below the belt, but he seemed very strong by the way he moved the gurney around, up and down, with no effort.

As soon as they entered the hospital, the emergency nurses took over, putting the young lady into Emergency One and Tony into Emergency Two.

In a moment, a gaunt doctor with only a fringe of hair around his bony skull, came in. He was brusque in manner. Looking down through reading glasses that hung on the end of his large nose, he examined Tony's arm. "Looks bad. It'll take stitches, and we'll want to keep you here overnight."

*　　*　　*

The next morning Tony awoke when a nurse brought in breakfast. He was still a little groggy. He had been given pain medication the night before, which made him sleep. His arm was bandaged and in a sling. He wasn't aware of the slight ache in his arm, but he was aware of a gnawing in his stomach. However, he lost his appetite when he took a bite of hospital food. Pushing the tray aside, he went into the bathroom and, with some difficulty, cleaned up. Finding his pants in a closet, he put them on and walked down to the nurses' station.

"Good morning," he said to a pleasantly plump nurse. Her partially gray hair stuck out in tufts around her cap.

She smiled through crooked teeth. "Good morning. How do you feel today?"

"I feel fine. But what about the girl I pulled from the river?"

"She's just fine, too. So you're the hero that saved her life?"

"Well, I don't know about the 'hero' part," he said, leaning closer and whispering, "What room is she in?"

"Right across the hall from you." Her eyes twinkled.

"Thanks." Tony winked as he walked away.

What do I say, he asked himself as he approached the open door, adjusting his sling. He found her wide awake and looking directly at him, when he stopped in the doorway.

"Good morning. Come in," she said with a devastating smile. She was sitting up in bed with a couple of pillows behind her, her long blond hair framing her face..

"How do you feel?" he asked awkwardly as he walked to the foot of her bed.

"Great!" she replied with a warm smile.

Her smile lit up the pools of deep violet blue and drew him in and engulfed him. *What do they say about the eyes*, he thought. *They're the windows of the soul. And I like these windows. I can't explain it, but I can feel it. Maybe I'm falling in love. Love at first sight, I guess. Ha! But then I have never believed in that. On the other hand...*

She interrupted his thoughts. "How do you feel? Looks like you were injured when you saved my life, and I want to thank you for that, for, uh... saving me, that is..." She groped for his name.

"The name is..." He almost blurted out Burt, but caught himself. "Tony, Tony Garber. But my arm is okay. Just hurts a little."

"I'm sorry."

What's your name?"

"Sandra Forrest."

"Anyone ever call you Sandy?"

"Sure, some of my friends do, and my father. But if Daddy calls me Sandra Lee, it means I'm in trouble, big trouble. At least that's the way it was when I was a kid." She laughed.

Her laugh is infectious, he thought, *and captivating, and coupled with her eyes....* He felt a little weak.

"Are you all right, Tony?" she asked with concern in her voice.

"Yeah, I'm all right. It's just that..." Tony fidgeted. He didn't know quite what to say. Then he spotted her untouched breakfast, and said, "I'm famished, but I just couldn't eat the hospital food."

"I couldn't either." She glanced at her breakfast tray.

"I've got a great idea. Are you getting out of here this morning, too?" When she nodded, he continued, "How about we go someplace and get some good food."

"Okay, as long as you let me pay for my own breakfast."

"I asked. I pay. You ask. You pay." Tony grinned.

Sandy grinned back. "Okay, you win. But next time it's on me."

"All right. But remember the rules; you have to ask."

"Okay, okay, okay." She laughed. "Now get out of here. My doctor will be here any minute, and I have to get prettied up."

Smiling, he said, "You got a thing for the doctor?"

"You just mind your own business." She smiled coyly.

"I'll see you in the lobby in a little while, and don't be late."

"Humph," was her retort.

Tony walked back to his room. In his mind he was rejoicing. *Yes. Yes. Yes,* he repeated, totally satisfied with the turn of events. He wasn't sure whether he had the moxie to handle this gal, though. *I really like her! I really like her!* he thought joyously.

*   *   *

At Sandy's suggestion they wound up at a quaint little place on the outskirts of Kankakee called The Greenhouse Restaurant and Inn. Behind the restaurant, a swimming pool surrounded by deck chairs and tables was centered inside a U-shaped inn.

As they entered, Tony noticed the greenhouse effect; lots of green tinted glass with greenery separating the rows of booths and tall potted plants of various kinds placed at the ends of each row. "I hope the food is as good as this place looks," Tony stated as they sat down.

"It is," she answered. "You'll notice the variety on the menu. There are dozens of different breakfasts, some with a Mexican flavor, some European, Hawaiian, and others as well."

"How about just good old American flavors?" he asked.

"They have those, too." She laughed.

The waitress interrupted to take their orders.

Sandy decided on the huevos rancheros and then looked up at Tony. Seeing the questioning expression on his face, she asked, "You've never had huevos rancheros?" When he shook his head, she added, "Try'em, you'll like 'em."

"Okay, I'll have the same," he told the waitress and glanced at Sandy again. He couldn't keep his eyes off her.

Sandy looked a little uncomfortable. "Why do you keep staring at me?"

"I guess I'm just nuts about you. I can't stop thinking about you. You're the Greek Goddess I've always dreamed about. That's why."

"You're crazy," she laughed. "Just crazy."

"Yes, crazy about you."

"Oh, nonsense."

"I'd go to the ends of the earth for you."

"If you don't stop it, I may ask you to do just that. Just to get away from you. Besides, you're embarrassing me." She had turned a light shade of pink.

"Okay, I'm sorry. But I'll stop only if you tell me a little about yourself."

"Now, that's a deal. But there isn't much to tell. I graduated from college, the University of Illinois, and recently passed my bar exam. I'm starting to work for a local law firm next week."

"You're a lawyer?" he exclaimed. "Wow! I would never have guessed it."

"Why, because I'm female?"

"No, no," he answered quickly. "I really don't know why I thought that. I'm sorry if it sounded that way."

"Well, I'm sorry, too. I shouldn't have reacted like that. It makes me sound like I'm one of those radical feminists."

"Naw. You're too sweet for that."

A little embarrassed, Sandy quickly asked, "Now, how about a little historical background on you?"

Tony had to think twice, since he was no longer Burt. "I graduated from the University of Indiana, where I majored in business. I started on my MBA, but my dad developed heart problems, so I had to go home and run his business for him, a hardware store.

"He died a couple of years ago, and Mom, a year later. I couldn't stand Gary, Indiana, anymore, so I sold the hardware store and headed South. That's when I met you. And that was the happiest day of my life," he finished with a smile.

He was expecting some kind of retort, but her response was soft and gentle. "It was a very happy day for me, too, except for smashing my car, and almost getting killed. But you saved my life and I'll always be in debt to you for that."

"I was glad to do it. But now I have another question. Since you're a lawyer, tell me what you think of the O.J. Simpson trial and verdict?"

She looked at him to see if he was serious. "I'm a neophyte," she explained. "I have no experience. I can't give you a credible explanation. Especially after all those expert lawyers the media hired to interpret every aspect of the trial."

"Sure you can. I don't know anything about the law, but I have an opinion."

"Opinions, I have."

"Okay, your opinion then."

"Well, I would have to say that by the evidence only, he should have been convicted. But you have to recognize the fact that there were a lot of factors involved. Oh, I know the jury is instructed to leave emotions out of their decision and base it on the facts, but that's impossible to do, totally. You especially have to remember where the blacks were coming from, and there were a number of them on the jury.

Tony leaned back in his seat, and looked seriously at her.

"The defense made sure that the race issue was involved. They certainly brought it out through that L.A. police detective who was supposed to have used the 'N' word. Bitterness still is prevalent in the black community. You can't really blame them. It's hard to get away from it, with as many racists as we have around. It takes only one rotten apple to spoil the barrel. These few racists perpetuate the problem. And the mainstream media unwittingly sustains it with their coverage of it.

"Then you have to take into consideration the 'Dream Team,' as they were so aptly labeled, some of the best lawyers in the country. And they're masters at taking the facts and coloring them, to raise doubts about them, constantly interjecting conspiracy. It was enough to confuse anyone.

Tony leaned forward again, and put his elbows on the table, resting his head in his hands.

"Lawyers are taught that there are not two sides to everything. There's only one, your side. All else is wrong. Every person you represent is innocent, regardless of the evidence. If, as a lawyer you have doubts about the innocence of your client, you'll probably lose the case. When you speak to a jury, you'd better do it with the confidence that the client is innocent.

"So you see Tony, it's not a simple thing. Many of those jurors wanted him to be innocent simply because he had been a hero to them. All those years on the gridiron; receiving the Heisman Trophy; many commercials on TV, like running through the airport and jumping over luggage. But if I had been on that jury, I think in the end I would have voted 'guilty,' because of the evidence."

Tony smiled at her. "And if I had been on that jury, I would have said 'not guilty'"

"See? You have just proven my point. You would have voted with your emotions, not with logic."

"Oh, but I am a very logical person." He grinned back. "But like you said, he was my hero. I watched him while he played football at U.S.C. and through his professional career. I didn't want him to be guilty."

"I rest my case." She laughed. Tony joined in.

They were both quiet for a moment. "Since you are without transportation, I would like to take you home. Where do you live?"

"In Champaign. Its quite a long drive, south of here."

"That's the way I was headed."

The food was served, piping hot and tantalizing.

*   *   *

Tony looked at Sandy's house with amazement. They had pulled up to the electronically controlled gate. "My 'clicker' to open the gate was in my car, so just press the button," she instructed.

He did.

"May I help you?" a female voice answered from within.

"Hi, Matty. It's Sandy," she yelled across Tony. "Open sesame."

There was a giggle from the speaker, then the gate slowly opened.

"That's my secret code with Matty, our house-keeper," Sandy informed him. "It really isn't a secret, but she knows I call it that in jest. I have a good rapport with her."

Tony didn't respond. He sat in awe as he slowly drove toward the biggest house he had ever seen. The concrete driveway cut a graceful swath through closely mowed grass, neatly trimmed hedges and a variety of beautifully nurtured rose-bushes. The house itself was a white, three-storied colonial style mansion with multiple steep gables across the roof. A lengthy veranda supported by tall, round pillars stretched across the front of the house. Sculptured flowers adorned the top and base of each pillar.

As Tony stopped in front of the entrance, he noticed three concrete steps leading up to the veranda, which was lined with used bricks. The custom crafted double doors contained beveled, frosted panes of glass. A large, brass bell hung on the right door jam and from it hung a twisted red rope.

"I've never seen anything like it, except in the movies," exclaimed Tony. Then he looked at her and continued, "It's a mansion. And you live here...in it?"

"Yes." She admitted with a smile. "I'd prefer something smaller for me. Much smaller. But this is Daddy's. It really represents him and his style. It's the kind of man he is: big, complicated and dignified."

Tony made up his mind at that moment. *Champaign is my new home. This is my new girl, beautiful and rich. What more could I ask for? And some day this is going to be my home.*

Sandy interrupted his musing. "Can you come to dinner tonight? I'm going to call Daddy. I'm sure he will cut his meetings short when he hears what happened to me, and he'll want to meet you. Will tonight about seven work out for you?"

"Sure. No problem. I've decided to settle down here. I'll probably look for a business here."

"Great!" Sandy almost shouted.

"And I hope I can see more of you, a lot more."

Smiling coyly, she purred, "Maybe. We'll see."

I really like him, Sandy thought. *At least, I think so. Of course, I don't know much about him, but I'd sure like to find out. All I know is I like being with him. Time will tell...time will tell.*

"See you tonight, then," she said, opening the front door.

"Okay, Sandy. Seven it is," he answered. "But one last thing. Could you recommend a good hotel?"

"The Chancellor Hotel is nice. It's part of the convention center; lots of activity going on there. I'm sure you'll like it. Get off U.S. Highway 74 at Neil St. and go south a few blocks. It's on the northwest corner."

CHAPTER FOUR

The imposing electronic gates gracefully swung open when Mr. G identified himself into the gate phone. As they drove in, a large brick house loomed before them. A formidable three story structure supported turrets at the north and south ends giving it a medieval appearance. Located in the posh Oak Park neighborhood, it had expansive lawns and flower beds. Several gardeners worked near the long driveway.

"Nice place," Karla remarked with amazement.

"Yes, it is. Just slightly larger than my place."

"You mean you live in one of these mansions, too?"

"Well, mine is a white colonial monstrosity, down in Champaign."

"I'd like to see it sometime."

Mr. G smiled. "I'd like that. Anytime you can get away."

They pulled up and parked beside a pearl white Sports car. "His daughter must be here. That's her Jag."

A middle-aged burly man with olive-colored skin opened Karla's door. He was dressed in a dark suit, shirt and tie. He did not smile. His black eyes stared at them as they got out of the car.

"Good afternoon, Mac," Mr. G said to the man.

"Uh," he grunted with no trace of recognition.

Always so personable, Mr. G mused. A log in the woods has more personality.

Karla paid no attention to the man. Hooking onto Mr. G's arm, she ascended the steps to the doorway filled with Mr. Fratenello.

"Sam and Karla," Sal beamed. "Welcome to my home. Come in. We'll go right out back to the patio for lunch. My granddaughter says she is famished. But that's not her word, it's mine. Actually she said, 'Gampa, Lisa hungry.'"

Sal laughed heartily. "She's a doll. Like my mother said the first time she held Lisa. She looked down at her little face and said, 'Bella, bella, bambino.'"

"Which means?" Karla asked.

Sal stopped abruptly in the spacious living room and looked deeply into Karla's eyes. "Italian for beautiful, beautiful, baby. That's what my dear mother said to her," Sal said softly as his gaze lingered on Karla. Then turning to Mr. G, he added. "You don't mind, Sam, do you? Or is she your special girl?"

Mr. G's face registered obvious embarrassment. "We haven't known each other long enough for anything like that."

Karla smiled warmly.

"That's okay, Sam. You'll get there." He turned and led them to a clover-leaf-shaped swimming pool surrounded by flagstone. At the far end a waterfall cascaded into one clover leaf. A second to the right contained the Jacuzzi, elevated slightly above the other three leaves with its warm water flowing into the center. In the left leaf, a small island, with a narrow arched bridge to it, an inlaid marble table with benches, connected them. The fourth leaf was directly in front of them. *This one must be for swimming,* Karla thought.

Karla turned her attention to the little island.

Sal said, "Don't worry. We're not going to have lunch out there. Although, if we were all in swimsuits, perhaps we would."

"No, I wasn't thinking about that, although that would be fun, but I was admiring the unique beauty of your back yard."

"Thank you. Ah, here they are. My beautiful daughter and granddaughter. Come, let me introduce you," Sal said expansively. "Karla, this is my daughter Kathy and my granddaughter Lisa. Kathy, this is Karla. Mr. Forrest you already know."

Kathy smiled demurely. The soft curls of her dark-chocolate hair framed a young attractive face with sparkling brown eyes. Her plump, mature figure was plentiful. "It's a pleasure," she said.

Two-year-old Lisa was dressed in a blue jumpsuit. She was a smaller and slimmer version of Kathy. She stuck her hand out. "Me, too."

"And me, too, to you, Lisa," Karla said, kneeling down and shaking hands. Then looking up at Sal she said, "She certainly isn't a shy one."

"No, she isn't. Takes after my dear departed wife. She was gregarious, too." Glancing around at everyone, Sal added, "Well, let's eat. And then while Sam and I have our little business meeting, you girls can go swimming or whatever."

"It's a little cool for swimming for me," Karla said, "I'll just wait here and enjoy this beautiful yard."

"We'll join you, Karla," Kathy said. "Won't we, Lisa?"

Lisa nodded delightfully.

*   *   *

Sal and Sam took their coffee in the library. Sal was sitting behind his mammoth mahogany desk in front of a large-paned window overlooking a multicolored rose garden. Mr. G had settled into an overstuffed chair in front of the desk. On the two opposite walls were floor to ceiling bookcases, filled with expensive-looking volumes. At the far end of the room, a large seascape painting depicting huge waves violently smashing a rocky shoreline hung on a rugged wall of jutting granite. An antique table with chairs was situated before it.

"I may have a problem, Sam."

"What kind?"

"I think Art Bocha is cookin' my books. Little things that don't add up. I don't want to flat out accuse him without evidence, because if I'm wrong, I could lose a good accountant. I know he's saved me a lot of tax money over the years, but on these other things...I just don't know."

"What do you want me to do?"

"I want you to look over my books; the real ones. They're here in the safe. As a banker, I figure you are a step above an accountant. Wanna take a look see?"

"Sure."

Sal moved to the end of the room. He stopped in front of a small bookcase and grabbed a hook shaped lamp on the wall, twisting it a quarter of a turn to the right. Mr. G heard an audible click, and when Sal pulled on the bookcase, it slid open. Behind it was a wall safe. Opening it, he pulled out two flat accounting ledgers and handed them to Mr. G.

Mr. G studied them for a good half hour and then looked up at Sal. "I've found at least three places where the figures could have been doctored, but I can't be sure until I have a lot more time to go over them. Could I take them back to my hotel to work on them?"

"No, no. It's too dangerous. Could you come back here tomorrow morning? Spend the whole day, if you need it. And when you finish I'll have something very nice for you, whichever way it goes. Okay?"

"Fine. I'll return first thing in the morning."

Sal looked relieved. "Great. Now let's join the ladies."

*   *   *

It was late afternoon when they left the estate. Mr. G eased his black Mercedes SL 500 into the street. He reached for Karla's hand and squeezed it gently. "You have one of the most fantastic figures I've ever seen, bar none."

"Flattery could get you in trouble."

He glanced into the rearview mirror. A sporty Black T-Bird had pulled out behind them. He made a quick turn at the corner, and grunted, "I work out almost every day, but as you said, the lack of a tan destroys the image."

After the abrupt turn, Karla looked at him. "Well, maybe we can work on that together."

Inwardly, Mr. G was pleased with that obvious invitation. Making another turn, he said, "I accept. I know I would enjoy it. Especially with you."

"I don't have a lot of time. You have to remember that I'm a working girl, too."

"Me, too, but I'll make the time," he answered, glancing in the rear mirror again. "Don't turn around, but I think we may have company."

Karla stared straight ahead. "Are you sure?"

"Yes. A car pulled out behind us as we left Sal's place. Every turn I've made, they've made. Let's see if they follow me up on the freeway."

The sign read, "U.S. 290 East." Mr. G accelerated up the ramp and merged with light traffic headed toward downtown Chicago. "They're still with us. Hang on. I guess we're going for a ride." He pointed toward the glove compartment. "There's a pistol in there. Would you hand it to me?"

She pulled out a Walthers PK, looked it over and handed it to him. " Why do you carry a gun?"

"As a banker I sometimes have to tote one." He set the weapon down between them and pulled around a car in his lane. Boxed in for a moment, he waited for his opportunity. Suddenly, the two cars behind him pulled off the freeway.

"Here they come," Mr. G said as he pressed the button to roll his window down. The cool May air rushed in, chilling them to the bone, but neither was aware of it. Placing his left hand at the twelve o'clock position on the steering wheel, he picked up the Walther in his right, holding it in the ready position as he glanced quickly at the chase car and the highway in front of him.

"If I can make it to the next exit, when they're almost parallel, I'll turn off. They should be trapped on the freeway."

He again glanced nervously back and forth between the freeway traffic and the black T-Bird. He could see that the passenger window was open and something was slowly emerging from it. "They've got a sawed-off shotgun," he shouted as he whipped his car toward the off-ramp.

The driver of the T-Bird slammed on his brakes and skidded in behind them, missing them by inches.

Staying in the left lane, Mr. G hit his brakes hard as he approached the yellow light at the underpass. The light turned red as he made his squealing turn beneath the freeway.

Looking back, he noticed that the T-Bird was still behind them, its body tilted to the right as it careened around the corner. Horns blared from angry motorists who had to slam on their brakes to avoid hitting the T-Bird.

Mr. G wove in and out of the staggered cars, but, half a block away, the light was red. Four cars waited for the green light when the left arrow blinked on. As Mr. G pulled into the parallel lane, the arrow turned red. Then he remembered what the fire engines do in similar circumstances. Slamming the palm of his hand on the horn and his foot down on the accelerator, the car leaped forward, horn blaring, as he quickly sped around the cars.

Now with two cars between them and the T-Bird, Mr. G felt slightly relieved. At the next corner he made a quick left turn onto Jackson Boulevard and cruised into Columbus Park. Seeing that the T-Bird was stopped in the left turn lane with another car in front, he swiftly made a decision. After going around a curve and out of sight of traffic to the rear, he pulled into a nearly full parking lot and parked the car at the far end.

"Let's go," Mr. G said, jumping out of the car. He slipped the pistol into his belt and buttoned his coat over it.

Karla followed.

Running quickly into a wooded area, he stepped behind a large tree and looked back. He held Karla's hand, keeping her behind him and out of sight. The T-Bird came around the bend and passed the entryway into the parking area, but moments later, it made a hasty U-turn and entered.

Tightly holding Karla's hand, Mr. G moved deeper into the woods, using the large trees as cover. Looking back, he saw two men in dark suits emerge from the T-Bird. They looked around the parking lot, turning full circle. One gestured toward the wooded area.

Mr. G stiffened. He pulled Karla close. Her trembling body aroused in him a curious blend of sexuality and desire mixed with the fear of the situation.

"They're coming. They've spotted my car. Come on, we'll circle back."

The two men entered the woods.

Mr. G and Karla turned and ran from tree to tree, dodging limbs and brambles that clutched and tore at their clothing.

Karla's breath came in short gasps.

One of the men caught a glimpse of Karla some 300 feet away as she slipped behind a tree. He raised his gun.

"Wait," the other one said. "I think they're circling back. We'll get them when they get closer to the parking lot."

Karla tugged on Mr. G's hand, "Stop a moment," she begged. "Let me catch my breath."

"No. We have to keep moving. These guys have guns. The sooner we get back to the car, the better off we'll be."

Mr. G and Karla neared the edge of the clearing that bordered the parking area. Staying just inside the tree line, they moved cautiously forward.

Mr. G stopped and listened as he pulled his gun. Minutes passed. Seeing and hearing nothing, he whispered to Karla, "Wait here, I'm going to take a look."

Warily, he stepped into the clearing. Seeing no one, he gestured to Karla, "Come on."

Karla ran to his side.

The two men jumped from the cover of the trees, guns poised.

Karla ran back toward the trees as Mr. G fired two quick rounds. Both shots hit one man squarely in the chest, knocking him backward. The shotgun flew out of his hands as he fell. The second man fired his pistol, grazing Mr. G's deltoid.

Mr. G cried out and dropped to one knee. He leveled his gun. "Drop it, Art!" he shouted.

Art dropped his pistol and bolted into the woods.

"Come on," he said to Karla, slipping his gun into his belt. We can't be here when the police arrive."

"You're hurt," she said with alarm. "We'd better get you to a hospital."

"No. No hospital."

"Why not?"

"How would it look for an upstanding, respected banker to be involved in a shoot out?"

As they reached his car, Mr. G was grateful that the people parked in the area were congregated at a Little League baseball game, shouting and cheering.

*   *   *

When they arrived at the hotel, the doorman opened Karla's door. Mr. G kicked his door open and exited, covering his left shoulder with his jacket.

Karla clasped his right arm and murmured, "Come up with me, darling. One last drink."

"Maybe we can order room service, too."

"Yes, yes, darling..." her voice trailed off as they walked into the lobby and into the elevators. If anyone had noticed their disheveled appearance, it wasn't obvious.

"Yours or mine?" she asked.

"Mine, I think. I have fresh clothing there. It's the tenth floor."

Karla punched the button for ten.

Once in the room, he tossed his jacket on the bed and sat down wearily.

With his right hand, he pulled off his tie as Karla unbuttoned his shirt and gently pulled it off. A lot of blood ran down his left arm. Bloody streaks had stained his white sleeve.

Karla dampened a towel in the bathroom, brought it out and carefully cleaned the arm, and gently dabbed at the open wound. She placed a wet washcloth over the wound and put his right hand over it. "Now you hold it like that until I return. I'm going down to the pharmacy to pick up a few things."

When she returned fifteen minutes later, he was still in the same position. She dumped the contents of a plastic bag on the table – tape, gauze, iodine, and a sling for his arm.

Picking up the iodine and removing the washcloth, she said matter-of-factly, "This is really going to hurt. So get ready."

"You couldn't find something that wouldn't hurt?" He teased.

"No. This is all they had, you big baby. Now come into the bathroom and put your arm over the sink."

He did what he was told, and when she poured the liquid iodine over the wound, he stiffened and gritted his teeth.

Blotting off the excess, Karla led him back to the chair, sat him down and dressed his wound. "Now how does that feel?" she asked.

"It's throbbing. But I can make it without any trouble. But now I am famished.

I wonder if everyone who gets shot also gets hungry."

"I don't know. I've never been shot. But if you'd like, I can order some food after I clean up this mess. In the meantime, I think you should lie down. So off with your clothes."

"That sounds interesting."

"Don't get any grandiose ideas, lover boy."

Stepping up in front of him, she unbuckled his belt, unzipped his pants and let them fall to the floor.

"Boy, I've never had service like that before."

"And you probably never will again." She smiled and winked.

Mr. G stood still, looking at her, not knowing what to expect. "What now?" .

"Nothing, except that you go directly to bed and you do not even pass 'go.'"

"Okay. But it seems that you're an expert at undressing men."

"First time," she said flatly.

"I'll bet."

"True."

Stepping out of his pants piled around his ankles, he sat down on the bed, asking, "Will you join me?"

"Absolutely not. I'm not that kind of girl. Besides, you need your rest."

"Yes, I suppose I do. I need to go back to Sal's place in the morning. I have work to do."

"I think you should rest for now, but if you have to go, I'll take you. You'll need help."

He knew he could handle it, but he did want her around, so he answered, "I guess I will need you. I hope you won't mind, and that you have the time."

"Like you said earlier, I'll just make the time."

"Why don't you come over for breakfast around seven?"

"Okay, but first I'll order some dinner for you, and then I'll see you tomorrow at seven."

*   *   *

"What in the world happened to you?" Sal questioned as he greeted Mr. G and Karla in the foyer of his home. Mr. G was wearing a sling tucked inside his jacket.

"A little shoot-out in Columbus Park after we left here yesterday. According to the paper, I killed one of them. I scared the other off, but not before he winged me. Can we talk privately?"

Sal nodded his head in the direction of the library. "Karla, go on into the kitchen over there." He pointed. "Kathy and Lisa are having breakfast. They like eating in there because Milly, my cook, spoils them with all the fattening foods they can eat. I tell them that one day they'll be big and fat like me."

Karla smiled and headed for the kitchen as Sal led the way into the library, asking over his shoulder, "Would you like some coffee or something?"

"No thanks, I'm fine." Again they sat down in the same places as the day before, Sal behind the desk and Mr. G in front. "Now, give it to me straight," Sal commanded.

"It was Arthur Bocha. I'm not sure why, but I know he was very jealous, even quite angry when you made me the bank manager. He felt he was more deserving and more qualified. And maybe he was."

"Maybe. But my friend Mooney Giancana made me promise I would put you in. He liked you; thought a lot of you. Besides, I liked you, too. Still do. A lot better than that slime-ball, Arthur."

"But why try to knock me off? He wouldn't gain. He's not in line for my job now, anyway."

"That may be true, but like you said, the question is: Why? I think he may be a little paranoid. He did always seem a little defensive. Maybe when I asked my son to pick up my books from him yesterday, he became suspicious."

"That could be. When Karla and I left yesterday, a black T-Bird followed us. At that time I didn't know who it was or even if they were following us, until I made a series of turns and they stayed with me."

"Well, Arthur's a dead man, now. Just leave him to me."

Mr. G didn't like knowing too much, but there was nothing he could do about it. Too much of the wrong kind of information could be very dangerous.

Mr. G tugged on his sling, "I guess I'd better get going on your books."

Sal's eyes narrowed. His forehead was pinched. "Not necessary now. He has already pled guilty."

Mr. G nodded his head. "I suppose you're right."

CHAPTER FIVE

Samuel G. Forrest sat on the edge of the bed and dialed Karla's room. After leaving Sal's estate, they had returned to their hotel to freshen up.

He had removed his sling and tossed it aside. He dressed in a fresh suit, shirt and tie and then had gone out for the evening with Karla. They had enjoyed a candlelight dinner at the Drury Lane South Theater in Evergreen Park and had returned to their rooms only an hour ago.

"I'm glad you called. I'm afraid I need to cancel breakfast tomorrow. I have to go to L.A. on an emergency business trip. I'm catching a seven-fifteen flight out of O'Hare and won't be back for a week. I hope you'll still be around."

"No, I can't stay. I was going to stay for a few extra days to be with you, but now I'll probably leave tomorrow afternoon."

"That's too bad. I'll give you my phone number for future use....well, in case you are in Chicago again sometime."

"Great. I'll give you a call next week. I'd love to have you come down to Champaign for a visit. I can show you off as my Chicago girlfriend."

As Karla chuckled over the phone, there was a light rapping on Mr. G's door. "Someone's at my door. Hang on a minute." He set the phone down on the night stand.

Wanting to quickly dispense with the interruption, he hurriedly stepped to the door. But as he opened it, it suddenly came crashing against him, knocking him to the floor. Arthur Bocha barged in, a Colt .45 automatic leveled at him. "Don't get up, Sam. Just stay there. And don't try any funny business, or it'll be your last." He elbowed the door shut. It swung to a position where the metal tumbler clicked against the strike plate but it didn't latch.

"Wait a minute, Art. We can work this out," Mr. G roared.

With snakelike-eyes, Arthur stared at him for a moment, a malevolent grin on his face. "You think you're so smart. I know what you're trying to do, and I won't let you."

"What are you talking about, Art?"

"What am I talking about? I'll tell you. First you steal the bank manager's job from me, that was rightfully mine. Now you're going over Sal's books trying to find any creative figuring. But even though you won't find any, because I'm much too clever, you'll lie to him, and that's all he needs. I'm dead meat. But before they get me, and they will eventually, I'm going to make sure you're in hell first."

Arthur took a couple of steps forward and took aim.

Mr. G squirmed a little to his left. "Are you crazy, Art? I have never tried to take anything from you.

I can't help what Sal does. He's the boss, not me. He controls everything, as you well know."

"Yes, but you make suggestions and recommendations that he listens to. And I'm sure that all of them favor you and make me look bad. Now, you'd better say your prayers, if you know how, because you have less than a minute." He straightened his arm. The big, black .45 automatic pointed toward the center of Mr. G's chest. The big black hole at the end of the barrel mesmerized Mr. G for a split second. Out of the corner of his eye, he noticed the door inching open. To distract Arthur, he held up one hand. "Wait a minute, Art. There is one thing you don't know."

"You're not going to trick me. Goodbye sucker," and started to squeeze the trigger.

Mr. G's eyes were glued to the slightest movement of Arthur's finger. He knew it was coming. He closed his eyes tightly. There was the explosion of the gun. He felt nothing. He shuddered.

"Sam," a soft voice broke through his moment of death. That voice was the most beautiful sound he had ever heard. He opened his eyes and saw Karla standing there, a small caliber pistol in her hand. Arthur lay at his feet with a gaping red hole in the back of his head. He had fallen forward, his head striking the floor between Mr. G's ankles. He pulled his legs away.

"You all right, Sam?" Karla asked. She knelt beside him.

"I'm pretty shaken. I didn't think you were going to get here on time," he whispered hoarsely. "That was too close."

"It was. I heard your conversation. I came as quickly as I could."

Mr. G was staring at her gun.

"It's a good thing I carry this, especially on business trips. You know what could happen to a woman alone on the road. But what do we do now?"

"I'll call Sal. He'll take care of it."

"Then I'm leaving, if you don't mind. I'd rather not be involved."

As the door clicked behind her, Mr. G got to his feet, and reached for the phone. *She probably wants to get away from all this*, he thought. *I don't blame her*.

After a half a dozen rings, a sleepy-voiced Mac answered. "Yeah?"

"This is Samuel Forrest. I need to talk to Sal."

"I'm sorry, I can't disturb him. He's asleep." His voice was curt and hard.

"This is an emergency, Mac. I know he will want to talk to me about this. "I'll take full responsibility for awakening him. Okay?"

"Well, okay. But it's your neck, not mine."

A few minutes later, Sal was on the line. "What's so important that you have to wake me in the middle of the night, Sam?" Sal was annoyed.

"I'm in my hotel room with a dead body."

"If you keep associating with these stiffs, you might wind up like them." Sal chuckled. "Who is it this time?"

"Art."

"Art Bocha?"

"One and the same. He came in here a little while ago with his big gun pointed right at me. If it hadn't been for Karla, I'd be dead now. She had to leave. Nervous, I guess. But what do we do with the body? It can't be found here."

"Okay, okay. I'll send Mac out. He'll take care of it. Wait in your room, and don't let anyone in."

"I don't think I'll have any callers. It's midnight."

"Just stay put. He'll knock once, then three times, and then once again. Got it?"

"Yes."

"Tomorrow, I mean today, when you get up, drive out here for a talk."

"Okay. And thanks, Sal. I really appreciate your help."

"We're family. Remember that. Good night, Sam."

"Good night."

*   *   *

Scarcely an hour and a half later, Mac arrived. He gave the secret knock, which Mr. G thought was a little silly. *But it's better to be safe than sorry,* he concluded.

Opening the door a crack, he eyeballed Mac. He was wearing a knit cap and light blue windbreaker, standing there with a laundry cart behind him. "You alone?" Mr. G whispered.

"Yeah. What d'ya think? I brought the cops?" Mac's sardonic voice seemed to echo down the hall.

"Shhhh..... keep your voice down and come in."

Mac stepped in, pulling the cart behind him and stopped just short of the body. "Never liked dis creep," he said, looking down at the corpse. "He got what's comin' to him, a real brainer."

Mr. G looked up quickly in surprise. If Mac had meant that as a pun, it didn't show in his stoic face. "What are you going to do with him?"

"Dump him in the Chicago River. But first you gotta help me load him."

Mac pulled some of the rumpled sheets from the top of the cart, bent over and easily picked up Arthur's upper torso. "You grab da feet," he said, motioning with his head.

Mr. G grabbed the ankles and lifted. They swung the body over the cart and dropped it in with a thud. He winced and grabbed his injured arm.

Mac didn't say a word, but immediately adjusted the body and legs so they all fit nicely in the laundry cart and then covered the body with the rumpled sheets. Then, pulling out a quart sized jar with clear liquid in it, he cleaned up the blood wherever he found it. Most of it was on the area rug; its flowered design helped disguise the spots left after cleaning.

"Sam," Mac said, "I'm gonna run innerference for you. I'm gonna lead, be in front of the cart. You push from behind, but you gotta wear dis cap, dis jacket and sunglasses. Okay?"

"Okay." Mr. G tried not to show his agitation.

"Yeah. Den nobody recognize ya."

Mac handed Mr. G the cap, the jacket, and sunglasses.

Moments later, Mac poked his head out into the hallway. He gestured for Mr. G to follow, then led the way to the service elevator. Mac pressed number "1" and waited.

When the elevator door opened on the ground level, the night watchman was standing there. He was in his late fifties, and overweight. The dark blue denim jacket that matched his pants was stretched to its limit. "What's going on here?" he questioned sharply. Before he could continue, Mac grabbed the night watchmen's neck and buried a fist deep into the man's protruding solar plexus. With a loud "oof," the man slipped to the floor, arms splayed.

"Come on," Mac ordered and led the way to his panel truck.

Following the speed limit carefully, Mac drove onto the Michigan Avenue bridge that spanned the Chicago River. He parked the truck on the bridge and turned off the lights and engine.

He rolled his window down and listened. It was quiet. No lights. No traffic. Nothing but dark, high-rise buildings and deserted streets on both sides of the river.

"Okay, let's do it," Mac commanded, getting out of the truck.

Mr. G's heart was pounding. He got out and went around to the back of the truck where Mac was already opening the doors. "We dump the whole thing, cart and all, on the count of three. How's dat arm?"

"I'll manage. Let's get this over with."

When Mac reached "three," Mr. G groaned as they lifted the cart onto the bridge railing and then gave it a shove. They watched it descend into the river below with a muffled splash.

Suddenly, fear gripped Mr. G. Headlights of an approaching car flicked on them. It had turned a corner two blocks away and was headed toward the bridge.

"Get in!" Mac yelled. "And duck down!"

Both men leaped into the truck and scrunched down as far as possible.

Mr. G could hear the car approach, slow down for a moment, and then move away from them. He realized that he had been holding his breath. "That was close," he muttered.

"Yeah. Now I take you out to the boss's house. You spend the night there and in the morning after you talk to him, I take you back to your hotel."

"I could just drive myself out there in the morning."

"How you gonna get in the hotel without being seen?"

"I see what you mean."

Mr. G didn't have a choice, besides Mac was already taking him out to Oak Park.

* * *

"I can't believe Art got past my two men. They were in your hotel lobby," Sal complained angrily. The morning sun shone through Sal's library window. Sal sat on the edge of his desk.

"Somehow he slipped by them," Mr. G reasoned. "He must have recognized them and come in the back way."

"Well, I'm glad it's over. You and your little lady did a great job. And for that reason, I have a little bonus for you." He handed him a fat envelope.

Without looking at it, he slipped the envelope into his jacket pocket. "Thanks, Sal. I appreciate that." Then shaking his head, Mr. G continued, "I thought I was a goner for sure. He caught me by surprise. I wasn't thinking when I opened the door. Good thing that Karla was armed. I knew if she had to call the police from her room, I'd be dead before anyone could get there."

"Probably so." Sal moved behind his desk and sat down heavily. "A lot of women today carry a piece. And I can't blame them, with all the weir-dos in the world."

The ringing of the phone interrupted them.

Sal answered, "Yeah?" He listened for a moment. "I have to go, Sam. Some other business. I'll have Mac take you back to your hotel. We'll talk more, the next time you come up. And keep up the good work."

CHAPTER SIX

It was late in the day when Samuel G. Forrest drove up his driveway. The afternoon sun slanted across his expansive lawn, casting long shadows that engulfed the front entrance to his house. It was a typically lazy spring day with bees buzzing and birds singing, but Mr. G was completely oblivious to it.

Earlier in the day when he had received the call from Sandy, his insides choked and fear had filled him, even though she had tried to reassure him that she was all right. She was his only child, a beautiful daughter. And after his wife died of cancer, he couldn't stand the thought of losing her. He wouldn't be totally free from fear and be able to relax until he had his darling daughter in his arms or in this case one arm. And now he had his good arm around her.

"What happened to you, Dad?" Sandy questioned with a worried expression on her face.

"I'm fine. I took a fall, but nothing serious. Just a torn ligament in the shoulder," he lied.

"Well, I'm glad we're both all right."

Tightening his grip around Sandy and pressing her head into his broad chest, he whispered compassionately, "I'm so relieved you're safe. The only fear I have in life is losing you. But you're unharmed and nothing else matters."

He pushed her out at arms length and looked at her tenderly, then wiped her tears away and for the first time noticed the young man standing in the doorway of the living room. "And who do we have here?" he asked.

Taking her father's arm, she said proudly, "Dad, this is Tony Garber. He's the one who saved my life."

"Well, young man," Samuel G. beamed as he walked over and took Tony's hand in both of his, "I certainly want to thank you, but that is not enough. There is no way I can express what I feel and how indebted I am to you. In fact, I owe you. I owe you big time!"

"No, sir. You don't owe me anything. I'm just glad she is safe, too," Tony answered looking at Sandy lovingly. "She's special to me, too, already."

Sam noticed the way they looked at each other, but pushed away the thoughts that followed. "However, I'll never forget what you did."

"Dad," Sandy broke in, "I've asked Tony to stay for dinner. That's all right, isn't it?"

"Of course. I'm glad you did. It gives me a chance to get to know him better."

"Great," Sandy said, "I'll go check on dinner then."

Both men watched as Sandy left the room. "Sit down. Tony. Would you like a drink of something?"

"No, thank you. Unless you're going to have something."

"I plan to have a glass of iced tea. Matty, our housekeeper, keeps a pitcher of it in this little refrigerator at the bar. I almost never drink alcohol. Only fools use it to alleviate their problems. All it really does is cause problems to escalate."

Tony ruminated for only a moment, then said, "Well as long as it's no trouble, I'll have a glass of iced tea, too."

"No trouble. Sugar and lemon?"

"I'll drink it any way you make it."

As Sam poured the ice tea, he asked, "What do you do, Tony?"

"I was running my father's hardware business. I was in school studying for my MBA when he had a heart attack, so I left school to help. But when my father died two years ago and my mother last year, I decided to sell the business and do something else. I haven't decided what, yet. But after meeting Sandy, I decided whatever it was I was going to do, it was going to be here in Champaign. I hope you don't mind."

"No, no. I don't mind. In fact, if there is anything that I can do to help, let me know."

"Actually, I hope you approve of my interest in Sandy."

"That would be Sandy's decision, not mine. But I do ask that you treat her with respect."

"Dinner is ready," Sandy announced. She had changed into a fresh, crisp, gingham dress with spaghetti straps.

Tony stared at her for a moment. *Stunning*, he thought, *just stunning! I can't believe the effect she has on me*. "Well, I'm famished," he admitted, standing and setting his glass on the table.

Sandy smiled. "Good," she said, "because we have plenty."

Mr. G. also smiled and stood. "After you, Tony."

*   *   *

With dinner complete, Sandy and Tony wandered out to the front of the house and sat side by side on the porch swing. The big orange ball of fire was sinking low in the west. High overhead a contrail streaked diagonally across the pale blue sky; its condensation beginning to spread as the vapors were blown askew by the jet stream.

Tony started to slip his arm around her, but was stopped as Sandy took his hand and held it in both of hers in her lap. "Not so fast young man," she said coyly, "we need to talk."

"About what?"

"Us."

"Okay. What about us?"

"Well, in the first place, I am very interested in you, but..."

"No buts," he interrupted. "I just..."

"Tony, listen. It's important to me."

"All right. Shoot."

"Look, we've only known each other a short time and I think you have an interest in me, too. Right?"

"Yes, big time."

"I think we should give it a little time, then we'll see. I imagine we could have a great time together."

"Me, too," he intoned passionately as he moved into position and started to pull her body close to his.

"Whoa," she said. "I think I've had enough excitement for one day."

"I think I'm falling in love with you."

"Maybe. It really is too soon to know. At least we have something to look forward to. Give it time. Then we'll see."

Sandy stood up, pulled him to his feet and walked an unhappy Tony to his car. He felt totally frustrated, but there was nothing he could do without losing her.

She reached up and gave him a peck on the cheek. *He looks so unhappy*, she thought. *But I have to be firm. It feels good, but....*

"I...I don't know what to say," he stammered.

"Just say good night, Tony. We need to make sure we're heading in the right direction."

"Okay. But...well..." Tony was definitely perplexed. "Can I call you tomorrow?"

"I certainly hope you will. Do you have any paper? I'll write down my phone number."

* * *

As Tony drove slowly down the driveway, Sandy watched the lights disappear around the bend. Her thoughts were pensive. She was not sure about her feelings. When she was with him her spirits soared. But now they were quiet and reflective. *He seems so right*, she thought, *but there is just something I can't put my finger on. Hmm... time will tell, I guess.*

* * *

Standing in the dark behind the sheer living room curtains, Mr. G. had watched Sandy and Tony. He hadn't liked Tony's reactions, but felt relieved when Tony had sat back again. He had mixed feelings. He was afraid Tony might try to go too far and for that reason he didn't trust Tony. He liked him, but when it came to his daughter he was extremely protective.

A hardened expression crossed his face as he thought, *I will do anything to protect her...anything.*

* * *

Tony was thinking, too. He didn't enjoy this frustration, either. *She's just too prudish,* he thought. *But I can break her down if given enough time.*

He smiled with the knowledge of his past conquests. *There were many and I had my way with almost all of them. My buddies used to laugh and call me, "Lover boy," because of my triumphs.*

Tony's smile increased as he drove toward Champaign, his new home.

CHAPTER SEVEN

The Chancellor Hotel was a multi-level brick structure with the highest level at seven stories. It was set back from Neil and Kirby Streets. Spotlights tucked behind shrubbery illuminated the building, giving it a warm, attractive appearance.

Tony checked in and went to his room. He was tired and confused. *I've got me a sweet little gal, even though she's a little goody two-shoes. But my biggest problem now is what to do. I could go back to school, but for what,* he thought, as he undressed for bed. *Now that I have all this dough, I don't want to work for someone else. I need a business of some kind. But what kind?*

He ran his hands over his face and through his hair. *I'll look for an apartment first, then get a newspaper and see which businesses are for sale.*

After brushing his teeth, he tried to switch on his night-light. It didn't work. *Must be burned out,* he thought. Ever since he was a child he had needed it. But tonight as he slipped into bed, he felt he was in trouble. *It's just an awareness,* he tried to convince himself, *so I won't trip when I have to go in the middle of the night.* He had always felt uneasy and disoriented in total darkness. The room seemed to close in on him. He had never been able to shake that feeling. He had tried to convince himself he had no problems with darkness, but the con had never worked.

The TV in the adjoining room went silent, and Tony lay on his back staring into the darkness. Only a sliver of light peeked in from a crack between the drapes. The total silence made it worse. He could almost hear his heart beating. The ever engulfing essence of silent darkness deepened his sense of loneliness, causing his apprehension to accelerate.

Every night as he lay in the dark, a phrase ran through his mind. "If I should die before I wake, I pray the Lord my soul to take." It haunted him whenever he was alone.

Tony tried to trivialize his thoughts. *How did that silly prayer go? Let's see.*

Now I lay me down to sleep.
I pray the Lord My soul to keep.
If I should die before I wake,
I pray the Lord my soul to take.

A stupid child's prayer. I've got to stop this, he scolded himself. *This is ridiculous. I'm a grown man, now.*

But one part of that prayer, "If I Should Die..." kept replaying over and over in his mind. What if I should die, he asked himself. He remembered what his mother had said about that.

"If you are a good boy," his mother tenderly declared, "you will go to heaven, but," and she always emphasized the "but," as she pushed the hair out of his eyes, "but if you are bad, you'll go to hell."

Tony knew he was going to hell, because he was always bad, not only as a child, but as an adult, too. At least I have to be honest about that, he admitted to himself. I lie to others all the time, but I'm usually honest with myself. Usually.

His thoughts and fears closed in on him until he realized he was gripping his pajamas and that he was bathed in sweat. He quickly jumped out of bed and opened the heavy drapes, but overcast skies and the large motionless trees outside allowed little light to enter the room.

He turned on the bathroom light, stripped, and stepped into the shower. He decided he'd leave the light on in the bathroom with the door partially open.

Later, with the light slanting across the foot of his bed, he slipped into a fitful sleep.

*   *   *

Late afternoon Tony finally called Sandy. Golden rays of sun filtered through the trees while birds sang their songs. A slight breeze rustled the leaves, making it difficult to spot the birds.

Tony had located a beautiful apartment to rent, but had not found a business that sounded interesting to him.

"Hello," came Sandy's sweet voice.

"Hi, Sandy. I'm at the Chancellor."

"Did you have a good night's sleep?"

"Yes," he lied. "And you?"

"Fine."

"Listen, Sandy, the Sunshine Dinner Playhouse, right here at the Chancellor Hotel, has a musical comedy performance tonight. What say we take it in?"

"Sounds great. What time?"

"We'll have dinner at six, then kick back and watch the show."

"Then I'd better get a move on, so I can be pretty for you."

"I'll bet you're always pretty, even in the morning."

"Maybe it's a good thing you haven't seen me in the morning."

"And just maybe some day I will. I'll pick you up at five-thirty. Okay?"

"See you then."

A play is not my first choice for a fun-filled evening, Tony thought as he hung up the phone, *but it's a good way to see her again. And just a short distance from my hotel.*

He felt a little embarrassed about his behavior when he was with Sandy yesterday. *What's wrong with me?* He asked himself. *I'm acting like a hard up school kid. I'm probably smothering her. I know better. I've always been successful with women when I've been laid back and relaxed and let the women be the aggressors. But then Sandy doesn't seem like the overly eager type, either.*

*   *   *

When Sandy answered the door, she was wearing a deep wine colored dress with white accents. Teasingly, she said, with a throaty impression of Greta Garbo, "Come in, Tony. You look very handsome."

He was wearing a navy blue jacket with a nautical emblem on the upper pocket, gray slacks, a pale pink shirt with a tie that had diagonal stripes of dark blue, reddish pink, and gray.

Now that she had stolen his thunder by complimenting him first, he didn't know what to say. Finally he blurted out, "You look good, too." Then warming up he added, "In fact you look ravishing. Those colors are you." "Thank you. They are especially good colors for blondes. And it's true that blondes have more fun, but not for the reasons most people believe. It's because we believe what we say."

Her smile broadened. "But where are my manners? Come in, Tony, come in."

He returned her smile. "Thank you," he said, bowing and then entering.

"My, but aren't we gallant tonight." She curtsied. "I shall runup stairs and powder my nose. I shouldn't be too long."

"Take as long as you like. I shall be refreshing myself after the long drive out here. Where are those needful little rooms?"

"There's one in Daddy's library over there." She pointed. "I don't think he's in there, but give a little knock first."

"Thank you, my dear," Tony said and strode off to knock.

Hearing no response, he entered, closing the door behind him. It was a large room with floor-to-ceiling bookcases on two sides. Enormous paintings decorated the wall near the door. On the far end a large cherrywood desk sat in front of a bay window, framed by blue flowered drapes. He then spotted the bathroom.

He was just putting the finishing touches to his hair, when he heard the outer library door open and then close. Tony couldn't see who had entered, but stuck his head out for a moment and recognized Sandy's father. He retreated quickly and continued combing his hair.

Samuel picked up the phone and dialed a number. A moment later he said, "Vinnie, this is Sam Forrest. What's this about my handling Cincinnati and Indianapolis money, too? I can't launder everybody's money. I'm already handling too much. It's too risky."

Tony's ears perked up. He moved closer to the door. A banker laundering money? Interesting. Very interesting.

When Tony stepped out of the restroom, Mr. G. stopped talking. "I'll call you back, Vinny."

Tony stood looking at Sandy's father with a slight grin.

"Do you always eavesdrop, Tony?"

"No, but I think a conversation about laundering money would catch anyone's attention. Maybe you should be a little more careful."

His eyes were steely gray as he looked hard at Tony. "My phones and this room are checked every day for bugs. And, no one ever uses my private bathroom."

"Oh, you don't have to worry. I won't say anything," Tony said insouciantly.

"I wasn't worried about you, Burt." That last word hung in the air in deadly silence.

Stunned, Tony took a sobering step backward. "What do you mean?"

"I know all about you, Burt. When we had iced tea together, I took the glass down to the chief of police, a very good friend of mine. It's amazing how fast they can get results back. Must be the new technology.

"You were in the Marines." Mr. G picked up the papers from his desk and scanning them, continued. "Four years. Anyway, as you know, the military always fingerprints you when you go in. Copies automatically go to the FBI. Hence, your record. In fact, the Chicago police are looking for you. It's very interesting."

Tony looked thoughtfully at him. "And now I know something interesting about you, too. It's a stand-off, I guess. So now what?"

"Now we talk. Not here. Not now, but tomorrow morning at the bank, in my office. Agreed?"

"Yes. Agreed."

"Two things before you go. First, the reason I didn't turn you in immediately was because of what you did by saving my daughter's life. Remember I said I owed you. Secondly, I'm very protective of my daughter. I don't mind your going out with her, as long as she wants to, but you'll respect her in every way. From what you've heard of my conversation on the phone, you must know I'm connected with the 'Outfit.' I just want you to know that if you ever hurt Sandy, I'll have you eliminated. And it won't be painless, either." His cold gray eyes never blinked.

He means it, Tony thought. A slight shiver ran up Tony's spine.

"Tomorrow I'll give you the reasons you don't want to try to take advantage of her in any way. And I might have an interesting proposal to offer you. I think you'll like it."

Tony wiped his sweaty palms on his pants. A lump formed in his throat. "Yes, Sir. I'll never hurt her. I think I'm falling in love with her. So you don't have to worry about me. I'll take good care of her, if she'll have me."

Tony turned to go. His knees trembled. Then nervously he said, "I'll see you in the morning, Sir."

*   *   *

Tony's demeanor had sobered considerably. Sandy seemed worried about him. "Are you all right, Tony?"

"Sure," he lied. "I'm okay. Just a little unsettled because of a business venture I'm considering." It's your father, he wanted to shout in her face, but he felt sure she didn't know what he was involved in, so why upset her, and ruin his chances?

I shouldn't have been such a pansy with Sandy's father, he thought as they drove into town. *On the other hand, I'll need to keep my trap shut, if he is what I think he is. He mentioned he was connected, the "Outfit," formerly called the Mob, the Syndicate, Cosa Nostra.* His thoughts stopped on that note, then continued. *He must be laundering money for the Outfit in Chicago. This is just great. Now what do I do?*

Sandy's voice filtered through his thoughts. "Tony, Tony! Are you listening?"

"Yeah. What's up?"

"You've been off in la-la land."

"I'm sorry. It's just that I have some important business on my mind. I guess I'm not good company tonight."

"You seemed happy when you first arrived at the house."

"Yeah, but I made a call from your house," he lied again. "And that's when the problem arose. It's too involved to explain. Maybe I'll tell you about it, sometime."

"Maybe we should put off our date until tomorrow night."

"But I don't want to disappoint you."

"Oh, I don't mind. I understand these things happen. It does all the time with Daddy. Besides, I'd rather have all your attention. So please turn this car around and take me back home. I'll plan to see you tomorrow night. Okay?"

"Okay," he sighed. "I should have it all settled by then."

Yeah, settled, he thought, *but how? I know too much.*

*   *   *

The Republic Bank of Champaign was a massive gray building adorned with round columns and decorative ornamentation. But Tony was unaware of his surroundings. He couldn't imagine what Samuel G. Forrest would be offering, if anything.

He asked for Mr. Forrest and was led to a secretary in the back part of the bank who instructed him to sit and wait.

It was a full five minutes before Mr. Forrest opened his office door. He smiled. "Come in, Tony," he said expansively, pulling Tony in with a handshake and closing the door behind him. "Have a seat." He motioned toward a plush leather chair in front of his desk.

Tony sat down, still feeling very inquisitive and apprehensive. "Thank you, Sir." The fear that started as a little knot in his stomach had grown to full stature, again. He knew he would say "yes" to whatever this man would ask.

"I hope that what I said last night was not too upsetting," Mr. Forrest stated after sitting down behind his desk. "It was meant as a warning only. In fact, Tony, I like you. You're an enterprising young man, just as I was at your age. I think we have much to offer each other."

I like you? Tony's thoughts questioned. *I don't believe that for a minute. It's gotta be a snow job. But, why?*

"But let me give you a little of my background so you know where I'm coming from," continued the banker. "My mother, God rest her soul, was one of the dancers at the Chez Paree, a first-class night club in Chicago, during World War Two.

"One night one of the waiters came to her dressing room and told her that Mooney Giancana wanted to meet her. But she didn't even know who he was. It's Samuel 'Mooney Giancana,' he told her. He was only the most powerful mobster in Chicago. She went out and met him, thinking he might help her career. Well, one thing led to another, and I was conceived.

"My mother told me that Mooney was proud of the fact that he finally had a boy. His wife, Angeline, produced three daughters, but no sons. That's why he doted on me so much. He wanted to groom me to take over some day, but Mamma made him promise not to get me into the 'Outfit.' Too many die, she said. So Mooney came up with this idea of having me become their banker. He took care of Mom and me. Not even his brother, Chuck, nor the inner circle of the 'Outfit' knew this.

"And that's where I got my name—Samuel Giancana Forrest.

Tony finally understood. That's why he goes by Mr. G.

"The only time he ever whipped me was when he caught me smoking," Mr. G continued. "A friend had sneaked a couple of cigarettes from his dad's pack. We took a few puffs, then threw them away. A few moments later, Mooney stopped by to see me and Mom. He picked me up, but then set me down hard. 'You been smoking!' he screamed at me. I was totally dumbfounded. I couldn't figure out how he knew. After he slapped my butt and I cried for a few minutes, I asked him how he knew. 'I know everything,' he told me. 'You're not gonna get away with anything with me. Understand?'

"Of course, I agreed with him. In fact, I always agreed with him.

Samuel G. sighed. "That's it."

"But why did you tell me all this?" Tony asked.

"Because," he answered, rising to his feet and starting to pace the floor. "I wanted to be open with you. I wanted you to know where I came from and what you'd be getting into if you should elect to accept my idea. There is nothing in what I've told you that you could use against me, except to muddy up my name or hurt my Sandy. She would be devastated if she knew what I was doing and with whom I am associated. But I don't think you would want to mess my life up that way, because of what you know I'd do to you. You can't enjoy life when you are wearing cement shoes at the bottom of Lake Michigan. And I believe you want to live your life to the fullest. Proof of that was when you pulled that big job up north. Sometime you'll have to fill me in on how you did it, exactly. But enough said about that for now."

Tony pressed his back up against the chair, wishing he could get away from this man.

"Now to my proposal, Mr. G said with a slight smile. "A friend of mine who owns a private detective agency just had a heart attack. His assistant is running the business now. This assistant is an excellent man, but has no money to buy the business. And this friend, Jonathan Holmes, needs to sell it to pay for medical expenses and retire. He knows who I am and does a lot of work for me, not all of which is legal. Oh, he hasn't taken too many chances, but...

"Anyway, I think this could be a great business for you, if you are interested. His assistant would be more than happy to train you personally. And I would continue to throw bank business your way, like skip and locates. That's one of our legitimate jobs, to find people who owe us and have skipped out on paying. There are plenty of others as well. If fact, they have over thirty agents now who do all types of investigations, for different insurance companies.

Samuel G stood and stepped behind his high backed, leather chair and rested his hands on it. He looked straight at Tony and said, "He wants half a million for the business, and it's worth every cent of it. He had a net-net of over a hundred grand after taxes, not counting what I paid him and what others paid him under the table."

Tony nodded, but didn't say anything.

"And here is the kicker. I'll launder all that money you have stashed someplace for ten cents on the dollar. The going rate is twenty. That'll save you a quarter of a million and pay for half your new business up-front.

"You may be asking why I would do that for you. Well, if another person bought the business and was totally legit, I might have a hard time finding someone I could trust without going to Chicago, and that's too far away. I believe I can trust you for obvious reasons.

"Now it's your turn." He sat down and waited for Tony's answer.

"I really like the idea, especially about laundering my money. I haven't been able to use any of it in sizable amounts. It's too dangerous. They're looking for someone buying with large amounts of cash. That's why I'll be renting an apartment, hopefully today. But I'm not sure about being a private cop. I have no experience."

"That's where Jonathan's assistant, Bobbyo, would come in," Samuel G. explained. "He has trained almost all the employees working there. When he finishes, you'd know the business like the back of your hand."

Tony looked at the back of his hand without actually thinking about it. "Okay. But before I make any final decision, I'll need to look over the business and the books."

"Of course. If it's all right with you, I'll call up Bobbyo and see if he's available. I did talk to him earlier this morning and said I might be up with someone who is interested. The business is located on the third floor of this bank building.

"Also, from now on you can call me Mr. G. All my associates do." He smiled magnanimously.

A few minutes later, they went out into the foyer of the bank building and took the elevator up to the third floor. The plaque on the door displayed, "Holmes Detective Agency ." After stepping inside, they were met by Bobbyo, who ushered them into his office. The brass nameplate on his desk was engraved Donald Bobbyo, Ass't. Mgr.

Bobbyo was an intimidating young man, probably in his early thirties. He was big, real big. Six feet seven, to be exact. His square head was topped with short brown hair, parted on the left side. His massive shoulders and chest declared his muscles, even under a white shirt with a tie hanging loosely from the throat. When Tony shook hands with him, his hand felt dwarfed.

He should be a guard for the Bears, he *thought. I'm just glad that I'm not the quarterback on the other team.*

Tony was expecting a guttural growl from Bobbyo, and was surprised by his lazy Texas drawl.

"Well, it's nice to meet you, Tony." The "well" sounded like "wahl," the way Jimmy Stewart would have said it.

Tony nodded as he looked around the office. Wood paneling decorated the wall behind the couch and large windows offered a view of the city. "Tell me about this business."

Samuel G. sat quietly as Bo, behind his desk, thoughtfully stroked his chin and explained the business to Tony. "We're a fee company. We primarily do insurance inspections. We've broken it up into three divisions. The first is domestic. It deals with the public generally; individuals who employ us in divorce cases, surveillance for one reason or another, and other types of investigations on a personal basis. It's the smaller stuff."

Bobbyo took a deep breath, then continued. "Secondly, we're hired by various insurance companies. We inspect various properties, like high-value dwellings, and businesses. The value on homes has to be five hundred thousand bucks and above, even into the multi-millions. The insurance companies want to know what the approximate replacement cost would be, such as all the extras like marble flooring, chandeliers, expensive counter tops, et cetera. Plus, what kind of security system they have. We have trained people to do this.

Tony nodded.

"Another thing. You know those medical-release slips you sign when applying for life insurance or medical insurance? Well, we use those to get medical records from the doctors. Our agent goes into the doctor's offices and copies all the records the doc has on the patient. Insurance companies pay us to do that, too.

"Also we do workman's comp claims, too. We investigate people collecting compensation to make sure they're entitled to it."

Bobbyo pulled on his chin again in thought. "We also do audits on businesses for the insurance companies. I think that's all for that division.

"Boy," Tony stated. "That's a lot of different types of inspections."

"But not all of it. Division three is the big stuff. We do employment investigations for high-profile jobs of large corporations and some government agencies such as the overflow from the FBI. We don't get the high security investigations from the FBI, but mostly people who are not exposed to top secret info.

"You'd be surprised at how much we can learn about a person today. We have the most sophisticated computer equipment available. We have six computer hacks that don't do anything but sit at their computers and spin out reams of info about people or businesses. They can penetrate most agencies, county, state or federal. You know about the Freedom of Information Act. Well, we use it all the time.

"Also, you remember the OJ Simpson trial? There was a lot of investigatory work done by the prosecution and the defense. We do the same. We don't do any for the DA's office, but a lot for the defense attorneys.

"That's just part of what we do. You have any questions?"

"Yes," Tony answered, "but first I want to say that was an excellent overview."

"Thank you."

"My only question is: Where are the books?"

"Right here. Knowing you might ask for them, I dug them out."

Bobbyo picked up a stack of large ledgers from a table next to him and set them in front of Tony, who glanced at them and picked out the current year and started to read.

It didn't take him long since he really didn't know what to look for. Looking up, he said, "I'm just looking at the bottom line, and it all looks good." Turning to Mr. G. he asked, "Have you looked these over, Mr. G?"

"Yes, I have. Jonathan asked me to check them out after his heart attack when he realized he wouldn't be able to do the work anymore. As a friend, I was happy to oblige."

"Is this a sound investment in your opinion?"

"Without a doubt. I figure the business to be worth about six hundred thousand dollars. But Jonathan said he would sell for five hundred thousand, to make a quick sale."

"With your endorsement, Mr. G, I accept. Just write it up, and I'll sign."

On the way down in the elevator, Mr. G turned to Tony. "You'll have to bring that money in."

"No problem. I'll have it for you in an hour. Then I'll have to establish a checking account. I'll need it to rent my new apartment."

"Hold off bringing the money in until tonight, around six-thirty. I'll tell my night watchman, Benny, to let you in. All of the others will be gone by then. I don't want too many eyes or ears around. Benny's okay. He's a little hard of hearing. By then I'll have a checking account opened for you and explain the rest."

CHAPTER EIGHT

That evening, the night watchman let Tony in. He was a man in his early fifties with lifeless gray hair combed straight back. Bushy gray eyebrows covered pale blue-gray eyes. *He's a gray nonentity*, Tony thought.

Benny went back to his sweeping.

Mr G came out of his office. "Would you like a cup of coffee, Tony?"

"Sure."

Mr. G poured the coffee, and went back into his office. Tony followed.

It took Mr.G almost an hour to count the money, even though he used a bank money counter. Finally he looked at Tony. "This is the way it works. Have you ever heard of the Internet?"

"Yes, but I don't know anything about it, except it's a large data base, accessed only by computer."

"That's right as far as it goes. But there's much more to it. The U.S. Defense Department set it up for their own purposes back in 1969 or 1970. They gave it the name of Advanced Research Project Agency. They knew that if all military information and communications poured through one computer location it was open to sabotage or nuclear destruction and a loss of all data. They believed that if they would set up a series of computer centers, one equal to the other, it would minimize or totally eradicate the chances of loss of data. If one is destroyed, the others still have the same info, thus the Internet.

"The National Science Foundation got into the act. They built a number of super computers. I think it was five, located in various parts of the country. This was in the nineteen eighties. They wanted to connect all the universities together for research purposes.

Mr. G loosened his tie, and continued. "When the universities started to use this system for mail between the universities, electronic mail, or E-mail was created.

Tony sipped his coffee.

"Next, businesses saw the potential and became involved. It wasn't long before all of them started coming together. It's been exploding ever since, and now we have a super-highway of electronic marvels.

Tony was impressed. "Amazing," he said.

"One group of entrepreneurs decided to start an Internet Bank, a depository for digital money. It's still in its infancy, but the possibilities are enormous. My bank here has just become involved with it. Most banks are coming on line. We'll be expediters. As a depositor, if you want to buy a house, car or just want some cash from your account, we would issue a cashiers check or plain good ol' cash.

"If this is agreeable with you, we'll put your money into the Internet Bank. It will be an invisible account, protected by cryptography, a process that scrambles information electronically so that no one, not even government experts, can de-code it. Only you will have access to your ac-count records through a program called PGP. In your encryption code you can use as many numbers and letters you want as a pass-word. Each letter indicates the corresponding num-ber that goes with it. For example, A equals 1, B equals 2, and so on all the way to Z, which equals 26. Your chances of winning the lottery are fourteen million to one, when you pick six of fifty-five numbers. If you used the Gettysburg Address, the odds would be in the billions. It's safe."

"That's awesome." Tony was shaking his head. "But how do you do it? Getting this money into that account."

"It's simple," Mr. G explained. "I'll open a num-bered account for you at the Internet Bank and transfer money from this bank into it. The amount transferred will be replaced with your money at this bank." He pointed to the counted piles on his desk. "Next, you insert your code, and it's done. No one will know about that account, but you. Even the people at Internet Bank will not know. It'll only be an account number to them."

"I like the idea. Let's do it." *Talk about being in the right place at the right time*, thought Tony, *I certainly was when I saved Sandy's life and met her father.*

Straightening his tie, Samuel G. said, "As I said I would, I have had temporary checks printed for you already. I will be depositing fifty thousand in your account for you. I also have drawn up a cashier's check for five hundred thousand for the purchase of your new business. I'll also need two signature cards from you, one for your personal account and one for the Holmes Detective Agency, so you can write checks on either account."

Mr. G pushed two signature cards in front of Tony.

"Looks like you have everything all set up," Tony remarked as he signed the cards.

Samuel G. nodded, then handed Tony the temporary checkbook and a deposit receipt for $1,695,000. "As you can see," he pointed with a pencil, "two and a half million to start. Two hundred fifty grand to me for my trouble; five hundred thousand for the business; fifty in your checking account; and a little over five you kept out in cash. Your balance, one mil, six hundred ninety-five grand, which will be in your Internet account. Any questions?"

"No," Tony said as he examined the receipt carefully. "That sure reduced my nest egg."

"You still have all of it, except for my fee, which really gives you two mil, two hundred fifty thousand in cash and equity. Not bad for a young man your age."

"I guess not," Tony said with a smile that expanded until it almost cracked his face.

*　　*　　*

The next morning Tony signed the lease agreement on the Maynard Lake Suite, a fancy apartment building overlooking the lake on the front side and the Lincolnshire Field Country Club and its rolling green fairways on the back side, between Lakeshore Drive and Stoney Brook Drive.

He loved the view, which Sandy was now admiring. "Two gorgeous panoramic pictures from your two balconies."

"That's true, but what I need now is an interior decorator to dress this place up. Have any ideas? If you aren't interested in doing it," he said, simpering. "I imagine you could recommend someone."

"Do you really mean that, Tony? You want me to decorate this...this beautiful place? I'd love to, but I've never done anything like this before. I don't think I could do it justice."

"Well, why don't you pick out someone with experience to help you? Kind of give you guidance, so to speak."

Sandy threw her arms around him, squealing with delight.

*　　*　　*

Later that morning, Tony was sitting behind his desk at the Holmes Detective Agency.

Bobbyo was sitting across from him, leaning forward and explaining what kind of inspections they would be doing. "First, I'm gonna audio tape today's work."

"Isn't that illegal?"

"Not if you agree to it, but we're gonna tape it so you can study it as long as you need to.

"We can start with the easiest ones, if it's okay with you. Then we'll work our way up the ladder to the hardest ones. They're a lot more complicated."

"That's fine with me. I need to learn them all, Bob. Or would you prefer Bobby or Bobbyo?"

"Why don't you call me Bo; most of my friends do."

"Okay, Bo. And you can call me Tony."

Tony liked Bo already and it seemed to be a mutual feeling between them. Nothing had been said about it. It just happened.

Bo was pulling on his chin again, in thought. Then he stood and said matter-of-factly, "You'll learn faster in the field than if I try to teach you verbally."

Tony followed Bo through the outer office. The various employees they passed smiled. Bo had introduced him to the staff earlier at a special get acquainted-meeting with coffee and doughnuts.

Bo drove his company car to the first stop, a small, single story, stucco home with a gravel roof. "This is it," Bo stated as he looked down at the insurance company's inquiry. "It's a skip and locate.'"

He pointed at the name. "Ronald Skinnerman, here, took out an unsecured note for five thousand dollars from the Northside Fidelity Loan Association. When his business went under, he skipped out, disappeared. And Fidelity wants its money back. We need to find out where he is and where he works. This place is his mother's home. I'll talk to her. You just listen."

Bo led the way up the short sidewalk that divided a sparse and patchy lawn and rang the bell. The old stucco surrounding the door was chipped off, exposing some of the lath underneath. At first Tony thought no one was at home, but finally he heard a shuffling behind the door. It opened a crack, and one eye and a thin nose poked out.

"What d'ya want?" a crotchety voice asked.

"Mrs. Skinnerman?"

"Yeah."

"Well, Ma'am, I'm an insurance inspector, and I need to get a hold of your son, Ronald."

"Well, I don't know where he is," she said harshly, still looking through the crack in the door.

"That's really too bad, because of the good news I have for him."

"Good news? What do you mean? You're not from the bank, are you?" She opened the door a little farther, revealing a woman in her sixties with a cadaverous body. Her gray hair was put up in bobby pins and she had a narrow, bony nose above thin lips.

"No, Ma'am. Like I said, I'm an insurance inspector. I don't work for any bank."

The woman gave a crooked-toothed smile as she said in a syrupy voice. "He got some money coming or something?"

"I can't divulge that information, Ma'am, but it is very important for him." Bo smiled warmly.

"How much's he gettin'?"

Again Bo was smiling. "I can't reveal that, either."

"Well, since you're not from the bank, I suppose I can tell you. You know how it is. People all the time stickin' their noses in where it's not wanted," she beamed now. "He lives over on First Street at eight oh five. Eight oh five First Street," she repeated."

"Great! I'll go right over and see him."

"You'll have to wait until tonight. He's at work now."

"That's too bad, because I can't go over there tonight. Maybe I should stop by where he works and take care of this."

"Sure. He works for the Thompson Computer Discount Outlet over on Ward Avenue and Halsey Boulevard. He's the foreman there. Tell him to call me."

"I'll do that, Ma'am. And thank you."

Back in the car, Tony exclaimed as they pulled away from the curb, "That was smooth, real smooth. I loved the way you guided her to get the info you wanted."

Bo was grinning from ear to ear. "I didn't say he was going to get any money. She assumed it. The rest was easy. When people get greedy they'll talk, even the smart ones.

"She was real cantankerous. Changed to sweetness when she thought her darling son was going to come into some money. And she probably thought it would be a lot of money, coming from an insurance company.

Tony held up his hand., "But you're a private eye or investigator, not an insurance inspector. And how can you say you're not working for the bank, when you are?"

"Actually, I work for you. I'm not employed by the bank. Secondly, we can label ourselves according to what we do, and we do insurance inspections, so..." he waved his hand. "So it's okay."

Tony nodded his head in understanding. But his mind kept going over the technique Bo had used. He realized how clever it was. This was something he knew he could do and do well.

"The next one," Bo explained after driving awhile, "is an insurance inspection. We've done all the work needed for the insurance company except we need to find out what kind of work he does. If it's something dangerous, they'll have to charge more premium. But the company he works for, the Arlington Aircraft Corporation, refuses to give us that information. It's their policy. So we'll have to find out from his wife. Again, just listen, okay?"

Tony didn't answer. He just nodded again, lost in thought until they pulled up in front of a two-story house, shaded with large oak trees. It had a three-car garage and a slate tiled roof. A middle-aged blond woman in white shorts and red blouse was watering her lawn, soaking up the sun's rays.

When they walked up to her, Tony could see that time was catching up to her; the lines splashing out from the corners of her eyes showed this; the beginnings of a double chin revealed it; and the thickness of her waist announced it, also. She had been a beauty once, but still was very attractive.

"Can I help you gentlemen?" She had an engaging smile.

"Yes, Ma'am. Are you Mrs. Lightman?"

"Yes." The smile was gone, replaced by curiosity.

"I'm an insurance inspector, Ma'am, and I was wondering if I could ask you a few questions."

"I'm sorry, but my husband told me not to answer any questions from insurance people or anyone else, unless I knew them."

"Oh, well, that's all right, Ma'am. I understand. Thanks, anyway."

Her smile reappeared as they turned to leave. Then suddenly Bo spun around and asked, "Just one thing. Your husband does work for Todd Company, doesn't he?"

"No. He's with Arlington Aircraft."

"Well, how long has he been there?"

"Nineteen years."

"And he tests their aircraft every day?"

"No, no. Maybe once a month, no more."

Bo gave her one of his disarming smiles and said, "Thanks again, Ma'am."

"And again, I'm sorry I couldn't help you."

"That's okay. You have a good day, Ma'am."

Bo was driving down the oak-lined street with a slight grin on his face, when Tony finally spoke. "You did it again, Bo, as slick as can be. She didn't even know what she was saying. She gave you exactly what you needed."

"That's right. There are a lot of tricks to the trade. And you'll learn them all before long. For example," Bo continued, "if she had not given me the info, I would come back a little later and talk to the neighbors. If they're friends with the insured, they'll know about his work. People like to brag. And a test pilot will let the neighbor know how dangerous his job is. It's as simple as that."

*   *   *

After lunch, Bo and Tony headed for their next stop. "This is a workmen's comp case," Bo expounded. "This man has been collecting from the insurance company a couple of years for a bad back. We need to find out if he's legit. If he is...fine. If not, we need some proof he's not. The insurance company thinks he's faking, but they have to be sure. They don't want any lawsuits."

Bo pulled to the curb in front of a narrow, three-story frame house.

Probably built in the 1920s, Tony thought. *In fact, every house on the street looks that old.*

"This is not where the insured lives," Bo explained. "He lives a few houses down and across the street. We won't talk to him, just to neighbors."

When the doorbell didn't work, Bo knocked on the door. A moment later, it was opened by a woman almost as wide as she was tall, wearing a large flowered tent that covered her adequately, but still did not hide her multiple rolling hills.

"Yeah?" she questioned briskly.

"We're insurance inspectors, Ma'am. And we're doing a follow-up on Mr. Haversham, just down the street. Do you know him?"

"Sure. Why?"

"Well, if you owned your own life insurance company, would you feel he was healthy enough so that you'd be willing to issue him a large life insurance policy?"

She hesitated a moment. You could almost see the wheels turning. "I'd issue him as much as he wanted. He's in real good shape, a fine gentleman."

"But what about that accident he was in a few months ago?"

"Oh, he's completely recovered now. No more problems. Last week he painted his whole house.

This week he's putting on a new roof. In fact, there he is," she said pointing to a man climbing a two-story extension ladder and carrying a fifty-pound bundle of roofing shingles.

Tony and Bo turned in unison and looked. Sure enough. The man had reached the roof and was removing the first shingle. A moment later he nailed it just above the previous shingle, near the peak of the roof.

"Well, I declare," Bo remarked as he returned to the fat lady. "That man sure must be in good health, like you say. You were absolutely right. And I want to thank you, Ma'am. You certainly have been a big help."

"I'm just glad I could," she snuffled as she wiped her nose on her sleeve. "He's a good man."

Back in the car, Bo pulled forward about fifty feet and stopped the car. He pulled out a video camera and pointed it at the man on the roof. Slowly the zoom lens moved in. "I need a closeup of his face," Bo muttered. "For identification purposes."

A few moments later Bo brought the camera back into the car, then waited until the man started down the ladder. As he neared the bottom rung, Bo started shooting again.

As Mr. Haversham stepped off the ladder, picked up another fifty-pound bundle of shingles and turned, he spotted Bo with the camera. "Hey," he shouted, dropping the bundle. "What're you doing?" He started to walk toward them in determination, quickening his pace.

Calmly, Bo put the camera down, put the car in gear and smoothly made a U-turn as the man ran after them, swearing and shaking his fist.

"Why run away, Bo? You could have handled him easily."

"Sure, but we try to stay away from physical contact. Because of who we are, we have to keep our noses clean to prevent the cancellation of our licenses. He's not worth the trouble."

"I suppose not. I guess it's just a matter of pride, with me."

"Well, pride can get you into a lot of trouble."

"Well, if I had your muscles, I'd have confronted that guy. He probably would have backed off when he saw how big you are."

"Maybe," Bo chuckled. "I'm a black belt. I know I could put him down without any problem. But it's better not to have any kind of confrontation."

"Did you say you're a black belt?"

"Yes. I've been studying martial arts for years.

"Do you work out a lot?"

"Sure. Most days."

"Do you think I...could sort of tag along sometime?"

"Of course. In fact, I'll be attending a session this afternoon. It's a lot of strenuous work, but after awhile you get use to it."

*   *   *

He was exhausted when he arrived home, and plopped down on his couch, placing his sore feet up on the coffee table. I'll just rest here for a minute before I shower. He closed his eyes and without realizing it drifted off to sleep.

It was dark when he bolted upright into his worst nightmare, his consuming fear of the dark. He was drenched in sweat, confused, not remembering where he was. Fear engulfed him. He took a step forward, tripped over the coffee table, stumbled, and hit his forehead a sharp blow on something, but he didn't know what. He grabbed his head. "Oh, my God, where am I?" He could feel the stickiness of what he assumed was blood. In a panic, he jumped up. His head began to spin violently, and he fell back to the floor. "I've got to find a light switch," he mumbled. "The door, the door. There's always one by the door."

Tony rolled over onto all fours, and began to crawl. His head pounded, and he could feel something dripping off his nose. Blood, I guess. I'm still dizzy. He bumped into a chair. Behind the chair, he found a wall, and followed it, until he came to a door. He put his hand out to feel it. Hinges. Other side. Door nob. Up and to the right. Ah... He flicked the switch, and the light exploded into his face. He was directly in front of a lamp, sitting on an end table.

Tony rolled over, and sat down on the floor, his back to the door, and looked at the blood on his hands. He was angry with himself. *Every time this happens to me, I swear I'll never let it happen again, but...*

*   *   *

They drove to their first inspection the next morning. Tony had used a light makeup on his face and the bruises didn't show much.

Bo glanced at Tony. "Marty, the martial arts instructor, told me you're a natural; you have good moves, learn fast, everything it takes to become a master. We're from the 'hard school,' which accents power and strength. The 'soft school' features speed and precision.

"Our style is called Aidido, which is more complex than most karate techniques. It is mainly used in self defense, but also helps to develop our coordination of mind and body. We are taught how to subdue an attacker without inflicting injuries."

"That's the part I want to learn."

"You need to study all of it. It'll help you mentally and physically, to put the whole man on track."

Tony thought about it a few moments. "That makes sense." *But he wasn't sure how he wanted to use it. However, more than anything he wanted to have it.*

Bo interrupted Tony's thoughts. "This is the street where our next victim lives." He chuckled. "Her name is Mona Shulty. She's collecting Workmen's Comp, too. Only it's her heart, not the back. This is routine. The insurance companies check on these people periodically. Why don't you take a crack at it. You game?"

"Sure, why not. Got to get my feet wet sometime."

Bo explained the general questions he needed to ask. "If you get stuck, just turn to me. I'll explain that you're a trainee. No problem."

As they walked up to the front porch of the house, which was a two-story frame dwelling, Tony noticed that the door was wide open. He leaned forward to ring the bell, but stopped suddenly as a frumpy woman in a flowered print dress, covered with an apron, vigorously stomped down the stairs from the second floor carrying a pail full of dirty water and a mop. Her straw-colored hair, which was pulled back into a bun with wisps falling loosely on the sides, surrounded a round, ruddy face. "I'll be with you young men in a minute," she said a little breathless. "An accident in one of my tenant's apartments upstairs."

Tony grunted in acknowledgment. Bo was standing slightly behind him and to his left. They watched as the woman entered a small bathroom off the hallway and emptied the bucket. A moment later she was quickly clomping her way up the stairs again. A few moments later, she was on her way down again.

After dumping the second pail, she set it down on the old wooden floor, puffing a little from her exercise. Wiping her hands on her apron she beamed, "Now, what can I do for you gentlemen?"

"We're insurance inspectors, Ma'am, and..." He stopped when he saw her expression. The smile disappeared and her face registered shock.

"Uh...uh," she mumbled. "I...I..." She staggered for a moment and then slipped to the floor in a heap.

Tony momentarily was startled and just stared at her, when Bo stepped past him and picked her up in his arms. He easily carried her through an open door off the hall and laid her on a couch.

"My pills," she whispered, pointing to her purse on the floor.

Tony had recovered by this time and brought the purse.

"Water," she murmured as she fumbled for her pills in the big, black purse.

"Do you want me to call nine-one-one?" Bo asked as he knelt next to her.

She looked up at him and nodded.

As the ambulance drove away with Mrs. Shulty, Tony said, "That has to be the biggest act I've ever seen. She's a phony." His voice registered disgust.

"I don't doubt it for a minute," Bo retorted, "but what if we accused her and then we found out it wasn't an act? In that case, she could have died, and it could have been our fault."

"Could have, shmud have. So what do we do now? Tell the insurance company that she's a phony?"

"Nope. We're not doctors. We're inspectors. We tell the insurance company exactly what happened and what she said and what we said. Nothin' more, nothin' less. We let them decide what to do, if anything. But my guess is that they'll order a thorough physical by their own company doctor, not her physician. Her fraudulent days are probably numbered." He laughed heartily and Tony joined him.

On the way back to the office, Bo stopped at his favorite bistro to have a bowl of chili con carne along with a cup of coffee. "You ought to try the chili. It's great."

"Naw," Tony said frowning. "I'll pass. I don't like the hot stuff, but I'll have a hamburger and a cup of coffee."

After ordering, Tony looked around the long narrow room. Tables were located on one side and a customer counter bar on the other. The cooks were visible behind an order window. The front window displayed the establishment's name in reverse, Bab's Beanery. On both sides of the door were red, blinking neon beer signs. "You always eat at these fancy places?" Tony laughed.

"Sometimes on a whim I'll eat at a less showy place. If I want to impress someone, though, I bring'em here."

"So that's why we came here. You just wanted to impress me."

"That's right." Both men were grinning.

The waitress brought their food. Her name was plainly etched on a name tag pinned to her blouse.. "Hello, Irene," Bo said with a big smile.

"Hi, there," she answered, returning his smile. Noticing their suits, she asked, "What do you guys do?"

"We're with the CID. A government agency," Bo answered.

"Oh," she responded. She abruptly scurried off when the cook called her name.

"What's with this CID stuff," Tony questioned?

"I was wondering about the cubic inch dis-placement of the engine of your car and CID just popped into my mind. Maybe we can have some fun with it." Bo held up his hand to stop another waitress with the name of Margaret on her nam-etag. "Excuse me, Margaret, but we want to play a little joke on our waitress, Irene. Could you tell us something about her? Like what she did last night, what her boyfriend's name is, the kind of car she drives, her boyfriend's car, and anything else you can think of."

"Okay, but I have to keep movin,' cause of my work, though."

"That's fine."

Margaret leaned over and disclosed the requested information, and every time she passed their table, she dropped a few more tidbits along with answering his added questions. They were very circumspect, to make sure Irene didn't observe them.

Finally when all the food was consumed, Irene brought the bill for the food.

"Will there be anything else? We have some fresh pies, if you're interested."

"No, no pie, but I just want to let you know that when we checked you out, we found you clean, so far."

She looked confused. "What do you mean?".

"Remember I told you we're with the CID government agency? Well, when we investigated you, we found nothing negative, but then we're not done, yet."

"Oh, come on. You're just kidding me. Aren't you?"

"We are never frivolous when it comes to our work. For example, we know you're Irene Dunston, you live in the Riverview tract. Your boyfriend's name is Dave Nettles. He drives a white pickup; you drive a green Pinto. You've worked here about two years, et cetera. Of course there's lots more."

Irene's mouth dropped wide open. She was stunned. Nervously she rushed away, looking at them over her shoulder. She approached Margaret and started to whisper excitedly.

Anxiously, she turned back toward Bo and Tony's table. Behind her, Margaret covered her mouth and laughed.

With an ashen face, Irene came back to their table, and asked, "Why are you guys investigating me? I don't understand."

Bo was a little ashamed of himself, "Look," he finally said with a little contrition, "I'm sorry if we frightened you. Actually, we haven't investigated you. We got all that information from the other waitress. It was all a joke. Okay?"

Irene couldn't believe it. Turning, she saw Margaret, still laughing. She turned back to Bo and Tony, her face filled with emotional anger, "That was despicable," she said through clenched teeth. "I can't believe you'd do that to me. I can't believe I bought it." She turned away and stormed to the back room, her eyes filled with tears..

"That really was mean," Bo admitted.

"Loosen up, man," Tony suggested. "Personally, I think it was funny.

Bo tripled his tip. Retribution, he mused.

*   *   *

That night Tony spent the evening taking a karate lesson from Marty, the karate instructor, and by the time he arrived in his room at the Chancellor Hotel, he was exhausted. He grabbed a quick shower and slipped gratefully under the sheets.

The night light was on, throwing weird shadows on the far wall.

He chuckled as he reflected upon the last stop he and Bo had made that afternoon. The subject of the investigation, a Mr. Juarez, would not meet them without his lawyer.

The lawyer's fancy office was located on the sixth floor of the Palomar Building with James A. McCawley Law Firm printed on the glass double doors. The doors opened into the foyer where the receptionist and secretaries sat at their computers, looking very competent and business-like, but feminine.

They had been ushered into Mr. McCawley's office. It was enormous. An oversized carved oak desk with neatly stacked piles of folders on each side and a tall swivel leather chair sat on deep pile, berber carpet. A floor-to-ceiling glass wall behind the desk overlooked the city.

The opulence brought an elegance to the man getting out of the chair. Sticking his hand out, he proudly announced, "I'm James McCawley, Mr. Juarez's lawyer." He had perfectly groomed gray hair with soft flowing waves. His flawless features, gray-green eyes, Roman nose and a square dimpled chin were aristocratic. His demeanor denoted a certain air of haughtiness.

"I'm Donald L. Bobbyo. I'm the manager of the Holmes Detective Agency, and this is the new owner, Mr. Anthony W. Garber.

After the amenities, the lawyer waved them toward an informal area in the corner of the office. There were four charcoal gray stuffed chairs, one occupied, surrounding an oval coffee table. "This is my client, Mr. Juarez," the lawyer stated indicating the man sitting in the chair. "I will be the one to make sure you gentlemen don't overstep my boundaries."

Everything about the lawyer irritated Tony. He bristled, but kept his mouth shut.

Mr. Juarez stood and shook hands. He was a relatively short man, not more than five feet six or seven. His hair was mousy gray and thinning. He wore a tan sports jacket and dark brown pants. Tieless, he sat with an open-collar white shirt , revealing a tuft of gray chest hair.

Mr. Juarez, "the lawyer began, "you may answer all their questions, unless I hold up my hand to stop you." Turning to Bo and Tony, he continued, "You may begin your questioning."

He certainly wants total control, Tony thought, infuriated.

In the beginning, when Bo asked a question, Mr. Juarez nervously looked at his lawyer's hands before answering. This went on for ten minutes before the hand finally went up.

"Uh, uh," the lawyer said, looking at Bo, but holding his palm toward Mr. Juarez. "Not a permissible area," he smirked.

The hand went up a total of four times during the interview. And the last time he stopped his client from speaking, he added smugly, "You gentlemen have to remember I'm a lawyer, and I know all your little tricks. No matter what devious lines of attack you use, I'll recognize it for what it is. It's just another plan of subterfuge and chicanery to extract the information you want."

Bo closed his notepad and put it away. "I must say you can read me like a book. But even though you counteracted my ability to obtain everything I wanted, I thank you for your time, at least."

James A. McCawley stood, indicating their dismissal. "And I want to thank you for your understanding. Good day, gentlemen."

Tony wanted to smash McCawley right in the nose. But in the elevator, Tony revealed his exasperation in another way. "He stopped you in every key area, Bo. You really got nothing. Nothing at all!"

Bo grinned with satisfaction. "I got everything I hoped for and more." He emphasized each word.

Tony was surprised. "What, for instance?"

"He stopped his client from answering four questions in four different areas."

"So?"

"So, my friend. Those are the four questions and the four areas I will be pursuing. They are my leads. I didn't have a clue in what direction to go, until Mr. Smarty-pants, the lawyer, told me. It's almost the same as giving me the answers." Bo's expression said it all. "I just wish I could personally thank him for his help. That would really deflate his bloated ego, but alas, I can't. I might have to see him again with another of his protected clients, and I might need just as much help from him. I wouldn't want to spoil it...for me." He laughed heartily.

That Bo is a genius, Tony was thinking, still lying in his bed at the Chancellor. *He amazes me.*

A shuffling noise came from the suite next door. A man and a woman. The man shouted, and the woman screamed. He couldn't understand their words, but it was obviously a big battle, with loud crashes and breaking glass.

Tony sat up, turned on his bed lamp, dialed the desk and reported the disturbance. "You'd better get someone up here fast, or who knows what will happen," Tony admonished. "It's still going on and getting worse." By the time he hung up the phone, his muscles tightened up into knots.

Ten minutes later, Tony heard footsteps in the outer hallway and a loud knocking on his neighbor's door. "Open up! This is the police!"

There was sudden silence. When they had evidently opened the door, Tony heard an authoritative voice ask, "What's going on here?" A heated exchange followed and finally the authoritative voice again. "We'll just have to settle all this downtown."

Moments later, all was quiet. Tony flicked out the light and lay down again. He stared unseeingly at the distorted shadows of a chair and table splashed across the opposite wall. Memories floated through his head. He remembered his stepfather coming home drunk, beating up his mother, and the blood streaming down her nose from the blow. When Tony tried to stop his stepfather, his stepfather slapped him hard, knocking him across the room. He grabbed him, almost yanking his little arm out of its socket and threw him into the pantry, closing the door. It was totally dark in the small pantry.

He could still hear his mother crying, his stepfather cursing, and the sounds of blows as they hit soft flesh. Lying on the cold linoleum floor, full of fear of the dark, he cried himself into a troubled sleep, only to be awakened from a nightmare, screaming out at some imaginary figment in monstrous fright, only to be enclosed again in total darkness.

CHAPTER NINE

Sandy stepped off the elevator at nine sharp and entered the offices of Lang, Blaine, Brindley, and Colton. This was her first day on the job and she wanted it to be perfect. Earlier at home she tried on four different outfits. None of them suited her. She finally selected a conservative suit. It was a navy-blue, wool gabardine, a new type of twilled fabric. It had diagonal ribs of black and blue fibers. Underneath her jacket she wore a white dickey. She stood in front of the full length mirror, twisting and turning to see the full effect. *The skirt is a little tight across the hips*, she thought. *I know the boys won't mind that, but I don't want to give them the wrong idea. Besides, this is all business. The only way I want to impress anyone is with my brains and my ability as an attorney.*

"Good morning," said the receptionist. "May I help you?" *She's a young girl, not more than twenty,* Sandy observed, noting her short, bobbed, brown hair that crowned a slender, smiling face.

"I'm Sandra Forrest. I'm reporting for work today."

"Oh, yes. We're expecting you. Have a seat, and I'll tell them you're here."

Minutes later, a young man in his late twenties emerged from a side door with the words Conference Room clearly printed on it.

"Good morning," he said in a gentle voice. "I'm Craig Colton." His large hand dwarfed Sandy's. He was tall and slender with reddish-brown hair parted on the left. He pushed a strand of it out of his eyes. "You must be Sandy Forrest?"

"Yes, sir."

"Call me Craig. Mister is too formal. Especially since we'll be working together. My father is one of the partners, not me, so we won't be handling anything exciting, just routine stuff."

Sandy smiled and shrugged.

"Come on," he said taking her by the arm. "I'll introduce you to our bosses."

Stepping into the conference room, Sandy noticed a long, highly polished, mahogany table in the center. The walls were paneled with rich, dark cherrywood, broken on one side by narrow windows. Four men at the table stood up. The meeting had evidently just concluded.

"Come in," a man with a resonant voice came around from the end of the table and extended his hand. "You must be Sandy, Mister G's daughter. I'm Marshall Lang." He had a firm grip. He was in his mid-fifties with a shock of gray hair. His round, florid face beamed as he shook hands. "Next," he acknowledged, stepping out of the way, "is John Brindley, our tax expert."

Sandy took a quick inventory of the man. *Late forties*, she surmised. Straight black hair, dark brown eyes, swarthy complexion with a middle-aged spread. No smile. He shook hands and nodded.

"And," continued Mr. Lang, "this is Donald Blaine, our corporate specialist."

His long bony fingers wrapped around Sandy's hand. She looked up into a kind face with large blue eyes. He was so thin that his suit jacket looked like it was draped over a hanger. His full brown wavy hair didn't seem to fit.

"It's nice meeting you, Sandy. And if there is anything I can do to make your job easier, just let me know."

"Now, last, but not least, is Tom Colton, Craig's father, who is a brilliant criminal and legal strategist."

He took her hand gently in his. *He's an older replica of Craig,* Sandy thought. His warm smile radiated as he spoke. "I don't know about the 'brilliant' part, but I wish I were Craig's age, working with this lovely young lady. I want to welcome you to this firm. I also offer you my help in any way I can, but I'm sure Craig will be the lucky one to help you. He is very competent, even if I have to say so as his father."

Craig looked at the floor, flushing, as each of the four men returned to their offices, Craig introduced Sandy to the rest of the staff, including Jenny, the receptionist; the eight legal aids; and the secretary, Pauline, whom she and Craig would share.

Pauline was rotund in all areas, face, upper torso, waist, hips, and legs. *She's the type,* Sandy thought, *who has had to fight weight all her life.*

The flowered dress and bright shiny face indicated a sunny disposition, though.

"She's a jewel," Craig said looking down at her. "She is always pleasant and has a positive outlook on life. We all love her."

Pauline blushed. "You always say the nicest things, Mr. Colton."

Taking Sandy by the arm again, he continued. "Now, let me show you your new office. It's right next to mine."

It was not very large, just enough to hold a computer and printer on the wing of the desk, one chair for her, two in front, shelves on the wall behind her for her law books, and one window opposite the door.

"Not much," Craig indicated with one hand. "But mine is the same size. It's big enough if you hold your breath a little."

They both chuckled.

"Try out your new desk," Craig suggested. "See how it fits."

"Thank you." She slipped behind it and settled into the comfortable chair. "It fits fine," she said looking around. "What I need now is to bring down my law books."

"Why don't you leave those at home to use when you take work home with you? We all take work home. One of our former colleagues, deceased now, had no family, so his books are still here. I'm sure you can use them here, if you'd like. The rest of us already have sets in our offices."

"Sounds great to me."

Craig sat down in front of her. His expression became more serious. "As I said before, we'll be working together. That is, we will work on separate cases in the same department; insurance claims. We are on retainers from a number of insurance companies. We will represent those companies in court or handle negotiations when they're sued. Our job is to keep claims to a minimum. You know how outrageous some of these suits are. All this is coordinated with the insurance company's claim managers." Craig leaned back. "Any questions?"

"No. In fact, I'm eager to get started."

"Excellent. "I'll have Pauline come in and brief you on what you'll be working on."

Sandy felt good about her small office. After a few minutes, Pauline brought in a stack of case files. "This is it," she stated apologetically, setting them on Sandy's desk. "Look the files over, and if you have any questions, just ask. Okay?" She smiled again.

"Sit down for a minute. Let's talk." Sandy suggested.

Pauline sat down and tugged on her dress to cover her knees. It was very tight at the hips when she settled down into the chair. "Anything in particular?" she asked.

"No. Just a get-acquainted talk. Are you married, have children? How long have you been here? What are your likes and dislikes?

"But let me begin with myself, first. I'm not married and just passed the bar exam. That's been my life. Not very exciting. Now, how about you?"

Pauline pursed her lips, stared at the pile of files she had just brought in and, looking up into Sandy's deep violet blue eyes, she answered. "My life hasn't been exciting, either. I'm not married, not even a boyfriend at present. I've been here a little over three years. And as far as my likes and dislikes...well I dislike all the sad things happening in the world, like bombings, killings, especially abuse of children, greed, and so on. I guess the things I like most are lots of peace and quiet and love. I was raised in a home full of fighting and hate. I couldn't wait to get out. At least now I have quietness in my little apartment." She looked up at Sandy again and smiled.

Sandy returned her smile. "Thank you. I'm sure we'll get along just fine. Now I'd better get to work. Nice talking with you, Pauline."

*   *   *

Looking into the decorative bathroom mirror in his hotel, Tony pulled his skin taut in one place and then another as he slid his electric razor over his chin, where the heaviest whiskers grew. He strongly felt this was the night. The very thought of having Sandy excited him. He couldn't wait.

Again Sandy had invited him over for dinner. Matty, she had said, would prepare one of her specialties. But more than that, Tony enjoyed the news that Daddy was out of town. *Alone!* He relished the thought. *Alone on the swing. Matty will be cleaning up the kitchen or going to her room. Perfect.*

Tony hummed one of the latest songs, "Making Out with Mandy." He changed the "M" to "S." "Making out with Sandy," he crooned as he looked at himself in admiration, arms widespread, while he bubbled with anticipation. He didn't care about anything except scoring.

Grooming his hair and hurriedly dressing, Tony headed out for his big evening. When he walked to his car, he was even aware of the chirping sparrows in the bushes and trees. It was a balmy evening, and he embraced it openly. He started to hum that tune again, "Making out with..". In the distance a train whistle shrieked, and somewhere behind him a woman laughed.

He slowly cruised out of the hotel parking lot, his big V8 engine rumbling under the hood. After he cleared the dip and entered the street, he floored the gas pedal. The tires screeched, burning rubber, as he fishtailed down the boulevard. *Stupid,* he thought with a big smile. *Like when I was a teenager. Too many cops around. I'm supposed to be a respected businessman. I'd better act like one.*

He slowed to the speed limit, and noticed a policeman stepping out from behind a parked car and pointing his radar gun at him. *That was close, he* thought. *A couple of blocks earlier, and he would have had me.*

Sandy, sitting on the porch swing, had been waiting for him. She wore a silky off-white dress that flowed with the curves of her body.

When he mounted the steps, Sandy rushed to him and gave him a hug. He returned the hug, his hands sliding down to her hips.

She quickly pulled away. "You're bad," she admonished, laughing. She grabbed his arm and pulling him toward the front door, continued, "We're not married, so you don't have that kind of freedom."

"Are you proposing?" he asked.

"No way. I like you Tony, but that's all."

As soon as he opened the door, he smelled the delicate odors of food emanating from the dining room. "The food's ready?" he questioned.

"Yes. You're a few minutes late. But it's not a problem. Let's sit down and eat."

"What're we having? It smells delicious."

"Well, let's see. We start out with spinach crab soup and salmon rice salad. The main course is stuffed pork chops, potatoes au gratin and artichokes with curry-mustard dip. And for dessert, it's...uh."

Matty walked into the dining room with a pot heaped with the potato dish and set it down. "Matty," Sandy asked, "what are we having for dessert?"

Matty looked at her while tucking a strand of gray hair behind her ear. "It's a whipped cream dessert with lots of fruit, like seedless green grapes, slices of tangelos, pineapples, bananas, cherries and other fruits. I call it Fruit Whip."

Tony dropped to one knee. "Matty," he said, "will you marry me?"

"Bosh," Matty growled. "You're a big time kidder. What you do if I say, 'Yes?'"

"With your cooking, I'd be in heaven. What a way to go."

That brought a smile to Matty's craggy face. "I think about it, maybe," she said, and pushed her way through the swinging door into the kitchen.

Sandy chuckled. "You came that close to getting married." She placed her index finger and thumb a half inch apart.

"Well, I wouldn't have asked her, if you hadn't turned me down," he said as he held the chair for her at the dining table.

"My, aren't you being a gentleman. Anyway, I haven't turned you down, because you've never asked me."

"I just might, a little later."

"Promises, promises."

*   *   *

After dinner while sipping coffee, Tony sighed and blurted out, "I'm stuffed. I don't even want to marry Matty, now. And if I did, I'd look like a very fat whale in a couple of months."

"Don't be so quick with your decisions. She knows how to cook to keep you healthy. She's studied nutrition. She only makes these fattening meals for special occasions. Like tonight."

Tony looked up suspiciously. "What's so special about tonight?"

"I have a big question to ask you," she admitted.

"Wait a minute. Isn't the boy supposed to pop that question?"

"Silly, I'm not going to ask you to marry me."

"Whew," Tony said wiping his brow. "That was close."

Snickering, Sandy came back with, "No, no. I just wanted to invite you to a symphony in the park tomorrow afternoon that would be really special for me."

Why did she have to include that "really special for me" part, he thought. *How can I say "no" to her now?*

He had never liked classical music, only jazz. His mind raced, but no excuses came, and finally, he agreed, just to make her happy.

In appreciation, Sandy slowly got up and walked over to where Tony was sitting. "Stand up, young man, and get your reward for the right answer."

When Tony stood, Sandy slid her arms around him and moved in close. He put his arms around her, too, and pulled her even closer. Becoming aroused, he guided her toward the front door and the porch swing.

Passionately kissing her on the swing, Tony's kindled fire flared. He was burning inside with desire. And she was responding. This caused his flame to erupt even more. Then he started to drag her down on the swaying swing.

"Whoa!" came the muffled cry from under him. "We can't! At least I can't!"

"But I love you." he murmured passionately. "And I know you love me."

"No, no, no," Sandy's muted cry came out. She was struggling as he attempted to hold her down. Suddenly the swing gave way and they both tumbled to the porch. In the scuffle, Sandy jumped up and brushed herself off, totally flustered. "I'm sorry, Tony. It was all my fault. I shouldn't have led you on. I'm sorry," she repeated. "Please forgive me."

Tony was still sitting on the porch floor, legs spread out, hands behind him, bracing his upper torso. *Forgive you?* he almost shouted. He was about to continue with, *Forgive you for teasing me half to death and then dumping on me? Shove it, sister.* But again he knew almost instantly that such talks would end their relationship. So instead, he repeated, calmly, "Forgive you? Of course I do." Standing and gently taking her in his arms, he continued, "But don't do that to me again. Please. I can't take it anymore. In fact, don't do it again, unless you plan to go all the way."

He looked into her face. Her eyes were down-cast. He knew he had her. *If she permits me to go as far as I just did, and she will,* he thought, *then...*

He smiled. "I'd better go."

Looking up sheepishly, Sandy asked, softly, "You will still go to the symphony with me, won't you?"

"I guess so."

"Pick me up at two for a late lunch?" she responded quickly.

"Sure."

"And don't forget, it's my treat."

CHAPTER TEN

Sandy and Tony had finished lunch and were relaxing over a cup of coffee, enjoying the ambience of the Dutch House Restaurant. Her hair was pulled back and tied with a yellow ribbon that matched her off-shoulder sundress. He could see the stares from men of all ages as they devoured her with their eyes. Even the women in the restaurant had their eyes on her, in envy.

They were sitting at a quiet corner table. Their dirty dishes were being cleared by the waitress, who was wearing a short, black, pleated skirt, flowered bibbed bodice with a sash pulled tightly around her waist. It was worn over a white blouse with puffy sleeves. On top of her blond hair sat a white starched Dutch hat.

The colorful room was decorated with wall murals of windmills in fields of red ad yellow tulips. A pair of wooden shoes hung over each of the doorways.

"We'll have to leave in about five minutes," Sandy reflected as she looked at her watch.

Tony picked up the check and started to reach into his pocket for his wallet.

"Whoa, young man," Sandy exclaimed, "this one is mine. Remember, I asked you."

Tony reluctantly handed her the check.

A commotion broke out at the table next to them. "You can't do this to me!" shouted an attractive woman in her mid thirties. "You'll regret, it if you do!"

A man in his early fifties, held up his hand, as if he were trying to say something, but she turned and stomped out before he could speak.

"That," Sandy whispered, "is the chief of police. He and his girlfriend, who just stormed out of here, have been having their difficulties. Everyone knows everyone's business in a small town like this. Now maybe you'll change your mind about settling down here."

"No way, young lady. Unless you move. Then I'd follow you anywhere, and you wouldn't even have to 'blow in my ear' for that."

Sandy was smiling when she glanced at her watch. "Uh, oh. We're gonna be a little late."

*   *   *

Tony was checking the Holmes Detective Agency books in his office when Samuel G. poked his head in the door. "You got a couple of minutes?"

"Sure. Come in, Mr. G. I was just going over the books. Wanna be positive I'm still solvent."

"I don't doubt that you are, Tony," he said as he closed the door. He sat down and crossed his legs. "I have a little proposition I'd like to go over with you. I think you'll like it."

"Okay. Coffee or something else?"

"No. I'm fine. Thank you." Uncrossing his legs and leaning forward, he began, "Now that you have the balance of all your money in your Internet account, what plans do you have for it?"

"I haven't come up with anything, yet. Do you have something in mind?"

"A business associate of mine, who is also connected, up in Chi, is a futures broker. He owns a large firm. He's privy to some significant information taking place on the Chicago Exchange. If we had that information, it could make us rich."

"But I'm already rich," Tony admitted with a smile.

"Yes, but money that sits stagnant diminishes in value, because of inflation. Your purchasing power decreases. You certainly would prefer more than less, isn't that right?"

"Yes, of course. Go on."

"This would be a three-way partnership. You for the capital, the broker for the information, and I would be the facilitator, because of my position in the bank."

"Why do you need me? Both of you must have enough capital to swing this without me."

"Unfortunately, that's not true. You have to remember I'm the front man, as the broker is, for the Outfit. I own the bank on paper. He owns the brokerage firm on paper. All our books, bank accounts, and spending is scrutinized by the Outfit's bookkeepers. Oh, they'll take care of us when we retire, but at a drastically reduced lifestyle, and that's not for me. Even my house belongs to them, even though it's in my name. I'm a wealthy banker only for show. The same is true for my associate, the broker."

Tony leaned back in his chair. The hinges squeaked in protest. *It is my money*, he mused. *He said he liked me, but it is my money. He doesn't really have any of his own to hide, and the Outfit keeps tabs on him, so he can't squirrel away any of theirs. Now he wants me to help make him rich. But that's okay with me as long as I get richer, too.*

"This is our opportunity, only because of the total anonymity in the Internet. If the Outfit found out about a special account, they would assume we were skimming, and we would be history. It's the only safe way we have. We offer you the opportunity to make money beyond your wildest dreams and for us to prosper as well. It's foolproof."

"But how does it work?"

"It's called 'trading ahead.' It means that we place orders, but not large ones, at different small exchanges around the country on futures before my associate, Roberto, in the Chicago Exchange places his large order for one of his customers. In other words, 'trading ahead.'"

"But isn't that illegal?"

"Of course. That's the beauty of this. Accounts are set up at these small exchanges by phone. Roberto cannot place these orders at the Chicago

Exchange, because there would be a paper trail that would incriminate him and put him in jail.

"There will only be an account number for you; no names. The money will be transferred by the Internet Bank to the brokers and all profits back to your private account number and ours at the Internet Bank. And Roberto will place all the orders from his personal computer through E-mail through the Internet to the small brokers. You really don't have to do anything; just sit back and count your money."

"How much capital do we need?"

"Twenty-five grand for each account. That's two hundred and fifty grand. But we don't have to start with ten accounts. If you would prefer, we can start with five and expand as we prosper."

"I think I'd be more comfortable with five to begin with."

"Okay. We'll make it five. But you'll have to transfer the money. I'll get back to you with the details."

Mr. G slowly stood up. His facial expression was changing. It was harder, lips turned down slightly and a narrowing of the eyes. The old knot of fear popped up in Tony's stomach again.

"There is another thing," Mr. G stated flatly, eyes blazing. "I have a job for you and Bo. It seems I have an informant in my bank. Someone who reports to Chicago. I realized this when I was questioned about the bank branching out on the Internet. There were no objections. No questions about my loyalty. And when I explained how the Internet works and how it would benefit them with the laundering of their money with no chance of being discovered, they were delighted.

"But the very fact that they found out about it from another source tells me they have a plant on my staff." The anger flashed in his eyes. "Find that person, Tony," he said through clenched teeth, and then added menacingly, "and I'll personally take care of him."

A lump formed in Tony's throat. "Yes, Sir. I'll get right on it," His anxiety did not begin to subside until Mr. G was gone. And then it receded slowly. Tony chided himself for this weakness. *I'm not much of a man*, he thought. *But I sure don't want to get on the wrong side of Mr. G.*

*   *   *

In his office the next morning, Tony explained the problem to Bo. "I've never seen Mr. G this angry. He really wants this guy...bad. What do we do?"

Bo was pulling on his chin again. "The first thing we need is a copy of all employee's records and employment aps. In fact, we did most of the employee investigations at the bank. We go through them with a fine-tooth comb, looking for any leads, such as names and addresses of next of kin. We interview the next of kin, but not immediate members. They're too close. We go to other family members under the guise that we're just getting background information because their relative is under consideration for advancement at the bank, but in the event they are not selected, we ask that the interview be held in confidence.

"We do the same with people they've listed as character references and former employers and schools attended, teachers, students they associated with, especially at colleges or universities."

"Brilliant, as usual."

"But it doesn't stop there. That's just the beginning."

Bo stopped stroking his chin and smiled at Tony. "In fact, before we do anything I just mentioned, we check our own computer files. We'll probably have records of some kind on all of them."

"You do?"

"Sure. If they have ever applied for life insurance, auto insurance, hospitalization, or if we've investigated them for any reason, like for employment, we'll have it. We also have files on most people in this fair city and access to other agencies we cooperate with."

"Wow. That's a lot of people."

"Yep. And there are a number of other things we'll be doing when we investigate these people. This is going to cost him a fortune. He probably has twenty to twenty-five on his staff. We'll also be checking their phone calls, bank statements, credit cards and other things, depending on what we find."

"I can see how easy it would be to get the bank statements. Probably from Mr. G, right?" When Bo nodded, Tony proceeded, "but how do you get copies of telephone statements? They're private, I thought."

"They are. But if you know the right people in the phone company and have a little money, there's no problem. Those are very important documents. They tell you who they have been talking to. This could tell us exactly what we want and point the finger for Mr. G."

Tony scratched his head. "There's an awful lot to learn in this business. I'm just glad you're running things. I still don't know what I'm doing."

"You will. It'll just take time. It took me years to learn what I know now, but I believe you will learn it a lot faster than I did."

"Thanks, but you don't have to butter me up. You're my only hope in this business."

"Believe me when I say I'm not buttering you up. I don't need to. I could get a good job anywhere in the state, but it would mean starting over. And besides I like living here. And all my friends are here, too. I was just making a statement of fact."

"Okay, I believe you." Tony stuck his hand out and Bo shook it.

"One more question to enlighten me. How do you get info from the credit card companies?"

"We do a credit report, using Experian, formerly TRW, and of course, the other agencies. This will tell us which credit card companies they're using, along with all other financial information on the subject. Our computer hacks take over after that. They can get into credit card company records."

"What does all this tell us?"

"When we're through, we'll have a thick file on everyone working at the bank. That file will reveal a total picture of that individual. We'll especially be looking for any irregularities, such as large deposits in the bank, large payoffs on credit card accounts that are inconsistent with income. If fact, we'll know more about them than they know about themselves. Most of the info we'll have, they'll have forgotten."

Bo was massaging his chin, again. "We'll also check their federal income tax returns."

"You mean you can get into the IRS files?"

"No. They have too many protections. Besides, if they caught us.... Well I don't even want to think about it. There are only a few tax preparers in Champaign. We have someone in one of the largest firms that works with us.

"I'm going to get started." Bo stood. "I'll keep you informed."

*   *   *

Mr. G waited in the front entrance on the steps of his palacial home. Karla was driving a new, deep cherry red Porsche 911.

When she stepped out of her car, he noticed she was wearing a clinging white blouse with a three-quarter-length mauve skirt that swished around her legs. Her black shining hair, parted in the middle, was held in place with a scarf that matched her skirt. She slowly pulled the scarf off as she took in the magnificent home in front of her.

When her eyes drifted to the figure in the doorway, she said, "Sam, it's a beautiful home. I like it much better than Sal's."

Mr. G was taking in her beauty as she walked toward him. *Ravishing*, he thought. *Just ravishing*. Then he took her in his arms and holding her close, he whispered in her ear, "Karla, I'm thrilled that you came."

She stepped back and held him at arm's length, and with a stony stare, she said coolly, "I just came to see your house. Nothing else. To see if it was as grand as you said. Believe me, your description didn't do it justice."

Mr. G didn't know what to think. Then with a delicious smile, the sparkle in her dark eyes returned, and he knew she was teasing, "Well," he said with relief, "I'm better at numbers than I am with words. But come on in. I'll have Jeeves, my butler get your luggage and put it in the guest room."

She sure is a good actress, he thought.

"'Jeeves'?" she laughed, bringing him back from his thoughts.

"Oh, that's what I call him. Actually, his real name is James. Let's go in. I'll ring for him later. He lives above the garage. Besides I want you to meet my daughter."

He led her through the foyer and into the great room. Sandy was seated on a dark blue love seat. "Sandy," Mr. G said, "I want you to meet a friend of mine from Chicago. This is Karla Zambini," he continued, and then turning to Karla, "And this is my daughter, Sandy."

"It's nice meeting you," Karla said.

"For me , too." Sandy studied her.

Directing Karla to a couch opposite Sandy's love seat, Mr. G explained, "Karla here is a dress designer who has just moved from New York to Chicago. And we met and have enjoyed each other's company."

"What do you do?" Karla asked Sandy.

"Well, I just graduated from law school and started my first job with a local law firm."

"Very impressive." Then turning to Mr. G, Karla continued, "Now, you have a lawyer in the family."

"Yes," he said pridefully.

"Did you design the outfit you're wearing, Karla?" Sandy asked.

"No. My designs are for more formal situations."

"Oh." Sandy let her word hang in the air.

"Listen," Mr. G came on quickly. "We're going out to dinner and maybe a night on the town, such as it is. Would you like to go with us?" It was almost apparent that he was hoping for a negative answer. And that's what he got.

"No," Sandy said, "you two go ahead. I already have plans. Tony will be here in a few minutes." She looked at her watch.

Standing, Mr. G asked, "Sandy, would you mind asking Jeeves to take Karla's luggage to the guest room?"

"No, I don't mind." *How long is she staying,* Sandy wondered.

Turning to Karla, Mr. G said, "Do you have your keys?"

"They're in the car."

"Then we're ready to go. Unless you feel you have to freshen up or something."

"No, I stopped and freshened up just before coming. I wanted to look nice for you." She smiled coyly.

"You always look good." Mr. G grinned.

As they walked out of the room, Sandy followed. "Have fun," she said as her father waved back. Moments later they drove away.

Sandy was still standing on the front porch, deep in thought, when Tony drove up. *Dad must have left the gate open,* she thought.

"Hi sweetheart," Tony sang out as he exited his car.

"Hi," she returned solemnly.

"What's wrong with you?" he asked as he stepped up to her on the porch.

"Nothing. I just met Dad's girlfriend from Chicago."

"Yeah. I saw them going the other way, but I couldn't see her. What does she look like?"

"Attractive, I suppose. But I'm worried."

"Why?"

"I don't know. I just feel upset."

"Maybe it bothers you to see your father with another woman other than your mother."

"Maybe," Sandy said, still not sure.

Tony put his arm around her and guided her into the house.

*   *   *

Mr. G was working at his massive desk in his bank office when there was a knock at the door. "Come," he said looking up.

Tony poked his head in the door. He had a big smile on his face. "I've got` some good news for ya."

"Good. I could use some. Come in. Sit down." he pointed to a chair in front of his desk.

"Well..." Tony began as he sat down. "the informant, the one giving all that info to Sal, is Benny. We're almost positive of it."

"That's hard to believe. Why do you believe it's him?"

"His recent spending habits. For the last two years, he's been spending more than he earns, by quite a bit. We discovered he has another checking account across town at your biggest competitor. He has been making large deposits of three to five thousand every month.

"Then we had our computer expert break into Benny's account and found out the checks were from Fratenello Enterprises."

"Why, that little..."

Tony interrupted. "What're you gonna do to him?"

"I'd like to confront him and then kill him slowly, but I can't. He is sort of under the protection of Mr. Fratenello. If I do, I'm in trouble."

"We could just work him over a little for ya."

"No. Then you and Bo would be in trouble. I think the only thing I can do at this time is lay him off. After a few months, he could just disappear."

"I better get going, Mr. G. I still have a lot to do."

"What do I owe you?"

"Whatever you think it's worth."

"You'll see how much I appreciate the job you're doing for me the next time you check your Internet account."

CHAPTER ELEVEN

Sandy walked the two blocks to the Empire State Life and Casualty claims office, located in a commercial complex designed for small businesses that didn't need street exposure. Cool air greeted her as she stepped into the receptionist area. An L-shaped counter blocked walk-ins from the office area of the business. The room, void of creature comforts, had two filing cabinets, a small desk with a telephone on it and a receptionist sitting behind the desk.

"Yes?" the receptionist questioned, looking up. Her hair was stringy and straight and dyed blond. Her dark roots were beginning to show. She seemed tired, evidenced by puffy, blue bags under her brown eyes.

"I'd like to see the manager, please. I'm an attorney representing Empire State."

That information seemed to bring a little life into her. Getting up quickly, she revealed tight designer jeans below her loose-fitting University of Illinois sweatshirt. "One moment. I'll call him."

In a few moments she returned, followed by a large smiling man in his forties. His round face smiled above a layered neck. The folds bounced in rhythm as he walked. His small blue eyes seemed almost lost in the excessive flesh. The gray pin-striped suit was rumpled, and his blue and gray striped tie hung twisted and loose. The open collar of his white shirt was soiled with sweat.

Sandy accepted his pudgy, moist handshake. "Welcome, Miss..uh...."

"Forrest," she filled in.

"Oh, yes. I'm Jonathan Wilbur. Won't you come in." He lifted the leaf in the counter. "First door on the right."

As Sandy stepped in, she noticed a large room with two desks in it. A young man sat at the far desk. He stood up as she entered.

"This is Nathan Musbraum. He's the insurance inspector for the company, but he doesn't handle claims. I do that. He does all the investigation work on new policy holders. Because this is such a small town, we work together.

"Nate, this is Miss Forrest."

Nathan, in his early thirties, did not move out from behind his desk. But he did nod, as did Sandy; only she did so with a smile.

"Have a seat, Miss Forrest," Jonathan said, indicating a chair in front of his desk. "How may I help you?"

I just received a new breaking-and-entering case I'm supposed to handle. So I thought I'd drop over to meet you and give you a copy of it."

"Oh, no, not another B and E."

"I'm new at Lang, Blaine, Brindley, and Colton. Maybe you could fill me in on your procedure."

"Be happy to. You'll handle all legal aspects of it, especially if we go to court. I will be handling any negotiations that might be needed for settlement."

"Is that all?"

"Basically, yes. But if you have any questions, feel free to call me anytime."

"I probably will have to do that until I become more familiar with all of this."

Standing, Sandy reluctantly offered her hand. "Thank you, Mr. Wilbur. I can find my way out."

As Sandy walked back to her office, she was going over what was said. Something was bothering her. Just as she entered her office building, it hit her. He had said, "Not another one." That means there have been more. "Hmm," she muttered.

*   *   *

At noon Craig popped his head in the door. "How about lunch?" he asked.

Deeply engrossed in her work, Sandy took a moment to realize what he'd asked. She looked at her watch, and finally answered. "Time got away from me, I guess. But now that you mention it, I do feel a little hungry."

"Good. If you like Italian, there is a nice place within walking distance. That okay with you?"

"Sure. Strictly business, of course, and if we can go Dutch."

"Spoken like a true women's libber." He laughed. "Next, you won't let me open the car door, or...or..."

Sandy looked at him askance, but with a twinkle in her eye. "I'll have you know that I'm not a 'libber.' And I would love it if you opened the door for me and all the other little things a gentleman enjoys doing. I enjoy being pampered a little, but don't like being a burden. That's why I insist on paying my share. Now, hypothetically, if you asked me for a date and took me to dinner, you could pay."

"Sounds like a great idea. Would Friday night be okay?"

"I wasn't suggesting that you ask me for a date. I was just trying to make a point."

"I understand that. But I still think it's a great idea. My question is: Would Friday night be okay?"

"No, Friday night will not be fine," she said adamantly with a slight grin. "We have to work together. I think it would be better to keep our relationship on a business level."

"I don't agree, but for the time being, so be it."

*   *   *

Craig held her chair for her at a table adorned with a red-and-white checked tablecloth. They both had hints of smiles on their faces."What do you think?" he asked.

"Nice. But I'll hold further comment until after I eat."

"Fair enough."

Sandy's eyes wandered around the restaurant. Deep wine-colored carpeting with matching drapes surrounded fake windows with plastic flowers in potted plants on the sills and painted backdrops of country scenes back-lighted by hidden lamps, giving an illusion of a beautiful panoramic view.

There was a flavor of the old country. Pictures of old, mustachioed Italian men with fishing boats in the background were displayed on the walls.

"What's the name of this place?" Sandy asked casually, still looking around the restaurant.

"Carmen's Fine Cuisine. And it really has good food. I'd recommend the spaghetti and meatballs. It's their specialty."

"Sounds delicious. I'll try it."

After ordering for the two of them, Craig put his elbows on the table, clasped his fingers together and looked directly into her blue eyes. "Do you know what?"

"What?" she asked suspiciously.

"We have something in common."

Sandy looked at him, perplexed. "We have? What?"

"Something in common."

"What?" she repeated.

The waiter interrupted with their coffees. When he was gone, Craig continued. "Well, last Sunday I saw you at the symphony."

"Then you must be a music lover, too."

"Yes, I am. You were sitting with a handsome young man. Is he your boyfriend or something?"

"I'm not sure, yet. More friend, for now, I guess.

Craig's face changed from a slight worried look to a pleasant one. "Well, then, maybe we could go to a concert sometime."

"I don't think so, Craig. I don't want to mix business with pleasure."

"I definitely disagree, so I'll keep trying until you change your mind."

Nothing more was said about it while they ate their meals.

*　　*　　*

Pauline looked at Sandy and Craig when they entered the office. Her expression said it all when she teasingly asked, "Did you two have a nice lunch?"

"Be nice," Sandy admonished. "It was strictly business."

"Here are your messages. Two of them. Both from a gorgeous voice with the name of Tony."

Craig glanced at Sandy.

Self-consciously Sandy looked at them. Her face reddened a little. "He's just a friend. The one I told you about at the restaurant," she explained.

Both Craig and Pauline grinned, but said nothing.

"Come on, you two. Stop it. Besides I have another point of business to discuss with you, Craig."

When they had entered her office, Sandy stopped in the doorway and turned toward Pauline. "I'm going to leave the door open, in case you thought...thought...whatever."

Pauline threw her hands up. "My thoughts are pure," she beamed, laughing.

Sandy decided to ignore her. Picking up a stack of files from her desk, she sat down. "These," she indicated, shaking them, "are all 'breaking and entering' cases from the same insurance company, Empire Life and Casualty. One of them I received from you yesterday. The other six I retrieved from our files when I got a little suspicious after talking to the claims adjuster. It seems they all have the same M.O., modus operandi."

"I know what M.O. means," he corrected gently with a grin.

"I'm sorry. I'm sure you do. It's just that when I saw seven high-value dwellings burgled in the same manner, my curiosity was peaked. What do I do now?"

"Well, first of all, I have to congratulate you on your thoroughness and perceptiveness. Not many people would have caught that. For instance, I may have handled the other six cases."

"You did." She hesitated, then added quickly, "I'm sorry. I didn't mean to put you down or indicate a lack of thoroughness on your part."

"Don't worry, I didn't take it that way. Although I think we do get a little sloppy when we have more than we can handle. We just try to get the work done as quickly as we can. That's been my problem. And that's why they hired you to help me."

Crossing his legs, Craig proceeded. "Now to answer your question. What we do now is turn it over to an investigative agency."

Sandy thought for a moment. Her face brightened. "How about the Holmes Detective Agency?"

"That's fine. We use them quite often, anyway."

*   *   *

An hour later, Sandy was sitting in Tony's office with the seven B and E files. She gripped the pile in her lap. "These breaking-and-entering cases are almost identical, in that the burglar or burglars operated the same way."

"You mean they have the same M.O."

"Here," Tony extended his hand and accepted the files "Let me have a look."

"Smells a little fishy to me."

Tony didn't answer, but began to read.

Ten minutes later, he looked up. "You're right. It sounds like it might be an inside job. If it was random casing, it would be different insurance companies, not one. The question is who would have that information? It could even be someone here at the Holmes Detective Agency. I just don't know, but I'll look into it."

Sandy put her hand out to shake, then embarrassed, retracted it. It would have seemed strange to shake Tony's hand, because of their relationship. "Thanks, Tony. I'll look forward to what you find out." Flustered, she turned and hurried out.

*   *   *

When Sandy was gone, Tony went to the supply room, poured a cup of coffee and took it back to his office. Setting the cup down, he leaned back again in his squeaky chair.

What are the possibilities here? He mused. Somebody had access to these files. Sitting up straight again, he said into his intercom, "Larry, could you come into my office for a moment?"

In a few moments, Larry walked in. His uncombed hair, parted in the middle, curled down in ringlets almost to his eyebrows. He was a typical typecast nerd; short, slight of build, pimpled face, sloppy clothes, but a genius on the computer.

"Sit down, Larry. I've got a job for you. Can you find out who did the inspections on these high-value dwellings?" Tony handed him the list, then sipped his coffee.

"Sure, Mr. Garber. No problem. Everyone who writes a report has to have a code number to get into the program. It'll only take few minutes to get this for you. Be right back."

True to his word, Larry was back in ten minutes. "Here they are, Mr. Garber."

"Thanks, Larry."

At a glance, Tony could see every report was done by different people, except for two. *Seven reports*, he thought, *investigated by five different people. Of course, anyone in this office has access to these reports. Could have been anyone, but I doubt it. The key element here is the fact that all were insured by the same company. If it had been someone in this office, they certainly would have been smart enough to have selected them from different companies. I would have.*

Tony rose to his feet, walked to the window and looked out over the city covered with bright sunlight. The mid-afternoon sun was casting sharp shadows on the east side of the buildings. The afternoon traffic seemed sluggish. Even the people crossing the streets walked slowly. *Must be the heat*, thought Tony. *Summer really is here. I guess it gets just as hot here as in Chi.*

He lifted his eyes toward the horizon, but it was lost in the gathering angry clouds approaching quickly. *Maybe that will cool things down tonight*, he thought.

Back to work. His mind mulled the facts over and over. *With Bo gone for a few days, I'll have to handle this. I should get my feet wet sometime. Might as well be now.*

Sitting down at his desk again, he called for Jerry, one of his top inspectors, according to Bo. Besides, Jerry did not handle high-value dwellings, the perfect one to handle this end.

Jerry stuck his head in the door. He was mid-dle-aged with wavy, sandy-gray hair. His face was square with bushy eyebrows and a mustache. "What you need, boss?"

"Come on in. Have a seat." Then Tony handed him the list. "This is confidential, Jerry. There were seven inspections done by five different people from this office,` and all of the homes have been burgled. I seriously doubt that any of our people had anything to do with break-ins, but we have to touch all bases to be sure. Think you can handle it? Find out if anyone is implicated?"

"Wow, this is heavy. Some of these people are my friends. I certainly don't want to offend them."

"If you'd rather not, I can find someone else, I suppose."

"If I have to step on some toes, I'll find out fast who is my friend, good friend, or not."

"Thanks, Jerry. Bo said you were the best, and I believe him." Except for Bo, Tony thought, picking up his coffee. It was cold.

*   *   *

Just as Tony dialed Sandy at her office, the storm broke. Large drops hit the window and in moments, began to cascade down in torrents. He picked up the phone and took it with him to the window. He could see lightning crashing all around the city. Thunder rumbled and exploded like cannons. Dark clouds raced by to take their destruction eastward.

When Sandy finally came on, Tony moved back to his desk and sat down. With one hand covering his exposed ear, he almost shouted, "Hi, Sweetheart. We're getting a heavy storm here."

"I know. Here, too. Isn't it exciting?"

"Yes, I suppose so." His mind was already moving to the problem he had called about. "I've been trying to figure out this burglary enigma. The question is, 'Who pulled the jobs?'"

"You haven't made any progress, yet?"

"No, not really. I don't really think it's anyone here, but I have my best man on it, just to be sure. It's got to be someone else. But who?"

"I don't have the foggiest...unless..." The thought came to her.

"Unless what?"

"Not what, but who? It just occurred to me that the Empire State and Casualty claims office sees all those reports, too. The insurance agents write the policies, then submit them to the company, which in turn has them inspected."

"Describe the people who are in that office."

"There's a total of three. A receptionist, but I don't think she would be involved, too mousy. And I can't see the other guy doing anything. He's far too fat. Couldn't crawl through a window without a lot of push from below." Sandy snickered. "Unless he had someone else doing it."

"What about the third person?"

"His name is Nathan Musbraum, their inspector. He could fit. He's a small, thin man with ginger-colored hair. Young enough. Looks capable. But who knows."

"I think I'll need to have someone from my office do a little surveillance tonight." Looking at his watch, he added, "It's almost four. I gotta go before everyone leaves for the day. See you later." He stood and hung up the phone.

CHAPTER TWELVE

A mantle of darkness had clothed the city. The silence was broken by the hum of traffic in the distance and an occasional horn honking. Tony sat in a dark sedan under a large elm tree across the street and a hundred feet south from Nathan Musbraum's house. Tonight, Tony was stuck with replacing the agent who went home sick, late this afternoon. Because there was no one else in the office, he had to fill in. He had started his surveillance from the time Musbraum had left his office, four hours ago. Now, he was bored, his patience sorely tested.

What am I supposed to do, sit here all night? he asked himself in exasperation. *Too bad I didn't have time to reassign it, but it was too late. My office staff was all gone for the day.*

Tony looked at his watch. Almost nine. He picked up his car phone and called Sandy. He didn't expect her to be home, but was pleasantly surprised when he heard her voice.

"This is the Forrest residence. May I help you?" Sandy asked.

"Hi, Sandy. I'm glad you're home."

"You are? Well, earlier today I was hoping you'd ask me out, but then you said you'd be doing some surveillance tonight at 122 Oak. So I resigned myself to being lonely."

"It just happens that I'm lonely, too. That's why I called. I've got an idea. Why don't you come down here for a while and keep me company. I sure could use it."

"It sounds like a great idea. Where are you?"

Tony gave her directions. "I'll see you in about half an hour. Wait...wait a minute. Bring some food, too. I'm famished. Maybe a sub and a drink. I'll pay you when you get here."

"Don't be silly. This'll be my treat." She hung up before he could protest.

*   *   *

Sandy pulled in behind him in twenty-five minutes. When she slipped into the seat next to him, he grabbed her and kissed her ferociously, squashing the sandwiches.

"Down, boy," she gasped. "I know you're lonely, but this is ridiculous. Slow down."

"I'm sorry, but I kept thinking of you while I was waiting and I just couldn't stop myself."

"I'm sure it was difficult." She laughed. "But if I'm going to be a distraction, I'm going to leave. You're supposed to be working."

"Sure, but..."

"No buts," she interrupted. "We have to do our job right. Right?"

Sandy didn't wait for an answer. "Did you have any problem recognizing Nathan Musbraum?"

"No. With your description of the three people working there, it was easy. He came out, and bingo, I had him. Been with him ever since. But I think he's settling down for the evening. I saw a light go on upstairs a few minutes ago. Probably his bedroom."

"Could he slip out the back?"

"Yeah, but I don't think he would. He'd have to climb over a fence into someone's back yard. It would be too chancy for him. And then he wouldn't have a car. I think he still feels safe. In any case, I guess I just wait."

Sandy reached into the bag for the food.

"I have to insist that you let me pay," Tony said flatly.

"Are you kidding? You can pay next time when the bill is much higher than this."

Tony smiled and put the money away.

*   *   *

Sandy noticed it was straight up one o'clock in the morning. The food had been consumed, the talking had slowed down, and Tony had slipped off into dreamland. She smiled as she looked at him and listened to his deep breathing. *I still don't know whether I love him or not*, she pondered. *I think I do, but...*

Her thoughts were interrupted when Tony started to mumble. "Mama, mama," then with fear sobbed, "No, Daddy, no." Finally he slipped back into a fitful sleep.

"Wake up, Tony. You're dreaming," she said, gently shaking him. "Tony, wake up."

Tony awoke with a start. "What?" he said in confusion, staightening up in his seat..

"You've been dreaming."

He looked at her a little blurry eyed. "I'm sorry. I must have dozed off."

Tony wiped his eyes.

"You were having a bad dream. You were crying and saying things like, 'Daddy and Mama' and 'No, Daddy.' Do you remember any of it?"

"My father, actually my stepfather, used to beat me and my mom all the time. I still dream about it. That's all it is...nothing to worry about."

"Well, I think you need help. I have a friend that I think could help."

"What? A shrink?"

"No. She's a behavioral therapist."

"Not interested."

"Please," Sandy implored. "It's really important."

"Naw, it's just a dream. Let's forget it."

"I think we should talk about..."

"Wait a minute," Tony intruded, "he's coming out."

Musbraum walked to his car and got in. He was wearing dark pants and dark shirt, and carrying a small black bag.

"Duck," Tony whispered. "He may be coming this way."

Backing out of his driveway, Musbraum turned his car in their direction, his headlights splashing over their heads. When he was past them, Tony turned the car around to follow.

At the corner, Musbraum turned right toward the interstate. When he had disappeared from sight, Tony put his headlights on. As they approached the Interstate 74 access, Musbraum entered the westbound on-ramp and exited on Prospect, went south to Kirby Avenue, turned right, and continued across Duncan Road, taking an immediate left onto Maynard Drive.

"He's headed into my neighborhood," Tony exclaimed. "Besides the condos, there are a lot of nice homes there, too."

"You think he's going to burglarize one of these homes?"

"I don't know. But we'll know soon enough."

Musbraum turned into a locked, gated community, stopped at the security box and punched in some numbers. As the gate slowly opened, Tony pulled in behind him and followed him in. When Musbraum turned right, Tony turned left, pulled into a driveway, turned off his lights, then backed out quickly to resume his surveillance.

After coming around a gentle curve, they spotted Musbraum parked in the driveway of a large, auspicious home. The first floor of the exterior was constructed with slump stone, the upper floor was white stucco with decorative redwood trim, painted a dark color. Three dormers broke the line of a mottled tan-tiled roof along with two chimneys, visible from the front.

Tony stopped and shut off the engine.

Stepping out of his car, Musbraum walked confidently toward the house, then casually around to the rear.

Somehow, he knows no one is home. Picking up his car phone, Tony dialed 911.

"Nine one one," came a female voice. "How may I help you?"

"This is Tony Garber, owner of the Holmes Detective Agency. I believe we've spotted a burglary in progress at twenty-eight forty-one New Pine Court."

"That's two eight four one New Pine Court?"

"Yes, Ma'am."

"Would you stay on the line, please?"

"Of course."

Tony handed the phone to Sandy. "Hang on to this. They want an open line to us."

"But what are you going to do?"

"I'm going in."

"Oh, Tony, don't" she pleaded. "It's too dangerous."

"Don't worry." He smiled. "I'll be careful."

"What if he has a gun?"

"So do I," he said quietly, then was off before she could object again.

Crouching, Tony ran to a row of trees that lined the north end of the property. Stopping by a large spruce tree, he looked at the house and listened. He yanked his gun out of his shoulder holster and released the safety. Seeing and hearing nothing, he dashed to a thick rose bush, covered with flowers. He crept forward, circling the house.

Stepping onto a narrow strip of grass, he approached a low hedge. Tony froze. He observed movement in his peripheral vision.

There he is, Tony thought. *He's on the other side of that trellis. Must be working on the burglar alarm system.*

Dropping to one knee, Tony pointed his gun directly at Musbraum. He lifted it when Musbraum moved to the French doors, broke the small window pane with his elbow, slipped his hand inside and entered the house.

Tony slowly backed off and retraced his steps. He knew the suspect would return to his car. *It's a good thing I didn't nab him when I was going to*, he thought. *He wouldn't have had the goods on him, but now when he comes out...*

Tony felt smug as he crept in behind Musbraum's car. Kneeling down by the trunk, he held his gun in the ready position. He listened. Nothing, not even rustling leaves or dogs barking. It was the quietest neighborhood Tony had ever been in.

But he only had to wait about ten minutes before he heard footsteps coming toward him, growing louder with each step. His muscles tightened, ready to spring. His eyes darted here, then there. It was hard to hold back. There was no fear in him, just an overwhelming emotion to move, to act. This feeling was almost exploding within him, when he heard the car door opening.

He leaped out onto the driveway, his legs in a spread-eagle position, gun gripped with two hands, arms outstretched, and shouted, "Freeze. You're under arrest! Hands up, feet back, hands on the top of the car."

Musbraum raised his hands, and turned toward Tony. Tony moved in closer to do a search. Then with what seemed like lightning speed Musbraum's arm came down, striking Tony's gun with his fist, knocking the gun to the ground. After kicking the gun under the car, Musbraum started to run.

Tony looked totally surprised. When he realized Musbraum was getting away, he bolted after him.

Musbraum tripped as he jumped a low hedge, but scrambled to his feet quickly. It was at this moment that Tony leaped headlong over the hedge, and with a flying tackle brought Musbraum down. Both men grunted as they hit the ground and rolled over. Musbraum wound up on top. He doubled his first and hit Tony on the side of his head, then scrambled to get up, but Tony caught his rear foot., pulling him back to the ground. This time Tony was on top, his fist found Murbraum's face with a solid blow. Musbraum ceased to resist.

Tony rolled him over and sat on him, pinning him to the ground, face down .

Two black and whites screeched to a stop. Four police officers cautiously emerged, guns drawn.

Tony held up his hands, face out. "I'm Tony Garber, owner of the Holmes Detective Agency." He stood up, straddling Musbraum. "This is the guy that just burgled this house."

"May I see some I.D., Sir? Slowly."

"Of course, Officer." Tony carefully handed him his private investigator's license. "I was tailing this man. He works for the Empire State Life and Casualty Company, and I have reason to believe he's been involved in the burglaries of many area homes insured by his company."

"Are you the one who called in?"

"Yes, Sir."

"Good job," the police officer stated as he handed back the license. "But you should have waited for us to arrive. It might have been safer for you."

"I understand, Officer, but I was afraid he might get away with the loot. Then it would have been hard to prosecute, if we had no evidence." Tony retrieved his gun, and put it into his holster.

"Do you have a permit for that?" one officer asked.

"Yes, Sir. Right here." He showed his license in his wallet next to his private eye license.

Sandy, who had been waiting in the car, came running up. "Are you all right, Tony?" she asked fearfully. "I've been so worried seeing you with that gun and everything."

Tony with his hair messed up, and his shirt partially pulled out of his pants, slipped his arm around her. "Everything's fine." He indicated Musbraum in handcuffs, being led away. "I got my man," he said with pride.

When Bo had first suggested he carry a gun in a shoulder holster and a smaller, unregistered, throw-away in an ankle holster, it gave him a nagging feeling of uneasiness. But now it was different. In fact, he had enjoyed it. It gave him a great feeling of power. *I like this,* he mused.

*   *   *

Tony was having another cup of coffee when Mr. G entered his office. "I have good news," he said as he closed the door behind him. "Those futures we invested in?"

"Yeah?" Tony answered with heightened interest.

"Well, our partner in Chi just called. On a special unlisted phone I have. So we don't have to worry about being bugged. Anyway, he says we have already tripled our original investment. Not bad, huh?"

"Great. But how are we paid?"

"That's the nice part about it. It's automatically deposited into your Internet account. However, and I hope you don't mind, I asked him to double our investment. We'll earn a lot of money a lot faster. The other third was deposited. All you have to do is take a look at your account. I'm sure he put the money in. He can deposit into your account, but not take it out or see anything on your statement."

"I sure appreciate it, Mr. G."

"I'm glad to do it. We're just scratching each other's backs. That way we both make money." With his hand on the doorknob, he concluded, "I have to go now, Tony. But why don't you ask Sandy to invite you to dinner again? We'd both like that."

"Thanks, Mr. G."

Tony slowly exhaled a long breath, after Mr. G was gone. He slumped down in his chair, relieved. *I always feel uptight around him,* he reflected. *But one thing for sure, I'll be checking my internet account regularly.*

*   *   *

A vigorous workout should get my blood moving, Tony thought. He had converted one of his bedrooms into a weight room. Now, he was watching himself in the floor-to-ceiling mirror as he curled twenty-five pound weights in each hand. Left then right, left then right. He was wearing swim trunks.

He was pleased with what he saw. His skin glistened as he perspired, showing the rippling effect on his abdominals, his deltoids developing enough to give an appearance of broader shoulders, how his pecs stood out in good definition and his lats flared out from the waist to armpits.

Tony put the weights on the carpet, turned around, picked up a hand mirror from a nearby table and viewed his back. When he flexed his muscles, he noticed the same rippling down his posterior.

He turned around again, faced the mirror, and smiled. Very good, he said to himself. It's too bad I have to wear suits to work. I wonder how my staff would react if I walked into the office with a tight T-shirt and shorts. He laughed at the imagined sight.

Putting the mirror back on the table, Tony glanced at his watch. Oh, oh. It's almost noon. I got to meet Sandy at the... What is it called? Oh, yes. The Krannert Art Museum over on Peabody Drive. I'd better get myself in gear.

Stepping into the shower, Tony vigorously lathered his body with soap. He began to sing, "Making out with Mandy..." He loved that tune. Someday, maybe he'd sing it for Sandy. *Ha. That'll be the day*, he thought. *She's such a prude, but...* Dropping the thought, he went back to singing his song.

Toweling off, he selected an off-white velour shirt with a deep opening at the neck, black Dockers, and for his feet, loafers.

It was Saturday and he didn't have to go into the office, but he needed to work on his books. Tony wanted to make sure he was operating in the black. He had been taking bookkeeping classes for the past few months and found out he was a whiz with numbers, according to the instructor. He really enjoyed doing it,

*   *   *

When Tony approached the museum, Sandy was standing next to the entrance. Taking the steps two at a time, Tony stopped in front of her. "Sorry if I'm a little late, but time got away from me."

"I haven't been here long. Just a few minutes. Are you ready to go in?"

"Sure, but I came to feast my eyes on you, not some freakin' paintings."

"Tony! Behave yourself. They're not just paintings. They're creations of artists. Regular painters paint houses, but artists paint with their hearts."

"Okay. Again I'm sorry. It's just that I'm not into this sort of thing."

"That's because you don't understand it. Maybe I can help in that respect. If I explain it to you, after awhile, you'll be a natural. Bo told me you're smart, learn fast, and you're without fear. Fear, he said, inhibits a person and causes that person to be less effective."

"Did he say that?" Tony asked, delight on this face.

"Yes, he did. He's been very impressed with you."

"He said nothing to me about it."

"Of course not. If he complimented you, it would sound like he was doing it, because you're the boss."

"I suppose so."

Tony paid the entrance fee, and they entered a large atrium. Paintings hung on all the walls. Sandy took his arm and guided him to the first one. Two couples stood in the way admiring it. When they moved on to the next painting, Sandy asked, "What do you think of it?" She studied the pamphlet she'd received at the door.

He glanced at it. "It looks like someone threwup and then slapped some colorful paint around it."

"Very good, Tony. It's called 'Regurgitation. It says here that the artist was sick with the flu when he did it. He just painted what he felt."

"And you call that art?"

"It's called abstract expressionism. It's what he was feeling at the time, his emotions."

"That's stupid with a capital S," he said, disgusted.

"Well, maybe this one is a little gross. But some people say it's a 'now' painting. It's down to earth or earthy."

"And it should be buried in the earth."

"It's certainly not my favorite, either. But maybe this next one will be more what you like."

They worked their way through a small crowd and stopped in front of a large vertical painting in an ornate gold frame. "Okay, Tony, what do you think this one is?"

"I don't have the foggiest. It means nothing to me."

"Don't you see the person in it, the human being?"

"No, but I do see something that could vaguely, very vaguely resemble a ghostly person. But it dosen't look human."

"It's called 'Fear and Pain.' The mauve mass near the top is the brain. The reason it's not shaped like a brain is because those irregular strokes emanating out from it show the frustration and suffering it's experiencing. The arms extending outward are warding off the attacks of the world and the cruelty of it. And the feet spread apart indicate he's trying to stand firm against the evils of the world. At least that's what the brochure says about it. I can see it and feel it. Can you?"

"The only thing I feel about it is that you and the art world have got to be kidding."

"You're hopeless. I'll tell you what. Let's move into the next room. It's more realistic."

Tony glanced at her and chuckled.

"What's so funny?" she asked.

"Your face when you try to pour some culture into me. You have this hopeful expression. I just think it's cute, adorable, fantastic..."

"You're impossible," she broke in. "If you don't want to do this, we can go."

"Oh, I don't want to go. I just want to see art that I can understand, not this weird stuff."

They moved into another room. "These," she said, "might be more to your liking."

She stopped in front of a three-foot by four-foot painting in a matted cherry frame. Underneath it was the title "Amber Afternoon."

Tony looked at it for a moment. "Now this is something I can understand. It's obviously a wet autumn day. There's an old, turn-of-the-century house, surrounded by red and yellow leaves on some trees and on the ground, representing autumn. And in the foreground they're burning a pile of those leaves."

"Very good, Tony. What else do you see?"

"All the lights are on."

"Yes, they are. The artist is a relatively newcomer to the world of art, but he is becoming more and more successful all the time. His name is Thomas Kinkade. And this brochure says, he is 'renowned for infusing light into his paintings, creating incredibly romantic and tranquil scenes. Known as "The painter of light," Kinkade has an almost uncanny ability to recreate dramatic effects of pictorial lighting in a way that makes the image seem to glow from within.'"

"That's nice," Tony said without enthusiasm.

"You still don't enjoy this, do you?"

On a score of one to ten," Tony stroked his chin, "it's a six or seven. But, and I emphasize the but,

I am really enjoying you. I always have, and I always will."

"Okay, then take my hand and enjoy me as I enjoy these paintings."

CHAPTER THIRTEEN

Bo called Monday morning from San Ysidro, California at 8:05. Tony was already in the office. He knew that he could accomplish a lot more work with no one else around.

"Hi, Tony," Bo's voice crackled, over a poor connection. "Having any problems there?"

"No," Tony answered.

"Well, it's not going smoothly here. I need help."

"What's the problem?"

"I need an accountant; somebody who knows bookkeeping."

"Don't they have their own accountants out there?"

"Yeah, but I don't trust them. I think they're frying the books, cooking 'em the way they want, to hide pilfering. And that's why Mr. Fratenello asked me to come down here. He thinks they're ripping him off, and I agree, but I'm not good with books. That's why I need someone else."

"Who's Mr. Fratenello?"

"He's a friend of Mr. G's from Chicago."

"Oh. So anyway, you need someone good with books?"

"Yes."

"Do you want me to come? I'm getting very good with bookkeeping. I'm sure that if they're doctoring them, I could spot it."

"Are you sure you could find it?" Bo sounded a little skeptical.

"I'm sure," Tony answered confidently.

"Okay, boss. I'll book you a room here in San Diego at the hotel where I'm staying, the Towne and Country.

"I'll grab the first flight outta here."

*   *   *

Where's the smog? Tony questioned in amazement as his plane flew through a clear cerulean sky over California. Houses and businesses whipped by below as the plane approached Lindbergh Field, the San Diego International Airport. The final descent was very angular, and Tony felt the plane was too close to the buildings, but very relieved when the wheels finally touched down with a screeching sound of rubber meeting the runway.

Bo met Tony as Tony exited the Boeing 757.

"Good flight?" he asked.

"Yes. Uneventful. The kind I like."

"The kind everyone likes."

"That's for sure."

They didn't talk again until they had picked up Tony's luggage and were on their way to their hotel on "Hotel Circle in San Diego." Bo was driving a rented black Ford Bronco. He headed north on Highway Five, then entered the on-ramp onto interstate Eight East into Hotel Circle. "Our hotel's not far from the airport. In fact, we're almost there."

"Okay. Now tell me about the case."

"It's fairly simple. Mr. Fratenello was very suspicious that this Mexican outfit was skimming some of the cream."

"What kind of cream are we talking about?" Tony asked.

"Drugs, various kinds, but mostly heroin."

"Drugs?"

"It's all right," Bo told him. "You don't have to worry. Everyone in authority on the Mexican side has been paid off. We will be safe, because we're not really involved. We're just looking at accounting books in a Tijuana office."

"How do they get the drugs into the U.S.?"

"With money. Lots of it. It's shipped in a variety of containers, like cheap ceramic figures, cute little stuffed animals, and other items the Mexicans ship across the border to outlets. The trucks go through the San Ysidro crossing. Certain border patrol guards with the INS are bought and paid for. They let them know when they're on duty, and that's when they send their special trucks through."

"How much is usually shipped on one truck?"

"It varies, depending on a number of things – the purity of the product and the types of drugs. One truckload would generally be in the tens of millions of dollars with a street value ten times that. Give or take a mil here or there."

"Wow!"

"Yeah, we're talking about a lot of money. That's why Mr. Fratenello is so concerned. A little skimming could mean millions out of his pocket."

While Tony was chewing on that, they arrived at the hotel.

After checking in, Bo asked, "Are you hungry?"

"No, I ate on the plane."

"Then maybe we can swing down to Tijuana. It's not far. About forty miles. You can take a look at the books."

"That's fine. I picked up three hours coming out here. It's still early for me."

*   *   *

An hour later, they crossed over into Mexico. Tony noticed the dirty streets and sidewalks and the general disrepair of some of the buildings.

Bo stopped in front of a dingy stucco, one-story building with a red tile roof. Some of the stucco was broken, exposing wire mesh.

Tony followed Bo into a shabby hallway that led to a large bustling room filled with people, computers, and other office machines. "This is the accounting firm. They handle books for a number of local businesses. But only one man handles Mr. Fratenello's books. He's the owner, over in the corner, behind that partition. Let's go see him."

"Mr. Ortega, I want you to meet an associate of mine, Tony Garber. Tony, this is Mr. Ortega." He was a good six inches shorter than Tony. His raven-colored hair crowned a porcine face and body. His black suit and tie were rumpled.

The two men shook hands. "So you're the one who's going to check my books. I really resent it, but if that's what Mr. Fratenello wants, that's what he gets," he said with aloofness.

"It's no reflection on you," Bo came back. "It's just an annual check. Like taking inventory."

"I still don't like it."

"We're just doing our job."

"You know where the books are." He pointed to a shelf behind him.

Bo moved around the desk and picked up the two account books. He walked out into the main room and over to a table by a back window. Tony followed.

When they were seated, Tony said, "He doesn't like us."

Bo laughed. "How could you tell?"

Tony smiled, then looked out the dirty window. The rear of the property was cluttered with rusting auto parts, rotting tires, and odd pieces of paper fluttering around. In the distance it was the same, except with a few dilapidated buildings thrown in.

Bo handed the books to Tony, then tilted his chair back against the wall and closed his eyes.

Tony pulled out a pocket calculator and checked the figures. He worked for over an hour, then said to Bo, "These figures all add up. But there are two sets. Is that one for the IRS and then the real ones?"

"No, actually one is in U.S. dollars, the other in pesos."

"Oh. That makes a lot of difference. But the figures are still accurate for both."

"So, how is he doing it?"

"I don't know, yet. But I'll figure it out."

"We don't have a lot of time. Mr. Fratenello wants it right away."

"Can we take these books with us?"

"He doesn't want them outta the building. And that's orders From Mr. F, himself. Besides why do you need them if all the figures add up?"

"I guess I don't."

Returning the books to Mr. Ortega, they headed back to the hotel, had dinner and went to bed. Tony's room was on the sixth floor, and Bo's on the eighth.

Lying on top of the bed in his boxer shorts, Tony couldn't sleep. He fitfully tossed and turned, going over the books in his mind with no success. It was just after midnight when realization hit him. Picking up the phone without thinking what time it was, he dialed Bo's room.

Bo's groggy voice responded, "Yeah?"

"Bo, this is Tony. I think I may have it figured out. About the books, I mean."

"Are you still awake?"

"Yes."

"But I wasn't. I'm glad you have it figured out, but can't it wait until morning?"

"I'm sorry, Bo. I wasn't thinking. Call me in the morning when you get up."

After hanging up, Tony realized that Bo probably would be calling him while he was still asleep. *Payback, I guess*, he thought.

*　　*　　*

Bo did call Tony when he was dead asleep. It was a little after 6:00 a.m. "Get dressed, buddy," he snickered. "By the time you get down to the coffee shop, I'll have breakfast for both of us. What do you want?"

"I don't care. I'll eat whatever you order. See you in a bit."

Thirty minutes later, they were drinking fresh orange juice and coffee and eating huevos rancheros.

"I was famished," Tony offered.

"Um," mumbled Bo. He was still chewing on a piece of toast. Then as he sipped his coffee, he said, "Why don't you explain what you were going to tell me in the middle of the night, while I finish my breakfast?"

"Okay. If I'm not mistaken, Mexico has been in a severe inflationary period for a number of years. Is that correct?"

"Yes."

"How much is the exchange today?"

"Probably around three thousand to one."

"That much?"

"Uh huh."

"Let's just say for the sake of easy figuring that it is three thousand to one today. In a couple of days it could be thirty-three hundred to one. Right?"

"Sure," Bo said, stroking his chin in thought.

"Now if he makes his exchange today on thirty million pesos, he would receive ten thousand American dollars. But if he waits for a few days to put it in the books and now the exchange is thirty-three hundred to one, it would show as nine thousand ninety dollars and change. He can then pocket almost one thousand bucks. If he does that every day, he earns about three hundred sixty thousand a year. And if I remember correctly from those books, that figure is low. I'll bet his take would be in the millions each year. But first, we need to get a copy of the exchange rate for last year."

Bo was still stroking his chin. Then he stopped and looked squarely at Tony. "Nice job, Tony. When you said you could come down and do the books, I had my doubts, but not anymore."

"Thanks, Bo."

"And I know where we can get a copy of what the exchange rates were over the past year. It's the bank that does all the transferring from here to Mr. F's bank."

After receiving the exchange rates, Bo and Tony returned to Mexico and Mr. Ortega's accounting office. Ortega looked at them with flinty eyes. The day before it was with indifference, but now his eyes were filled with hate. He handed the books to Tony, but didn't say anything.

When they sat down again at the same table, Tony murmured, "It might be an old cliché, but if looks could kill, we'd be dead."

"I guess we would. But I don't understand why the sudden change."

"Maybe he thinks we're on to him," Tony answered, already checking the books with the exchange rate copy.

Bo leaned back again, but this time his eyes were open. He was deep in thought about the change in Ortega.

A few minutes later, Tony said, "That's it. That's exactly what he's been doing. I don't know how much, because it would take weeks to go through all of this. But I'm sure that's how he did it."

"Now, we take 'em. The books, I mean. I'm sure Mr. Fratenello would agree, too. We'll take 'em back with us and show him how it's been done. He'll take it from there."

"What do you think will happen to Mr. Ortega?"

"He won't be around much longer. He'll be taking a one-way trip to I don't know where, and I don't care. I just wouldn't want to be in his boots."

"No way." Tony shivered at the thought.

"Come on. Let's get outta here."

They hurried through the office and were approaching their car when Mr. Ortega and two rough-looking men stepped from around the corner of the building pointing Colt .45s at them. "Just a minute, gentlemen," Ortega said through gritted teeth. "I can't let you leave with those books. Step through that door next to my office entrance, please." He motioned with the index finger of his free hand.

One of the gunmen with greasy hair and a cold, hard look in his eyes preceded them. He turned around as he entered, keeping his weapon on them at all times. The other man and then Mr. Ortega followed.

"How did you know?" Bo asked, trying to buy time.

"The banker that I introduced you to a couple of days ago who gave you the copy of the exchange rate is one of my most trusted men. He called me as soon as you left the bank. I knew then that you'd figured it out and that I had to take care of you."

"So now what?"

"You'll be found dead in an alley. An apparent mugging gone wrong."

"It won't work, Ortega. Mr. Fratenello will just send someone else down here."

"But by that time I will have redone the books to correct what you found out." Then turning to his two gunmen, he added, "You boys know what to do."

Mr. Ortega left abruptly. One of the gunmen screwed a noise suppressor to the barrel of his gun. The other man kept his gun trained on them. As soon as the first man had finished, the second one began to mount his silencer.

Bo knew if the men were going to do anything, it would have to be soon. These two were very alert, and Bo rejected every idea that came to him.

Tony, not more than five feet away, appeared to be at a loss, too.

Then it happened, the one moment he needed. A backfiring car outside, distracted the men just for an instant, but long enough for Bo to react. His leg came up in an arc, kicking the first man's wrist. There was a cracking sound as the Carpal bone snapped. Then he grabbed the man and twisted him around just as the other man turned and fired. The man Bo held took the slug in the stomach. He cried out, his hands clutching his abdomen. Blood trickled out between his fingers as he slumped to the floor.

The moment the gun fired, Tony instinctively responded. His foot swiftly came up, catching the second man in the groin. As the man doubled over in excruciating pain, Tony took one step forward, brought his knee up with all the strength he could muster and caught the man full in the face. The man flipped over on his back, the gun flying out of his hand. He struck his head on the cement floor with such force that even Tony winced at the sound.

Congratulating each other with a handshake, they stepped cautiously out into the street, looked around, saw no one, and quickly drove away and back to the good ole U.S. of A.

CHAPTER FOURTEEN

Feeling a little squeamish, Tony glanced around as he used the brass hand knocker. The townhouse was impressive. The modern gray exterior with white trim was nestled in rolling hills of neatly mowed and edged lawns. A light cool breeze blew. Spring was pushing its way back in, although at that moment, Tony wasn't aware of it. He had received a rather cryptic phone call just an hour ago. The male voice had identified himself as Roger Thornfield, the chief of police for Champaign, and had asked him to come to his residence. That's when Tony started to get a little angry. When he asked the chief what it was all about, the chief grew edgy. "Not on the phone. I'll explain when you get here."

In the back of his mind, Tony had the feeling the chief was after his money, too. This thought disturbed him even more. At least with Mr. G, I've received something in return. If this loser wants a piece of my pie, I'll... I'll ... I don't know what I'll do.

When the door finally opened, Tony was looking at the man he and Sandy had seen in the restaurant. He was a little more than six feet tall, with a shock of taffy-colored hair. He was wearing his full uniform and a beaming smile. "Come in, young man. I've heard much about you from my good friend, Mr. G."

Not too much, Tony hoped.

"Come into my study and have a seat. And excuse the uniform. I have a formal function I have to attend after we have our little talk."

Tony followed him through double sliding oak doors just off the foyer. It was a large room with an oval oriental rug in the center. The chief moved toward a massive desk, sitting just off the rug. Paintings and book cases lined the walls. The two elongated windows were up high, near the beamed, angled ceiling, giving some light but also privacy.

Pulling out his high backed leather chair, the chief stopped. "Would you care for a drink? I'm going to have one. It's almost five. I have most anything."

"Sure. A bourbon on the rocks," Tony answered, still uneasy.

The chief unbuttoned his profusely medaled jacket, took it off and neatly laid it on the arm of an overstuffed couch. "My well-stocked bar is in this little alcove, out of sight from some of my 'tee-totaling' friends. If they see you have one drink, they believe you're an alcoholic. Ridiculous."

Tony didn't say anything. He stared at the big desk, its glass surface interrupted with only a small green shaded lamp, a large clean green ashtray and one lone sheet of paper, directly in its center.

"You may need this." The chief said as he handed a drink to Tony, and sat down behind his desk.

Tony looked directly into the chief's gray eyes. "What's this all about, Mr. Thornfield?"

"You can call me chief. Everyone else does," he stated calmly. But now the smile was gone. "Mr. G came to me with your fingerprints on a drinking glass. I ran them through the FBI and found out you're a wanted man. Your real name is..." He looked at the paper on his desk, placing his finger near the top and then continued, "Burton Alexander Helmsley."

I knew it, Tony thought, his temper flaring. He felt his blood start to boil, his face begin to flush with rage.

Slowly raising his eyes from the paper on his desk, the chief proceeded, ignoring the malevolent expression on Tony's face. "Now we can get down to the nitty gritty that you've been so anxious to get to. When I apprised Mr. G of your real name and that you were wanted for a two-and-a-half million-dollar robbery and gave him a copy of this rap sheet," the chief said, picking up the paper, then placing it neatly back in the center of his desk, "He asked me to keep it under my hat. That he had some plans for you. I did what he asked, because Mr. G and I are friends, but a few days ago I asked myself, 'What's in it for me?' I should get a piece of the action, I reasoned. And that's why I invited you here, alone, without witnesses."

"Why should I give you anything?" Tony growled, his anger erupting. "I took all the risks! You've done nothing!"

"But I will be protecting you. I'll be keeping you out of jail."

The chief's smile increased Tony's fury.

"Look," the chief said, "After paying me two hundred grand, you'll still have plenty left for yourself."

Tony's anger exploded, sending him into an uncontrollable rage. He jumped to this feet, arms flailing. His mind snapped. "You...you...you!!" he screamed. He reached down pulled out his Smith & Wesson from his ankle holster, and fired it twice. The chief's face registered shock and disbelief as two red holes appeared in his chest, clustered square in the middle of his shirt pocket. He slumped forward onto the desk.

Not comprehending what he had done, Tony sat down for a minute, just staring at the chief. When reality slowly returned, he got up, went around the desk and felt the chief's carotid artery. No pulse.

What am I going to do? his mind shrieked. What? What? First, I'm going to settle down, get control of myself and think. Think...think, he pleaded, but to no avail. He was pacing the floor over the oriental rug and back to the edge of the desk when a metallic sound interrupted his desperate thoughts.

Someone was at the front door with a key. He quietly crept over to the door of the study, pressing himself against the wall.

"Where are you, Sweetheart?" a female voice questioned. "Oh, there you are." High heels clicked on the marble floor as she approached the study. One step inside the room, and she stopped, a perplexed look on her face. Tony swung the gun, grazing her over her right ear. Her facial expression went blank as she fainted and slumped to the floor on her back.

My God, it's that woman from the restaurant, his girlfriend! He remembered their vociferous argument. An idea germinated in Tony's mind. He picked her up, carried her to the same chair he had occupied minutes before and placed her in it. Searching the drawers of the desk, he found some Scotch tape, using it to wrap her arms to the armrests and her legs to the chair legs. Next he wiped the fingerprints off his throw-away gun. He pressed the gun into her hand. Then he let the pistol drop onto the rug.

Wait a minute, a thought came to him. *A paraffin test would show I've fired a gun recently, and she hasn't.*

He took the tape off her right arm and putting the gun back in her hand, he pointed it at the ceiling and fired it, then taped her arm to the chair again.

He gazed at the scene, reviewing it in his mind. He picked up the ashtray from the desk and dropped it onto the rug, close by, and then kicked the gun under the desk. His heart beating wildly, he grabbed the phone and started to dial 911.

Tony stopped short when he realized he had almost forgotten a very important item. Returning the phone to its cradle, he grabbed the rap sheet, took it into the bathroom, burned it, and carefully flushed the ashes down the toilet. Then he completed his 911 call.

*　　　*　　　*

"Give it to me again, Mr. Garber," softly commanded Lieutenant Daniel Moynahan, the lead detective in the Champaign Homicide Division. He had a square, pugged face, topped with a crew cut. They were standing in the foyer, while a forensics team worked in the chief's study.

"How many times do I have to tell it?" Tony asked, a little irritated.

"As many times as asked."

"Okay, okay," Tony replied, realizing his position. He knew he had to be cool and co-operate fully. "It's like I said, I was having a business meeting with the chief..." "What kind of business?" the Lieutenant interrupted.

"Personal."

"Tell me about it."

"It's confidential."

"Not anymore. The chief's dead," Lt. Moynahan came back.

Tony thought for a moment, then shrugged. "Okay. He wanted me to place his old girlfriend, whatever her name, under surveillance, to find out where she goes, what she does and who she sees. Also to dig into her past as much and as fast as possible. Especially to find out anything he could use to get her off his back. That last part is a direct quote."

"Her name is Nancy Idenhauer."

"Whatever. Anyway, that's what we were discussing when I excused myself and went to replenish my drink. He had told me to help myself anytime, so I did."

"The one off his study?" queried the lieutenant.

"Yes."

"Then what happened?" the lieutenant was quickly scribbling notes in his little black book.

"I was wiping my hands on a napkin when I heard the front door open. She must have had her own key. I was about to come out, when in she storms, shouting, almost screaming, 'You dumped me like a bag of dirty laundry! You can't do this to me! I won't let you. I'll kill you first!' Or something to that effect.

"That's when I noticed she had a gun in her hand. She pointed it at his chest. I ran toward her, but before I could get there, she pulled the trigger. Twice, I think. I grabbed her wrists. She was a wild cat, screaming, kicking and trying to get loose. Another shot went off, then."

Tony took a quick breath and continued. "Holding on with one hand, I grabbed the first thing I could. It was the ashtray, and I hit her with it. And that's it. The chair I had been sitting in was behind her. She fell almost directly into it. I kicked the gun she had dropped under the desk, picked up the tape off the chief's desk, taped her to the chair and called nine one one."

"Did the chief say anything to her?"

"No. He just put up one hand, like trying to stop her or get her not to do it. I'm not sure."

The lieutenant studied his notes a minute, then looked up. "All right for now. We've taken her to the hospital. You must have hit her pretty hard. She's still unconscious. May have a concussion."

"Well, I was desperate when I hit her. She was trying to kill me."

"Maybe so. But we won't be able to talk to her until she comes around."

"May I leave now, Lieutenant?" Tony asked politely. "I have a lot of work to do."

"Sure, but we may have some more questions later. And we certainly will need you as a witness."

"No problem, Lieutenant. One last thing. She did threaten the chief at the Dutch Restaurant a couple of days ago. Mr. G's daughter, and I and other people witnessed it."

*   *   *

Tony stepped out of the chief's house into a brisk evening breeze. His mind, however, was in a turmoil. Several police cars were scattered around the driveway. He hoped he had not forgotten anything. He knew the smallest detail could trip him up. Besides, he also knew that when the chief's girlfriend came to, she would shout her innocence.

He smiled slightly when he pictured her screaming "I didn't do it!"

His smile increased when he realized how clever he had been, his quick response to the situation after he heard her coming in and his concocted story. *Keep it simple*, he remembered thinking when interviewed by the lieutenant. *Keep it simple. Less to remember.*

*   *   *

That night Tony tossed and turned, twisting the blankets tightly around him until he felt claustrophobic and bound up, like in a cocoon. He awoke in a cold sweat. His recurring nightmare hung heavily over him. He just couldn't shake it as much as he tried. Someone, and he couldn't remember who, had told him he had to make a decision that he wasn't going to have those dreams again, and keep saying it and believing it.

"I'm not going to have that dream anymore," he repeated to himself, trying to believe. But it didn't work. Then he remembered something else someone had said, from Shakespeare: *'Me thinks you protest too much.'*

Now, I feel very confused. Maybe I should do what Sandy suggested, but I just don't like the idea of going to a shrink, he thought in disgust. *She said this friend isn't a psychoanalyst, but a behavioral therapist. And I really need help, I guess.*

*   *   *

Dr. Michelle Seigelwitz sat in her high-backed chair behind a desk void of papers or anything else, except for a lamp and a pen, which she picked up from its cradle in the base of the lamp. The decor in the room was simple, a few chairs and a couch. Charts, cryptic drawings, and framed diplomas hung on the walls. Tony was staring at one of the drawings. He couldn't figure it out. *Looks like a bat with something in its mouth.*

His eyes dropped down from the drawing to the couch beneath it. Then he wondered if she was going to ask him to lie down on it. *No way,* he said to himself.

Dr. Seigelwitz smiled. Then almost as if she were reading his mind, she said, "Don't worry. I don't ask patients to lie down. We'll just talk while you're seated where you are. Is that okay?"

"Sure," he answered in relief, finally looking at her. *Attractive,* he thought, *in a severe way.* Her dark brown hair was pulled back and braided, then coiled into a bun. Her even features were still smiling.

Again Tony's eyes dropped. *Nice body*, he thought, *At least from what I can see.* She was smartly dressed in a dark gray, pinstriped suit with a high-necked white blouse. Her chocolate brown eyes seemed to penetrate his soul.

"Let's use first names, if you don't mind. Mine's Michelle. Okay?"

"Okay," he responded nervously. *This is kind of stupid,* he kept thinking. *I never should have come. I know one thing. When I get outta here, I'm gone, forever.*

"Now, Tony, I want you to go back as far as you can remember. Back to your earliest memories. Okay?"

"But I don't know exactly what I remember or what I was told afterward."

"That's all right. Just do the best you can."

"When I was a little guy, maybe four or five," Tony said in deep thought as he stared at the lamp on her desk, "my mother took me to Belmont Harbor in Lake Michigan, on the north side of Chicago. Not far from where we lived. She sat on a bench at the top of the beach, knitting or sewing or something like that. I played in the shallow water, maybe seventy or eighty feet away, where she could keep an eye on me. The water was quite calm in the harbor.

"On this one day, I was playing like I was swimming. I was in water less than a foot deep. I kicked my feet and took a stroke with one hand, while the other propelled me along by digging into the sand. I remember thinking that people will think I'm really swimming. I was real proud.

"But what I didn't realize was that I was moving farther and farther down the beach. And my mother was a little too engrossed in her knitting, I guess.

"When I had finished swimming, I came out of the water and ran up to where I thought my mother was sitting, not realizing I had swum down a couple hundred feet. My mother wasn't at that bench. Other people were sitting there. I looked around checking a few of the other benches, but not far enough to where she still sat.

"I guess I thought maybe she had gone home without me. I began to cry and walk toward home. But I had to get to the other side of Lake Shore Drive, a very busy thoroughfare. As I stood there crying, some kind gentleman asked me if I wanted to go across the street. When I nodded, yes, he picked me up, wet bathing suit and all, and carried me over.

"I walked west on Belmont Avenue. As I passed a Catholic church, two nuns and a priest were about to enter their car when one of the nuns spotted me. She asked me what was wrong. Between sobs, I told her I couldn't find my mommy. Then she asked, 'Where do you live?' And I told her on Clifton Avenue. So she said, 'C'mon, we'll take you home.'"

"When we approached my street, she asked, 'This way?' and I nodded. As we drew near,

I pointed out the house I lived in and they let me out."

"Did they take you to the door?" Dr. Seigelwitz interrupted.

"No. I can't remember why. Maybe I just jumped out and ran toward the house. I don't know."

"Okay. Go on."

"When I got inside the front hall, I rang the bell and hammered on the door of our apartment, but got no answer. I was scared. Really scared. I sat down on the floor and hugged my knees. I guess I cried again.

"I don't know how long it was before our mailman found me. He rang the bell for the people on the second floor, but they weren't home. But the woman on the third floor was. She was a very kind, understanding elderly lady, who took me in and fed me milk and cookies to get my mind off my problem.

"Meanwhile, I was told later in life, that my mom had the authorities dragging the lake and police searching the beach and surrounding neighborhoods. She had also called my father, an electrician, and he came down to Belmont Harbor and tried to comfort Mom, but he was afraid, too..

"Later, the police told my parents to go home, and if they found out anything, they'd call or come by to tell them.

"I was watching out the front window of the third floor apartment and saw my parents drive up.

I ran down the stairs to greet them. And I'm sure they cried when they saw I was alive and well.

"And that's as far back as I can remember."

"Very good, Tony. We'll pick up there the next time you come. But first, I want to explain some things to you, such as postraumatic stress disorder and flooding." She talked briefly about this and then Tony left, feeling more at ease.

That was easy. A piece of cake, Tony thought as he left. *Maybe I will come back. I'll talk to Sandy about it when I see her for lunch.*

*   *   *

Sandy had been very pleased when she heard from her friend, Dr. Seigelwitz, that Tony had gone into her office for a session. "What do you think, Michelle?" Sandy asked when they talked on the phone.

A thought popped up in the back of Sandy's mind. *What was it that my psych prof said in class last week? Something about abused children. Oh, yes--most abused children grow up to be abusers. That's a bit scary considering my present relation-ship with Tony.*

"I can't say." Dr. Seigelwitz said, "As you know our sessions are confidential."

"I know that. But what I have to know for me is if he would be a good father to our children, if things go that far.

"I understand. But it's much too early to come to any conclusions. When that time comes, if there is a problem, I will be able to warn you. Ethically, I can't reveal any of the details, but the circumstances would allow me to suggest that marriage would not be a good thing, until certain problems had been cleared up."

Sandy mulled this over in her mind as she waited for Tony in their favorite restaurant, the Blue Lagoon. She was hungry, but also eager to hear what Tony thought about Dr. Seigelwitz. I hope he was responsive, in a positive sense.

As he approached the table, the expression on his face indicated nothing. In fact, he looked a little somber.

He sat down heavily. He had already decided to tease her. He immediately saw that he was being successful. The disappointment was evident in her face. "Hi, Honey," she said. "How did it go with the doctor?"

"Oh, fine. It wasn't all bad. All I had to do was talk about myself, and that's easy."

"Are you going back?" She asked, hopefully.

A big grin creeped across Tony's face. He couldn't tease her anymore. "Yes, yes, yes. I'm going back. I don't want anyone else to know about it, but I really enjoyed it. She has a way that relaxes me."

"Tell me all about it," she bubbled.

"Well, let's see. What did she call it? Something like, 'acute and chronic Posttraumatic Stress Disorder.' Or something like that. Anyway, it's obvious, according to her, by my recurring nightmares.

She knows all about it. She's smart, really smart. At least about those things. Things like what happened to me as a kid can persist for years. That's why I still have a little problem now. But she said it's not bad, nothing that can't be cured. I can't wait."

"Did she say how it can be treated?"

"Yeah. It's called 'Flooding.' And what they do is desensitize you by talking about it. After you do it long enough the problem fades. How fast depends on the individual and how deeply seated the problem is. It's kind of interesting. She also mentioned behavior modification. It's a replacement thing. She replaces the bad with the good. I don't know much about it, but this substitution is something that can be learned, and I'm a good learner."

"I know you are," she said enthusiastically.

"It's like restructuring the mind. We first go into a relaxation mode, to get the body and mind to relax. Then we just talk. "When we were done, I was so relaxed I just wanted to go home and take a nap, but I wanted to see you first and tell you all about it."

"I'm so proud of you, Tony," she uttered, nearly in tears. "You did something not many people would have the courage or intelligence to do." She reached across the table, took Tony's hand in hers, and caressed it tenderly.

CHAPTER FIFTEEN

Bo was looking at him speculatively as Tony explained the murder situation ."I guess she's been denying it all over the place,"

"Vehemently," Bo responded. "In fact, I'm told she sounds quite convincing. It's your word against hers. But she has a motive, you don't."

Before Tony could continue, Mr. G knocked on the door and opened it. "May I come in? I have a big job for you two. Or am I interrupting something?"

"No, no," Tony answered. "We were just discussing that Nancy something-or-other murder case."

"What is her last name?" Mr. G asked.

"Nancy Idenhauer," Bo answered.

"Oh, yeah. Tony, you were a witness. Isn't that right?"

"Yes, sir. I saw the whole thing."

He looked thoughtful for a moment, then said, "Well, back to business. Tony, I want you to meet my boss. Bo, he knows. And if you impress him, he'll have a job for you, a big one."

Meet his boss? Tony's mind raced. *I don't know if I want to have anything to do with this guy. He could be dangerous.*

"Sure thing, Mr. G," Bo replied before Tony could object.

"I'll pick the two of you up at seven tomorrow morning," Mr. G responded as he left the room.

Tony watched as Mr. G walked through the outer office.

"Why did you do that?" Tony asked.

"Do what?"

"Agree for us to go up to Chi. I don't know if I want to go. Those are dangerous people up there."

"I agree with you. But what could we do, say 'no' to Mr. G, or worse yet, to his boss?"

Tony slowly shook his head. "I guess not."

*   *   *

Mr. G identified himself at the wrought iron gates that protected the entrance to the expansive estate. The electronically controlled gates opened smoothly. Mr. G's sleek limousine wound its way up the circular drive that cut through neatly trimmed rose gardens, and manicured lawns. The imposing structure ahead loomed up before them. There were men working in the flower beds and around the front entrance of the house.

"Nice place," Tony muttered.

No one else said anything as they rolled to a stop in front of the mansion. An olive-skinned young man with dark curly hair opened the car door. Standing in the doorway of the house, a short burly man, probably in his early sixties, with arms opened wide, gave Mr. G a hug and a kiss on both cheeks. "It is good to see you, Sam. And who do we have here?"

"Mr. Fratenello, I want you to meet Tony Garber, the owner of the Holmes Detective Agency. You already know Donald Bobbyo. And this, gentlemen, is Salvatore Fratenello."

"So you're the boys that done that nice job in TJ."

"Yes, sir," Tony and Bo said in unison.

"Come in, come in." They shook hands.

Tony stared in amazement when he stepped into the foyer. It was the largest entryway he had ever seen. The off-white walls were at least twenty feet high and trimmed in gold. In the center of the ceiling hung a very large, sparkling chandelier. Deep-piled, burgundy carpets led to a large circular staircase with the same carpeting and brass railings to the upper floor.

"Over here, Tony," called Bo as he followed the other two toward the back of the house.

Getting his bearings again, Tony caught up with them as they passed through a large pantry area off the kitchen and out onto a patio surrounding a cloverleaf swimming pool.

"Sit," Sal barked, pointing to the patio chairs. "Now what would you like to drink? I know, it's iced tea for you, Sam. But what about you guys?"

"The same," they both answered at the same time, then looked at each other in surprise.

As Sal left for the drinks, Tony's attention was drawn to the young woman playing with a child, not more than two years old, in the shallow end of the pool.

Sal returned with the iced tea and noticed they were all looking at the two in the pool. "That's my daughter, Kathy," Sal indicated with a wave of his hand, "and my beautiful granddaughter, little Lisa. We named her after my late wife. God rest her soul. "Kathy," he called out. "Come over here and meet my friends.

Acknowledging her father's request, Kathy picked up her daughter and stepped out of the pool, put a small white, terry cloth robe on Lisa and wrapped a larger one around herself. She walked up to them, holding the child by her tiny hand and giving everyone a friendly smile.

Tony had noticed Kathy's curvaceous body, clothed in an old-fashioned one-piece bathing suit. As she held the robe closed with one hand, he looked up into her large, brown eyes. *Beautiful*, he thought.

After the introductions, Kathy took her young daughter and disappeared into the house.

"Now we can talk. Get down to business," Sal said, looking around at each of them. "I asked you to come up here because I always like to meet the people I hire. Get to know them a little. Isn't that right, Sam?"

"That's right, Sal," Mr. G responded. Then turning toward Tony and Bo, he continued, "It gives Sal a better perspective and ..."

"Yeah," Sal cut in. "I don't like the phones. Person to person is better. Straight from the shoulder."

Bo nodded, "We understand."

"Okay, okay. This is the way it is." He was looking back and forth from Tony to Bo. "It's nothing illegal. All I want you to do is break into a house and steal something for me."

Sal looked at the young men expectantly, then burst into laughter. "I'm pullin' your leg," he chuckled. "What I want you to get for me belongs to me. That makes it all right, capisce?"

"You bet," Bo returned, leaning forward attentively.

Tony hadn't said anything. He had been nervous around Mr. G, but with this guy he was inwardly stricken.

A couple of months ago," Sal went on, "a former associate steals my books, account books. The real ones. If the cops get them, I'll be gone a long time. Up the river as they say. And I'm not a young man anymore. I don't want to spend the rest of my life in the joint. This associate joins forces with one of my competitors, Joseph Tattelone, better known as Big Joe in Detroit. Then this Big Joe has the gall to tell me he only wants my account books to protect him and his territory. As if I wanted his territory. At one time, maybe, but not now.

"So anyway, he says they're in a safe place. Yeah," he sneered. "They're in a safe place. In his puny wall safe, a cracker box in his study. It cost me to find out. Got it from one of his own boys.

"I've got it all figured out, the how and when. I'll give you a hundred and fifty G's, but you pay the expenses. Sound fair?"

"Of course," Bo answered without hesitation.

"What about you?" Sal pointed at Tony.

"Yes, Sir. It sounds fair to me," Tony responded.

Sal was still looking intently at them. "Now you might be asking yourselves, 'Why doesn't he use some of his own men instead of us, outsiders?' Well, that's all part of the plan. We're having a meeting with Big Joe and his people at a neutral place, probably South Bend. And if my men are with me, I can deny I had anything to do with the theft. Make sure you take more than just my books. I'm sure you understand why. And the nice thing about it, for you, is that most of their men will be with Big Joe at the meeting. There will only be a few men to deal with. Make sense?"

"Yeah. It sure does," Bo admitted. "That takes care of the 'when,' but what about the 'how?'"

"Before you leave, I'll give you Big Joe's house plans. That'll give you the 'how.' I'm sure you can figure out the rest."

*   *   *

Back at Champaign, Mr. G dropped Tony and Bo off at the Holmes Detective Agency. When they were alone and seated in Tony's office, Tony finally spoke up. "What have we gotten ourselves into, Bo?"

"Calm down, Tony."

"Calm down? How can I? We just agreed to break into the ... the ... Tattelone compound. Now that's what I call stupid. A death wish."

"No, it isn't!" Bo stated. "Listen to me for a moment. I'm not too happy about it, either. But we didn't have a choice. You don't say 'no' to these guys. Besides, we're going to have help."

"What kind of help?"

"Two of my friends who have nerves of steel and the expertise to go with it. We'll be a team of four."

Tony knew how chicken-hearted he sounded. He didn't want Bo to think of him that way. He'd seen Bo in action and was very impressed by him. *He's smart and tough*, he thought. *Smart enough to figure out the best, safest way to do this. Odds are we'll be all right. And with the backup...well...*

"Believe me," Bo interrupted Tony's thoughts, "we're not going to take any chances. It'll all be planned out to the nth degree."

"Okay, Bo."

Tony felt negative, but didn't want Bo to know about it. He wasn't afraid of ordinary people, but these people were tough and tenacious killers. Like elephants, they don't forget; they get even, or they'd lose the respect of others, and that meant losing control. Without control, they had nothing.

They project fear, count on it; vicious fear that paralyzes.

"Let's sleep on it, Tony. You'll feel more confident in the morning. I'll work out some of the details and run it by you at lunch tomorrow."

*   *   *

The four men lay in a prone position on the hill behind the Tattleone estate. They hid from view by the cover of darkness and the tall trees of Grosse Pointe Woods. Propped up on their elbows, they had an excellent view of the compound through their night scopes. They observed that the front of the house faced the shoreline of Lake St. Clair. To the south they could see the city lights reflecting off low clouds scudding over Detroit. The only sound was the gentle breeze rustling the leaves in the trees overhead.

Bo and Tony had already decided the easiest and safest approach would be from the lake.

The Tattelone family had left an hour earlier in four vehicles for a three hour drive to South Bend for their meeting with the Fratenello group.

"There are two men patrolling along the lakeside with dogs," Bo pointed out to his two friends. The one on his left, J.J. Phillips, was a squat fellow with a rusty- colored crewcut. On his right was Guy Towers with long, black, straight hair parted in the middle and hanging down below his shoulders.

"We'll all approach the property from the lake. You two move toward the outer perimeters of the property and take out the guards and dogs when they reach opposite ends of their walk," Bo explained. "Remember, it's a zero-kill mission, if at all possible."

"We understand," JJ answered. "We only use deadly force if we have to."

"That's correct. Tony and I will time ourselves to move in through the middle of the property after you have taken out your objectives. A simple, 'guard one's out and guard two's out,' is all we'll need to hear in our transmitters. Stay off the radios as much as possible."

"Won't the water ruin these radios?" asked Guy.

"No. They're waterproof," Bo answered.

Tony looked from one to the other, but did not say anything. *This is Bo's show,* he thought, *He planned it and I'll just follow instructions like the others.*

"Near as Tony and I can tell there are at least a couple men in the house," Bo continued. "Guy, you circle around to the rear and come in from the back. Tony and I will move into the midsection of the house from the lakefront. Guy and J.J. will come in from a forty-five degree angle from the left and right. Just be very careful. Don't rush things. Any questions?"

Both men shook their heads.

"Then let's move out," Bo said.

*   *   *

Kneeling in the lake with heads just above water, Tony and Bo listened intently. There was silence, except for the lapping of water around them. Then they removed their flippers and unwrapped their .45 automatics with silencers already mounted. The weapons had been brought ashore in waterproof bags.

The guards had paused for a moment to chat. The German shepherds sat in obedience, alert.

To the south of Tony and Bo, JJ had slithered across the beach and hidden behind a large piece of driftwood. *If the guard follows his usual path,* JJ reasoned, *he should make his turn about fifty feet from me. The breeze off the lake shouldn't carry to the dog. He won't smell me.*

A couple hundred feet north of JJ lay Guy, snuggling into the sand behind a slight knoll. He was more exposed than his partner and upwind from the guard's turning point, about seventy-five feet away.

I'm going to have to take out the dog first, Guy concluded. He's going to get a whiff of me too soon. This is going to be close. He held his dart rifle in his right hand and the backup 45 with silencer tucked into his belt.

Before Guy could get comfortable with his position, the guards started back, each in his own direction.

Within a few feet of their turn, one German shepherd raised his head from sniffing the sand and smelled the air in different directions, then began straining against his leash. The guard became a little wary, looking around toward the house, then back out over the lake.

Guy laid absolutely still, his dart gun making only the slightest move as it followed the dog.

On the other side, JJ smoothly took out his man. The guard slumped to the ground almost immediately after slapping his neck where the dart had entered. The German shepherd circled around his master in confusion. JJ quickly inserted another dart into the chamber. He raised his rifle again and fired. The dog gave a short yelp when the dart hit him, then slowly curled up.

"Guard one is out," he whispered into his transmitter.

Back on the other side, the wary guard reached down to release the dog when Guy fired. The dog yipped, but before it went down, Guy commanded softly, but firmly, "Hold it right there, Mister, or I'll blow a hole right through you."

The man froze in position, looking around, trying to see where the voice came from. Then when he spotted Guy he dropped to a crouch and pulled out his weapon. The man's confusion had given Guy just enough time to reload and fire his dart gun. As the guard spun around and dropped, Guy muttered, "Sweet dreams, fella."

"Guard two is out. Bow Wow's sleeping peacefully," came the transmission.

"Acknowledged," Bo said quietly.

Bo waved Tony forward. Stealthily, they moved out of the water and stopped behind a hedge at the edge of the lawn. They hastily discarded their swim gear and took their dart guns from another waterproof bag. They loaded them quickly. They were still three hundred feet from the house, most of which was wide open space.

Bo motioned for Tony to move to the right side of the long veranda facing the lake. Tony raced across the lawn, his eyes darting in all directions. He stopped momentarily behind a large oak tree and was about to sprint to a hyacinth bush near the side of the porch when a match flared. Someone was lighting a cigarette. A man. The glow on his face was so brief that Tony didn't get a good look at his features, but more importantly, he knew exactly where the man was standing. Staring at the location, Tony could finally see a dark shadow move as the man lifted his cigarette up for another drag.

On the next puff, Tony thought, *I'll get him*.

He didn't have to wait long. Just as the glow started to show, Tony pulled the trigger. He missed. The man moved at the last second, then he turned toward the sound as the dart hit the house. The man turned toward Tony pulling his gun out as Tony fired his .45. There was a little spit sound. This time Tony did not miss. The man reached out and grabbed air as he crashed into the bushes. Tony waited and listened. Nothing. Keeping his gun pointed at the shadowy heap, he cautiously moved toward him. He nudged the body with his foot. The man's arm flopped. Tony knew the man was dead. Trepidation was the name of the game. It seemed to him that this was par for the course of late. He was moving in the wrong direction, being sucked into a vortex that just kept pulling him down.

At the opposite side of the veranda, Bo had made it to the house without any problems. He was next to a large window, its light spilling out onto a stone-lined flower bed. Gingerly, he stepped onto the blossoms and peeked through the window. Two men were playing cards on a coffee table set in front of a pale green sectional couch in the far corner of the room.

Bo retreated to the grass. "Tony," he whispered and waved him over.

As Tony approached, Bo picked up a rock from the flower bed and pointed toward the window. "There are two of them in there. At the same time I crash through the door, you throw this rock through that window over there. Then take out the man on your left. I'll get the other one. Understand?"

Tony nodded and took the rock out of Bo's hand. Silently, they moved onto the porch. Inside, they could hear the men arguing about something. "On three," Bo muttered.

As Bo's body swayed in motion toward the door, Tony swung the rock. On the count of three, Tony released the rock as Bo's large, muscular body crashed through the door. The two men jumped up when Tony fired, expressions of astonishment on their faces. Almost without delay, Bo, getting his balance quickly, fired. Both men fell backward, crashing to the floor simultaneously.

Tony's feet crunched on broken glass as he stepped through the smashed door.

Bo put a finger to his lips and cocked his head, listening. There was noise at the other end of the house. Snapping off the lights, he bolted toward the door leading into a back room. Slowly, he glanced around the doorjamb, his .45 poised, his dart gun was empty.

"Hold it right there," he barked, flipping on the lights in the room.

"It's us," JJ spoke with alarm, hoping it was Bo or Tony.

The relief on their faces brought a rare smile to Bo's face. Again he held up his hand, then put a finger to his lips, listening. There was nothing but silence in the house.

*   *   *

"Stupido," Sal bellowed when he heard the news, standing behind his desk in his study. His son, Mario, a rangy fellow with dark curly hair, was on the phone. Tony and Bo were the only others in the room. "If Big Joe finds out, it's a gonna be war," he continued to shout. 'No killing,' I said. But you guys don't listen to me. An' I don't like it, when someone don't listen to me!"

"It couldn't be helped," Tony lied. "Just as I fired the Thoralen dart, the man moved. He was pulling out his gun when I fired my forty-five. If I hadn't, I'd be dead, and the whole operation would have blown up. Then Mr. Tattelone maybe would have figured out you were involved for sure."

"Dad," Sal's son broke in as he put the phone back in its cradle, "I was talking to our man, Vinnie, in Detroit. He says that Big Joe thinks someone else got your books. He's afraid you are going to find out about it and then it's going to hit the fan."

The frown was replaced with a toothy grin. "Maybe," Sal declared, "maybe it'll all work out. If he's worried about me finding out, I'll have him on the defensive. And that's where I want him."

He turned toward Mario. "Give 'em the money."

CHAPTER SIXTEEN

Tony confessed quietly, "God, I hope he doesn't want to hire us again." He was not praying, he was referring to their caper in Detroit. Tony was seated behind his desk with Bo slouching on the couch.

"I doubt he will," Bo affirmed. "We didn't exactly follow orders. But if he asks, there is nothing we can do, but go. As I said before, you don't say 'no' to someone like that."

"I suppose not."

"At least we got an extra fifty grand out of it, from the safe, I mean."

"Yeah. I like that part. All tax free."

"And another thing," Bo said with a grin. "I made copies of Sal Fratenello's books. It's just a little protection for us."

"Or our execution."

"No, no, Tony. I have 'em in a very safe place. And if anything happens to us, they go to the D.A. Besides, I'm not going to say anything to Sal about this, unless I have to, to protect us. So don't worry. What he doesn't know won't hurt us."

"Okay," Tony grunted as he looked at his watch. "What time is that lawyer coming in?"

"Should be at any time." Bo sat up straight. "Speak of the devil..."

The receptionist led in a gray-haired man in his fifties. His Brooks Brother's suit fit a lean, agile body. She introduced him. "Mr. Garber and Mr. Bobbyo, this is Mr. Colton of Lang, Blaine, Brindley, and Colton. And Mr. Colton, this is Mr. Garber and Mr. Bobbyo."

"Let's use first names, if you don't mind. I'm Tom; Bo I already know; and from the sign on your door, I assume you're Tony." He shook hands.

Tony answered, "Yes. Won't you have a seat, Mr... uh...Tom."

"Thank you." As Tom sat down, he continued addressing Tony. "I've used the Holmes Detective Agency for years, for most of my investigative work. I've been and am a friend of Jonathan's, the former owner. And knowing Bo for the same amount of time, I'm sure your company will continue to do the excellent work it has in the past."

"I'm sure we will, Tom," Tony reassured him.

"Of course, we will," added Bo. "What's the case?"

"It's been in all the papers. You've probably seen it; the murder of Rodney Marquette. My client, Marlene Marquette, his wife, has been charged with his murder. I'm certain she's innocent. I want you to find the real killer and bring him or her to justice. The police are not looking for any other suspects. They feel they have an iron-clad case against her. And they do. Motive? Rod and Marlene had a prenuptial agreement that she would get practically nothing if they were divorced. He was already filing for it. Opportunity? She was heard arguing with him just minutes before he was shot. And he was shot with her gun with only her fingerprints on it. It was left next to the body."

"Doesn't look good," Bo said. "We'll need to talk to her and the detective handling the case."

"No problem. I'll also get you into the apartment where the murder took place. And supply you with any depositions we take and all pictures or other info the D.A. may come up with. It's called 'Discovery,' full disclosure, as you may already know."

Standing, Tom concluded with, "I'll make the arrangements for you to interview her. Also, if anyone refuses to cooperate, let me know."

*   *   *

The four storied, gray courthouse and jail with a chiseled date of 1923 on the wall took up an entire city block. The room designated for the interviewing of prisoners, was square, high-ceilinged, off-white, containing only a long table and three chairs. The late afternoon sun slanted in through two mesh-wire windows.

Tony and Bo sat on one side of the table and watched through a glass door as Marlene Marquette entered. The guard closed the door behind her. She sat her sylph-like body down opposite them. She wore a wrinkled, drab, prison dress.

Her anxiety showed when her lower lip twitched nervously. Her only crowning glory came from her long ebony hair that cascaded around her stooped shoulders. It had a shine to it; It was obviously well cared for, as if she brushed it by the hours. Her slender fingers were intertwined with her soiled handkerchief.

"I'm Bo, and this is Tony. We'd like to ask a few questions. Do you feel up to it?"

Her nod was almost imperceptible. She was looking down at the table, too embarrassed to look into their eyes.

"Relax, Mrs. Marquette," Bo almost whispered. "We're here to help, not to badger you. Okay?"

Marlene slowly looked up, and whispered back, "Okay," then lowered her eyes back to the table again.

Tony switched on the tape recorder. "We'd like to tape the session if it's okay with you," Bo said softly.

"Sure."

Bo knew he had to be gentle. He had to move into the real questions from an oblique angle. "Mrs. Marquette, how long have you been...were you... married to the...uh... deceased?"

With only a slight hesitation, she answered, "Almost eight years."

Bo continued. "Where were you married?"

"At First Christian Church a few blocks from here." She was looking at Bo now, but seemed to be in a daze, mindless of her surroundings.

"Did you sign a pre-nuptial agreement before marrying Rodney?"

She looked at Bo, then at Tony, before answering. "Yes, I did."

"What did the agreement contain?"

"That if I left him or if we were divorced, I'd get nothing. But I didn't kill him. I never even thought of it."

"I'm not saying you did. I just had to know if you understood it."

"Yes, I did...do." She was becoming a little more alert.

"I understand you were having marital problems. Is that correct?"

"Yes."

"Tell me about it."

Marlene glanced out the window for a moment as if in thought, then began. "As I said, we have been married almost eight years. And they were happy years, until about six months ago.

"One night we were at a party when a handsome young man asked me to dance, and after a few minutes he danced me out onto the patio, then tried to kiss me. I was trying to push him away, when Rod came out. He believed I wasn't resisting. He became very angry and turned and hurriedly left through the bushes, out to the car and drove away, leaving me stranded. The young man offered to take me home, but I refused and called for a cab.

"When I got home, we had a big fight. And from that point on, he was very suspicious. I had to account to him every time I went out, but when I told him what I'd been doing, he wouldn't believe me. I don't know what had come over him.

"Then he hired a private detective to follow me. When the detective reported I had gone to see a girlfriend, he suspected I was meeting some man there. It was crazy.

"The next thing I know he's talking about getting a divorce. And to be honest with you, I was beginning to think that might be best, because of his suspicions. I was beside myself, miserable, but I never even thought of doing anything to him. I couldn't do that kind of thing."

Bo finally popped the big question. "All right, tell us about that night. I need to know everything."

Her face contorted as she pulled tightly on the mangled hanky. "A few weeks ago, he suggested I move out of the apartment. I was only too happy to accommodate. I couldn't go on with all the fighting and bickering. I moved into a small furnished condo on second street and got my old job back as a receptionist. I kept thinking he would get over this problem, and we could get back together again, like it used to be. He had been a great husband then, and I was hoping... wishful thinking, I guess."

The corners of her eyes filled and she dabbed at them with her wrinkled handkerchief. After an audible sigh, she continued. "But the day before yesterday, late in the evening, there was a knock on my door. When I opened it, I was handed divorce papers by a man I'd never seen before.

After he was gone, I sat down and read the papers and cried. But before long, I got angry instead. So I decided to go and have it out with him.

"I almost backed out when I was standing in front of his door, the door that used to be my home, too. And that made me mad all over again, so I pounded on it.

"I think he was surprised to see me, at first. I pushed him all the way into the living room and onto a couch, and I confronted him. I asked him, 'Why?' But all he did was jump up and shout at me and make accusations. He told me to leave and pointed at the open front door. I guess I had left it open when I pushed my way in. And then I left, closing the door behind me. That's all. He was very much alive when I left."

"And where did you go from there?"

"Home. The next morning, the police came and arrested me. And according to my lawyer, they have my gun with my fingerprints on it, and they found it next to Rod's body. And I don't have the slightest idea how it got there."

"When was the last time you saw the gun?"

"I don't know, exactly. Probably a couple of weeks before we split up. I always kept it in the drawer of the small table next to the front door."

"Who knew about the gun being there?"

"All of our friends and business associates. Rod thought it was funny that I'd wanted a gun. He laughingly showed it to them, when I first got it."

"Do you know the name of the private detective who followed you?"

"No."

"Do you know of anyone else who might have wanted your husband dead?"

"There were lots of them. His partner, for one. When Rod and I were arguing, he shouted, 'With Wally probably stealing from me, I don't need this, too.' I guess Wally, that's Walter Nystrom, has taken some of the firm's money and disappeared with it. Rod and Wally are investment brokers. Or were. I mean Rod was. Oh, I don't know what I mean. Anyway, they took peoples' money and invested it for them. They are very good at what they do... did."

She threw her hands up in confusion, then continued. "Another person that hated Rodney's guts was Brian Folleta. Rod used to work for him, but they had a falling out. Rod took all his customers with him and opened his own office, along with Walter. Both of them had been with Brian. That's another reason why Brian hates him.

"Then there is Mark Houser, one of his competitors. He's been jealous of Rodney's success, but I don't know if that was sufficient motive or not.

"That's all I can think of, but I'm sure there are more."

Bo stood up. Tony put his papers in a manila folder and arose also. "If you can remember anything else," Bo said. "You can let us know through your attorney, Mr. Colton."

Outside, Bo asked Tony, "What do you think?"

"She sounds good, but the evidence definitely points to her."

"True. But we've only just begun," Bo said with a smile.

CHAPTER SEVENTEEN

Dr. Seigelwitz said hesitantly "Now, Tony..." as if in thought. Her dark brown hair was not in a bun as it usually was. Instead it was combed out and flowed gently down her back.

Much better, Tony thought. *Makes her look younger and a lot sexier.*

"Now, Tony," she repeated, "I want you to go as far back as you can remember about your stepfather and tell me about him."

"Okay," he said reflectively, his eyes looking off toward the far wall. "I can remember the first time I met him. I was only five or six. My mother evidently had been dating him for sometime. How long, I don't know. But when he had come to pick her up for those dates, I guess I was already in bed for the night or was shoved off to my grandmothers house.

"But that day, Mother said, 'Burt....'"

"Burt?" Dr. Seigelwitz popped in, eyebrows raised.

Immediately, Tony realized his mistake. But he had already thought this out. He knew that someday he might make that mistake. "Yes," he continued glibly, "I was given the name of my real father when I was born, but my stepfather knew him and hated him. He said he never wanted to hear his name or be reminded of him. So, he said my name had to be changed. He decided on Anthony Garber. Even though my mother strenuously objected, it was to no avail. He was adamant. And when he said something had to be, it was without question. I only remember this vaguely. But my mother, on her deathbed, you know she died of a brain tumor, probably from the many blows she took from his big fists, she explained it to me when he wasn't around. By this time I was in college, paid for, I might add, by my grandmother. My stepfather wouldn't give me a nickel."

"All right, Tony. Go on with your story."

"When my mother first introduced me?"

Dr. Seigelwitz nodded her head.

"This is a mixture of what I can remember and what my mother told me when I was older.

"I was staying at Grandma's at the time..."

*　　*　　*

"Burt, I want you to meet your new father. His name is Albert Spore," Beth Spore said. "We were just married. That's why you've been staying with Grandma for the past week while we were on our honeymoon."

"I know. Grandma told me," he said as he looked up at the tall man with a crewcut who towered over him.

The man glared down with a stony face. "Burt," Albert Spore said sternly, "I'm sure we'll get along just fine, as long as you're obedient, which I'm sure you will be."

Burt had his little arms wrapped around his mother's leg, looking up at the man shyly. He hadn't really heard what the man had said. All he knew was he wished the man would go away.

Beth kneeled next to her son and hugged him. "We're going to be a happy family. And we're going to have lots of fun. Okay?"

When the frightened boy didn't speak right away, his new stepfather firmly said, "Answer your mother when she speaks to you."

"It's all right, Albert," Beth said, "This is all new to him. He'll be all right when he gets used to you."

"Used to me," he bellowed. Then looking at Burt he continued. "Stand up, young man and be a man. Young boys should strive to be as manly as they can. Do you understand?"

Again when Burt didn't answer immediately, he frowned and commanded, "Speak up! Or can't you speak?"

Quickly, Beth whispered in Burt's ear, "Nod your head and say, 'Yes, Sir.'"

Doing what his mother had asked, he nodded twice and said, "Yes, Sir," but so softly he could barely be heard.

"Okay," Albert said, "but you'll need to learn to speak up, so people can hear you. We'll work on that. Now it's time to go!" He waved his hand at Beth as if to say take care of it.

*   *   *

The following Sunday when Burt had returned from a neighbor's house, Albert looked at him sharply and asked, "You been playing next door again?"

"Uh-huh," he answered, tentatively.

"Don't use 'uh-huh.' That's for uneducated people. Say, 'Yes, Sir or Yes, Father or Yes, Daddy."

Timidly, Burt said, "But...but you're not my real father. He's dead."

Albert's hand flashed out and struck Burt on the side of his head. His little feet flew out from under him as he slammed to the floor, his head hitting the carpet with such force it made him dizzy. When Burt tried to get up, he fell to the floor again.

"Don't ever say that again. And remember that I am your father, now!" Albert said through clenched teeth and stomped away.

Burt didn't cry at first. He was too stunned and too dizzy. But when he was finally able to stand again, he stumbled to his room, flopped down on his bed and cried himself to sleep.

Later, his mother, who had been grocery shopping and didn't know about the incident, shook him. He was lying in a fetal position "Wake up sleepyhead. It's time for dinner."

Burt opened his eyes then closed them quickly. "My head hurts, Mommy," he said, wincing.

"Do you have a headache?"

Without thinking, he nodded his head. "Ouch," he responded in pain. "Yes, it hurts."

"I'm sorry, darling," she said gently caressing his face with her hand, "I'll get you something for it."

As Burt turned toward her to answer, his mother noticed the swelling. "Your face. What happened?"

Hesitating for just a moment, he replied, "Daddy."

Returning in a moment, she gave him a glass of water along with the aspirin. "I'll be back in a few minutes," She said gently.

After she entered the kitchen, Burt quietly opened the door a crack. Albert was chug-a-lugging his beer. He walked over to the refrigerator and pulled out another bottle of beer.

"Albert Spore," she said, her face flushed with anger, "Why did you hit Burt? You have no right to abuse my son. I'll not have it. If you do I'll...I'll..."

Turning slowly toward her and slurring his words, he said sarcastically, "Or you'll do what? This, maybe?" His left jab hit her directly in the mouth. She staggered back, but his second blow struck her just below the left eye, knocking her into the table, where she slid to the floor, unconscious. Burt wanted to run to her side, but fear of his stepfather stopped him.

Looking down at Burt's mother without compassion, Albert muttered, "No. You'll never do that to me." Then he turned and staggered toward the room Burt was in. He used his hands to steady himself as he passed table and chairs. When opposite Burt's door, his hand smashed into it. It swung wildly back, crashing into the wall as Albert, with total loss of balance, banged into the door jamb.

Burt had moved back from the door so it did not hit him, but his heart raced and his head throbbed. He was about to scream, when Albert continued to reel down the hallway.

Cautiously, Burt looked out the door to see his stepfather head out the front door. Only then did he feel safe enough to go to his mother. "Mommy, wake up," he pleaded. When there was no response, he put his head on her chest and cried.

*　　　*　　　*

Tony opened his eyes and wiped away tears.

Dr. Seigelwitz looked at Tony gently and said. "That'll be it for today, Tony. It was a very good session."

"Yeah, but also uncomfortable."

"Yes, I'm sure it was. You see, Tony, what you have been doing is blocking out all that pain and trying to live with it all bottled up inside of you. That's not good. It can cause you many problems. It surfaces in various ways at different times. What we're doing now is bringing it out in the open, so we can deal with it. The more you talk about it, and we discuss it, the more release you'll have in this area."

"You really think so, Doc? Even those night things?" He couldn't bring himself to use the word fear. It wasn't manly to say he had fears.

"I know so, Tony. I've done it many times with many people."

"You know, I do feel a little better."

"Good. We'll talk further at your next session."

*   *   *

That night at dinner, Tony freely disclosed to Sandy what had happened at the therapist's office. He didn't repeat it in its entirety, but he painted a picture that made it clear.

"That's wonderful, Tony. I'm very proud of you."

They were in a downtown restaurant, Gordon's Steak House, just finishing their meals. Sandy had had a cobb salad and Tony a large slab of prime rib, and a big baked potato, stuffed with butter, cheese and bacon bits.

"Do you really think it's helping you?" Sandy questioned.

"Sure. Like I told her, it may be hell remembering that period of my life, but after I tell her about it, it takes some of the load off me."

"That's what it's all about. When you bring it out in the open, you can see the problem and then deal with it. You can see it for what it is."

"I know what it is. Boy do I know," he said bitterly. "In fact, if I knew where he lived, I'd confront him and then beat the you-know-what out of him."

"That's not very nice, Tony."

"Sorry. But I would beat the pulp out of him, just like he did to my mom and me."

"Maybe we should talk about something else. You're getting too riled up."

Tony stared at the tablecloth a few moments, letting himself cool down. He didn't want to spoil a good evening with his special girl. When he looked up, he had a smile on his face as the bitterness subsided.

"Now, that's better."

"Thank you. Now let's see," he mused. "What to talk about. I know. Let's talk about you, not me. How is your job going, and what are you working on?"

"The job is great. I love it. And the case I'm working on is very interesting. I'm representing a real estate broker who is being sued by a woman who purchased a house through him. In fact, she is not only suing him, but also the broker whose office listed the property and the two agents who worked for the two brokers and the seller of the house. In other words, she is suing everyone she can."

"What is she suing for?"

"For a new roof, a cost of fifteen thousand dollars plus for the inconvenience of replacing it. She claims that she looked up in the attic and saw pinpoints of light showing through the shake roof.

A roofing contractor I talked to said that is natural with shake roofs. I could win this case for my client, but it would cost a lot more in court than it will to settle it out of court. I'm waiting for my client to decide which way to go. My guess is that he'll decide to settle. In the long run, it'll save four or five thousand dollars."

"I would fight it out. I wouldn't give in to her. It's the principle of the thing."

"I would agree with you, but it's not my money. But the kicker is, she has three other lawsuits going on at the same time. And a history of suing people or businesses for the past ten years, and she's only thirty years old. I guess you could call her a professional suer. But that 'suer' should be spelled, 's-e-w-e-r' and all her law suits should be flushed down that sewer.

"In one case, a neighbor saw her fall while getting into her car and was a little alarmed until he saw her get up and get into the vehicle and drive away. An attorney for the Shop and Save Market believes, though he can't prove it, that she drove straight to the store, entered, went to a deserted area and supposedly fell and injured herself. She sued for one hundred thousand dollars, but settled the case out of court. For how much, I don't know. That's the type of person she is.

Tony just shook his head.

"In another case that's still going on, she sued her father-in-law and mother-in-law when her husband died of a heart attack. She evidently believed that they were going to cut her out of their will, which wasn't true, according to relatives.

"Her in-laws owned the house she had been living in for more than five years with her husband. In fact, she still lives there. Her claim was called adverse possession. What it means is that if a person lives on a property and pays the property taxes on it for five or more years, they can lay claim to ownership. She lived there that long and did pay the taxes, but the taxes were reimbursed by her in-laws. However, she claims the money she received was for repairs on the property, not for taxes. Now, since the elderly in-laws have passed away, it complicates the situation and helps her.

"She's trying to steal the inheritance of the other three children surviving, two sons and one daughter.

"She isn't going to get away with it, is she?"

"Well, she's added a couple of other suits against the heirs and the estate. This has clouded the issue further. All this has been going on for a couple of years."

"In other words, only the lawyers are going to get anything out of the estate."

Rather sheepishly, Sandy admitted that was probably true. "I wouldn't handle it that way," she said defensively. "I will always try to be up-front with my clients and have their interests at heart, not my pocketbook."

"That's because you're an honest person."

"Hi, Tony," a middle-aged man said, interrupting. He was tall and slender, wearing a dark blue suit and tie. He had a sallow, but smooth complexion with a flat nose. He had straight black hair parted in the middle.

"Hi, Gordy." Tony smiled up at him and rose to shake the man's hand. "This is my true love, Sandy. Sandy meet Gordon Richolli, the owner of this place." Tony waved his hand around. "We call him 'Gordy' at the club. He swings a mean golf club. I won't play against him. I want him for my partner on the links."

"It's nice finally meeting you, Sandy. I've known your father from the club and at Rotary for a number of years. Welcome to my establishment. We're honored to have you. Was your food satisfactory?"

"Yes. It was delicious."

"Bull," Tony interjected. "She would have said that even she had been poisoned by your food."

"Tony!" she said sharply, leaving the rest unsaid.

Both men laughed.

"Sit and have a drink with us, Gordy."

"I'd be happy to, but only for a moment. I don't want to interfere with your evening. However, I do have a little job for you, Tony. If you're interested."

"I'm always interested in making money, Gordy."

"Well, one of my bartenders is ripping me off. Probably the new guy that's on duty now. Only I don't know how he does it. Of course, he never tries when I'm around. What I'd like you to do, Tony, is find out for sure who is doing it. I'm losing over two grand a month."

"Sure, Gordy. We'll go to the bar after we finish eating. We're almost done now."

*   *   *

A few minutes later, Tony guided Sandy into the lounge and sat her down on a stool at the end of the bar. They were facing each other, looking lovingly at one another. From this position, with only a slight turn of his head, he could see everything the bartender was doing.

"May I help you?" the bartender intoned. He was a small, slight of build young man in his late twenties. He had lost most of his wispy brown hair on top. His pencil-thin mustache followed his lip perfectly, undulating when he spoke.

Without looking away from Sandy, Tony said, breathlessly, "Excuse me a minute, Darling." Then turning to the bartender, said, "I'll have a bourbon and Seven, and she'll have a Margarita blank."

"Blank?"

"Yes, blank...without alcohol."

"Oh. I've never heard it expressed that way. We always call it a 'virgin.'"

"Yes, she is, but how did you know?"

Flustered, he shook his head. "No, I'm not talking about the lady."

"But I am. She is a virgin, and she does want a margarita blank."

"I do like the name, Sir. I'll get her one and your drink also, Sir." He scurried away.

Sandy was covering her mouth with her hand, trying to keep from laughing. "You're bad, Tony. And mean. You totally confused and intimidated him."

"I did that on purpose. You watch. After he serves us our drinks, he won't even look down this way. In fact, I don't want him watching us. He might catch me watching him."

Sandy thought for a moment. "That's smart. I never would have reasoned it that way. You're turning into a real detective."

Tony observed the bartender for more than an hour, until his shift ended. The replacement bartender was much older. Tony shrugged his shoulders and said, "When we finish these drinks we'll go. Okay?"

"Fine," Sandy answered. "I do feel a little tired."

A few minutes later, Tony gulped down the rest of his drink. As he started to pick up his change from the bar, he stopped short. He turned toward Sandy, and said almost in a whisper, "I just figured out how it's being done."

Sandy looked surprised. "How?"

"Let's go find Gordy, and I'll explain."

Gordy was in his office. "Sit," he said, indicating the two chairs in front of his desk.

"Gordy, my friend, I just figured it out."

"Already? That's amazing."

"Not really. But it's not who you think it is. It's the man who just came on duty."

"Harry? But he's been with me for years. I've never had trouble with him. My losses didn't start until this new guy went to work for me."

"I watched the young guy for over an hour, and nothing. We were about to leave, when the old guy came on. I spotted it almost immediately. I gave him a twenty to pay for our drinks and I told him to keep a buck for himself. He said thanks for the tip loud enough so that other patrons could hear. Then he put the twenty above the money drawer as he made change, gave me the change, returned to the cash register, picked up the twenty, said thanks again, and put the twenty into his tip glass. By saying thanks again, it drew attention to his face, not his hands. He's very slick."

"But why start now?"

"What better timing? A new bartender starts working, and that's when money starts disappearing. You certainly wouldn't suspect someone who has been tried and true. You look at the new man."

"Very good, Tony. Send me a bill."

"You bet I will. It'll be for two more meals like the ones we had tonight."

With a big smile on his swarthy face, Gordon stood and shook Tony's hand. "You got it. Any time you and your lady want it."

Tony gave him a thumbs-up as he and Sandy left.

CHAPTER EIGHTEEN

The name on the door read, Lt. Daniel Moynahan. *Strange*, Tony thought, *the same detective is handling this case and Nancy Idenhauer's.* He expunged the slight feeling of guilt for what he had done to Nancy as he and Bo entered the lieutenant's office.

"Good morning, gentlemen. I've been expecting you," the lieutenant said, waving them to chairs in front of a messy desk piled with papers. He was in shirt sleeves with a dark blue stringy tie pulled down at an open collar. "The Marlene Marquette case. Am I right?"

"Yes, Sir," Bo answered. Again Tony was taking a back seat. *I'm just learning*, he thought, *but my day will come.*

"We have an open-and-shut case. She had a good solid motive and the opportunity, in fact she even admits to being there, at least just before the shot was heard. We also have a witness that places her there at that time. And we have her gun, which was found next to the body. What more could I ask?"

"Any other suspects?" Bo asked.

"No. We don't need any. We have our man, or woman in this case. It's air-tight."

"But why would Mrs. Marquette kill her husband and leave her gun behind? That would be stupid, especially with her fingerprints on it."

"It's simple, she panicked."

Bo mulled that over for a moment, then asked, "What's the neighbor's name?"

Moynahan got up and pulled a little black book from the inside pocket of his jacket that hung limply on a clothes rack. Sitting down again and finding the right page, he answered, "Jack Mueller."

"Anything else you can tell us?"

"Yes. We ran ballistics on her gun, and it is the murder weapon. Her husband died from a single shot to the head. Anything else?"

"We'd like to examine the site and talk to the neighbor."

"No problem. The officer on duty now is Sergeant Bostwick. I'll give him a call."

*   *   *

"Has everything been dusted?" Bo asked Sergeant Bostwick as the Sergeant let them into apartment 712.

"Yes. But don't disturb anything," he admonished.

"Don't worry. I understand."

Stepping inside, Bo stopped quickly and Tony bumped into him. "Sorry," Tony said. Bo hadn't heard him. He was studying the suite. To his immediate right he noticed an open door to what appeared to be a study or office area. To his left was an open hallway, probably leading to the bedrooms, then a breakfast bar with the kitchen directly behind it. In front of him was the living room. He walked into it and noted that there was a conversational area with overstuffed couches and chairs in a flowered pattern up against the back wall. On the far wall were sliding glass doors opening onto a balcony and to the left of that, the dining room with a heavy, ornate table and chairs and a large cut glass chandelier hanging from above.

In front of the flowered couch, the police had taped off the body's position on the mauve carpet. The blood in the head area had turned a rusty brown. Tony stared at it. "So this is where it happened."

"Yep," Bo answered, deep in thought. He was stroking his chin again. "The murderer had to be standing about where you are. If I remember what Mrs. Marguette said, she indicated she was facing the couch when they argued, not from over there where you are."

"She could have moved."

"True." He removed his hand from his chin and stepped out onto the balcony. The view was spectacular from the seventh floor. The traffic moved sluggishly in the distance. Turning toward Tony, he continued, "Let's see if the neighbor is home."

Mr. Mueller was a tall slender man in his late sixties. His short, gray hair lay flat on each side of his part. Tony and Bo accepted his bony, but firm handshake as they introduced themselves.

"Come on in," he invited. "Let's sit at the table."

Bo noticed that the floor plans were identical. The rug was light tan and most of the massive furniture was brown leather. The thick glass table had a scrolled design on the edges. There were coffee cup rings on the table in front of Mr. Mueller. "I'm going to warm up my coffee. Want any?"

Tony shook his head as Bo answered, "No, thank you."

Mueller turned and picked up the steaming pot from the coffeemaker and topped off his cup. "I suppose you have some questions about the murder next door?"

"Yes. Could you tell us what you heard and saw?"

"I didn't see anything, but I heard everything."

"Okay. What time did it all start, and what did you hear?"

Mueller set his cup down and looked at the ceiling. "Well, it was about nine-thirty that night. I was sitting on my balcony, enjoying the evening. On a clear night, I can see all of the city lights twinkling. It's beautiful. Anyway, I was sitting there, like I said, sipping my coffee, when I first heard the shouting. Their balcony door was open, too.

"I could tell it was the Marquettes. I'd know their voices anywhere. They were arguing. No, I should say they were shouting at each other. I don't think either one of them was listening to the other. She kept asking, 'Why?' And he kept saying, 'You know why.' Much of the shouting was overlapped, so it was hard to understand. Besides, I wasn't trying to hear what they were saying. All I know is that it was a shouting match, and they were both extremely mad. A few minutes later, I heard the shot. That's it. I know it looks bad for Mrs. Marquette, but there is nothing I can do. I'm just telling the truth as I remember it."

"Thanks, Mr. Mueller. We appreciate your time. And if there is anything you can remember later, call me at this number." Bo handed the neighbor a business card.

*   *   *

Rodney Marquette's office was located in the Rogers Mercantile Building on the top floor, number 506, a corner suite. Thick carpeting, shiny, ornate furniture, large oil paintings, and beautiful secretaries created an atmosphere of wealth. The name plate on the front desk identified Jenny Marlow as the receptionist smiling up at them. Her blond hair, coifed in braids, wound into circles and piled on her head was very attractive. She was wearing a soft white Angora sweater with a flowing, navy blue skirt over an ample body.

When she spoke, Tony and Bo were surprised that she didn't have a Scandinavian accent. "May I help you gentlemen?"

Handing her one of his cards, Bo said, "I'm Robert Bobbyo and this is Tony Garber, the owner of the Holmes Detective Agency. We've been employed by Mrs. Marquette to try to clear her name. We need to check out Mr. Marquette's office. We probably won't find anything, but you never know. You can check with Mr. Colton, her lawyer, if you'd like."

"No, I'm sure it'll be all right," she said sympathetically. "Right behind me. Through that door." She pointed.

His office was large and impressive. His highly polished mammoth desk sat directly across from the entrance. Behind it, against the wall, was his computer work station.

Bo sat at the desk, opened drawers and checked out their contents.

Tony poked around the bookshelves and cabinets lining the walls.

They were completely absorbed in their snooping when the office door opened abruptly.

"What are you two doing?" sternly questioned a lanky man standing with arms akimbo in the entrance. He was wearing a gray pinstriped suit and black polished shoes. His dark brown hair was parted in the middle.

Bo explained who they were and what they were doing, then asked, "But who are you?"

"I'm Walter Nystrom, formerly a partner, but now the owner, since poor Rod was murdered."

Bo stroked his chin for a moment. "Could we talk? We only have a few questions we need to ask."

"Sure. As long as you don't mind letting me sit at my desk."

"Sorry. I thought this was..."

"It was Rod's, but he doesn't need it anymore, and I need the space, now that I'm in charge."

"I see," Bo said. He moved to a chair in front of the desk. "How is it that you own the business now?"

"Simple. Rod and I had partner insurance. If one died the remaining partner got the business and the deceased's widow got the insurance money. In this case, five hundred thousand dollars. But if Marlene is convicted, she won't see any of that."

"Ummm," Bo muttered, pursing his lips. "But I understood that you had disappeared, and there was some concern about missing funds."

"That's all been cleared up. A week or so ago, Rod and I had a falling out. I stomped out of here as angry as can be. I didn't want to talk to anyone in this business, so I left town for a few days. I needed to be alone. I had to think things through.

"I was expecting some important papers, so I had the post office forward my mail. A couple of days ago, I received a letter from Rod. He found the missing money in another account, and he apologized. He said we were a great team and good friends and should forget about the argument, but before I could get in touch with him, he was murdered."

"May I see the letter?"

"It's in my other office. I haven't completely moved in here, yet. If you'll excuse me. I'll get it for you."

In a moment he was back and handed the letter to Bo, who read it quickly. "Is this his normal signature?"

"No. He scribbled the large letter 'M' for inner office memos or other letters to close associates."

"When did you receive this letter?" Bo asked as he handed it to Tony.

"I found it in my mailbox night before last, when I got home. It was about midnight. Too late to call Rod."

Bo reached for the letter again and looked at it. "The date on this doesn't mean anything."

"Oh, I guess not. Here, maybe this'll help," Nystrom said, handing him the envelope.

Bo looked closely at the date on it. "Postmarked three days ago. And you got it two days ago at midnight. Correct?"

"Yes."

Handing the letter and envelope back, Bo stated quietly, "I guess that eliminates any motive you might have had, unless you wanted to own the business outright."

"I'd rather have Rod back, business-wise. He was sixty to seventy percent of it. Actually, I'll probably make less money, now. But the real reason I'd want him back is because he was my friend, a good friend. I'll miss him."

*   *   *

While driving back to the office, Tony asked Bo, "What do you think? Was he telling the truth or was he lying?"

"If he wasn't telling the truth, he is an awfully good liar. The clincher for him is that letter. It certainly seems to clear him."

"What do we do now?"

"Go back to the office and think this through. I like to use a blackboard, put everything on it. It helps me organize my thinking."

"We can keep a running list on the board in the conference room."

Bo was nodding his head. "Let's do it."

*   *   *

Later that night, Sandy and Tony drove onto the graveled parking lot by the Sangamon River. Their tires crunched to a stop in front of a dark, single-story building nestled among a stand of trees. A neon sign on the peak of the roof read Lake of the Woods Inn.

"The place seems to be jumpin'," Tony commented, observing all the parked cars.

"It always is. A lot of the college kids hang out here."

Tony came around to help Sandy out of the car.

"Still being a gentleman, I see. I like that."

"I hope so. I don't do that for everyone." He laughed.

Tony opened the heavy oak door and ushered Sandy inside.

They were greeted by the maitre d', who picked up two menus and asked, "Two?"

Tony nodded.

The maitre d' continued, "Smoking or non?" He was wearing a white shirt with a black tie, pants and vest.

"Non," Tony answered, "And could we have a table by a window?"

"Certainly, Sir. We have one that was just cleaned up. This way, please."

When they were seated the maitre d' handed them menus. "Your waiter will be with you shortly."

"Come here often?" Tony asked.

"No. Once in a while when I was still a student."

"With boyfriends?"

Sandy smiled. "With a bunch of girls from school. Never with a boy."

"Good. You know, I really like this place," Tony expounded with a pleased look on his face. "It has a great atmosphere." Then he glanced out the window. Bright lights splayed soft beams across the lawn, bushes and trees, right down to the dark river that meandered through the park.

"I love it, too," Sandy said. "I always have. It's such a peaceful place, especially during the day. We ought to have a picnic here someday."

"I'd like that, too."

The waiter arrived, dressed like the maitre d', except for the short white apron around his waist. "Are you ready to order?"

"No." Tony replied. "We've been talking too much."

"That's quite all right, sir. Take your time. I'll be back."

When the waiter returned, Sandy ordered first. "I'll have the Oriental Chicken Salad with rice pilaf and whatever dressing comes with it."

"And I'll have a New York steak, rare. The thickest they have. Baked potato with sour cream and chives."

"Anything to drink? Wine? Cocktails?"

Tony looked at Sandy with a question on his face.

"I'm like my father. I don't drink. But I'd like some coffee."

"Make it two coffees."

After the waiter left, Tony proudly announced, "I have a new case. And this one is really big. Something I can get my teeth into."

"Tell me about it," she said excitedly.

"Well, I'm sure you've heard about the Rodney Marquette murder. His wife is being charged with it."

"Yes, my office is handling the case. That's all people are talking about."

Tony explained the information he and Bo had, and finished with the motive the police have.

"And I, as a lawyer, would have to agree with the police. They do seem to have an air tight case."

Tony doctored his coffee and took a sip. Somewhere near the kitchen a dish crashed, disrupting his train of thought for a moment. "But I thought I had a suspect that had just as good a motive. Rodney's partner, Walter Nystrom."

"Wally?"

"Do you know him?"

"Yes. Well, no. That is, he belongs to the country club. I've met him there, but I don't really know him well."

Tony explained the information about the letter that exonerated him.

"Oh. So you did talk to him."

"Oh, yeah. But Rodney had found the mistake and apologized, asking him to come back, et cetera."

"Have any other suspects?"

"It seems he wasn't liked by very many people, except his clients. And they may have put up with him, because he was making them a lot of money. Makes sense.

"Brian Folleta hated his guts. Seems Rodney quit and took all of Folleta's clients with him, plus he invited Wally to join him, which, as you know, he did. This was a sizable amount of Folletta's business, almost half, I understand. Bo and I will try to see Folletta in the morning."

The food arrived and Tony and Sandy focused on it.

CHAPTER NINETEEN

A cool spring breeze drifted in through the open car window, ruffling Bo's hair. He was seated on the driver's side. Tony was in the passenger seat. They had backed into a parking space more than an hour before to get a better view of Brian Foletta's office building. It was a two-story brick building with his office prominently located in the front corner, next to the main boulevard.

Bo had called the man to set up an appointment, but he refused to meet. Then Bo called attorney Colton and by midmorning had picked up a subpoena to serve Foletta. Now all they had to do was wait.

Around noon, Foletta drove up in a new black BMW 450SL. He was a short, handsome man. It reminded Tony of some of the male Hollywood movie stars whose female counterparts were taller. He wore gray slacks with a dark blue blazer, his white collar open at the neck. Before he could retrieve his briefcase out of the back seat, Bo and Tony approached him.

"We have something for you, Mr. Foletta," Bo said with a smile, waving the subpoena.

Brian Foletta glared at them harshly and snatched the paper out of Bo's hand. "What's this all about?" he growled.

"The defense is calling you as a witness in the State of Illinois versus Mrs. Marlene Marquette."

"But why? I don't know anything about that."

"Well, when you refused to meet with Mr. Garber and me, Marlene's attorney felt you may have something to hide. Hence, a subpoena. In court you'll be forced to answer his questions."

"What if I change my mind and talk to you now?"

"Then he may not have to call you as a witness. But there are no guarantees."

"Okay. But let's do it in my car. I don't want anyone in my office to know about this."

The man slipped back into the front seat of his car as Tony got in on the other side. Bo sat in the rear seat and leaned on the front back rest.

"When did Rodney Marquette leave your company?" Tony asked for starters.

"About two years ago. And when he left, he also took another one of my top salespeople, Walter Nystrom and all his customers, too."

"Did that make you angry?"

"Of course. I was furious with him."

"You hated him?"

"Yes!"

"Enough to kill him?"

"No! Don't be silly. I may have disliked the man intensely, but not enough to commit murder. I'm just a businessman, not a killer."

"Where were you the night before last between nine and eleven?"

"In my office. I was working late."

"Anyone else working with you?"

"No. I was alone. The others had gone home."

Bo stroked his chin, elbow on the head-rest. "So you have no alibi for that night?"

"I guess not. But then I'm not the one under arrest."

"True," Tony replied. *Where do we go from here?* he asked himself. Then as an afterthought, he asked, "No one saw you?"

"Nope. Not that I can re...wait a minute. The cleaning lady came in but she excused herself when she saw I was working late. I'd forgotten."

"What time was that?"

"Oh, I don't know. Around nine, I suppose. You'll have to ask her."

"All right, Mr. Foletta. We're through, but if we have any more questions, we'll be in touch. One last thing. What's the cleaning lady's name?"

"I don't know for sure. I think it's Carmella. She's the only one who cleans my offices. You'd have to ask my secretary. My secretary handles that. On second thought, I'll find out and give you a call. I don't want my people discussing whether I'm involved, or not."

"I understand," Bo said. "And thank you for your help."

"You're welcome. And by the way, if you're looking for a good suspect, I'd talk to Rod's first wife. She's living with another man, but couldn't marry him, or she'd lose her alimony. The arrangement was if he died first, she'd get a lump sum from the estate.

"How do you know this?"

"His first wife and I were pretty close at one time. Now does that interest you?"

"Yes, it does," Bo answered, taking out a little black book and nodding his head. "And what's her name and where does she live?"

"Barbara Houston. And the last I heard, she and her lover were living at the Greenwood Manor over on Paramount Boulevard."

"Thanks again."

*   *   *

The Greenwood Manor was a high rise, at least for Champaign, Illinois. It actually rose ten stories with balconies jutting out from each apartment. Made up of mostly glass and shiny steel beams, it sparkled in the late morning sun as Tony and Bo entered.

A security guard seated behind a small desk in the lobby looked up. He was probably in his early sixties with tufts of gray sticking out around his visor hat sitting jauntily on the back of his head. His olive green uniform stretched over an ample mid-section. A smile on a road map face greeted them. "Good morning, Gentlemen. How may I help you?"

Bo squinted at the man's name tag. "Good morning, Arthur." We're here to see Ms. Houston. What apartment is she in?"

"I'll have to call to announce you, but I don't think she's in. Your names?"

Miraculously, a twenty-dollar bill popped up between Bo's right forefinger and thumb. "We'd prefer not to be announced. We want to surprise Babs, as I like to call her."

"I understand, Sir. That's apartment Ten forty-four. Top floor to the right." Arthur smiled as he plucked the twenty and slipped it into his shirt pocket. "If you gentlemen will excuse me, I'll just go and check something in the maintenance room."

Bo pushed the buzzer to no avail. "Like the man said, 'I don't think she's in.'"

Bo gave the buzzer one more shot, holding the button in for a full fifteen seconds, knowing if anyone was in there, it might irritate enough to get an answer. Bo smiled and said, "We'll just have to return later."

*   *   *

When they returned to Paramount Boulevard later in the day, the sun had set in the western sky. The night was chilly, accented by a brisk breeze. Tony and Bo, both hunched over to fend off the cool air, approached the Greenwood Manor. "Just follow my lead," Bo said as he wrapped his arms around himself for more protection. "And take lots of notes."

"Okay," Tony answered. The guard was nowhere to be seen.

Moments later, after punching the buzzer at apartment Ten forty-four, the door opened. A woman in her early forties with long blond hair hanging loosely around her shoulders greeted them. She had a narrow nose, pale blue eyes and a slender face. She wore a dark blue, wraparound skirt, a white silk blouse, and a lengthy strand of pearls.

A very attractive woman, Tony thought. *At least for her age.*

"May I help you?" she asked suspiciously.

Bo nonchalantly flashed his badge. As he slipped it back into his pocket, he said phlegmatically, "I'm Robert Bobbyo and this is my partner, Tony Garber. We just have a few questions we need to ask about your ex, Rodney Marquette."

Her eyes narrowed. "What kind of questions?"

"The usual about his life and so on. May we come in?"

"I guess." She stepped out of the way to admit them, then led the way into an expansive living room. The walls, a very pale green, were covered with large scenic oil paintings with mountains, jungles, and log cabins surrounded with lush green woods. The heavily flowered brocade furniture, couches, and recliner, sitting on a pale green carpet, were arranged for conversation.

"Would you like to sit down, Gentlemen?" she asked politely, indicating one of the couches.

She sat on the edge of an ottoman, suggesting they wouldn't be there long.

"Thank you." Bo smiled benignly. Both of them sat on the couch.

"Now, ask away," she encouraged.

Bo stroked his chin. "When was your divorce?"

"Be three years the second of next month."

Tony began to write in a small notebook.

Bo continued, "How often have you seen him since then?"

"Not very often. Once in a while, we run into each other at the club. A nod of the head in passing, that's all. We never talk. Nothing to talk about. It was a nasty divorce. I've lived up to my end, and he to his."

"What was the arrangement of the divorce?"

"I don't think that is any of your business," she retorted.

"I'm not interested in how much he paid you, Ms...Houston. Is that your maiden name?"

"Yes. I certainly didn't want to use his name anymore."

"What was the reason for your divorce?"

"Incompatibility. Total incompatibility. We couldn't even stand the sight of each other."

"I see. Now, Ms. Houston, getting back to the mechanics of your divorce, not how much, but just what arrangements were made, or agreements settled on?"

"Well, he was supposed to relinquish certain properties to me and pay me a stipulated amount monthly until I died or remarried."

"Is that why you haven't remarried?"

A smile settled on her face. "Very perceptive, Lieutenant. It is Lieutenant, isn't it?"

"No Ma'am. Please just call me Bo."

"Not Lieutenant. Is it Sergeant? Or let me ask you this," she asked. "Are you with the police?"

"Again, no Ma'am. We're private investigators."

Bounding to her feet, she almost shouted, "This interview is over! You misled me!"

"No, Ma'am. I showed you my badge, but you jumped to your own conclusions. That is not my fault."

"You're right. I should have looked more closely. Now, if you don't mind, I'd like you to leave. Immediately!"

"Of course," Bo said remorsefully, looking at the floor. Then lifting his eyes, he continued, "But let me ask just this. What happens to your alimony, now that Rodney is dead?"

Her eyes flashed.

'If looks could kill, Bo thought.

"Get out!" she bellowed, pointing at the front door. "Get Out!"

Tony and Bo moved toward the front door. Abruptly, Bo stopped, turned and looked her squarely in the eyes. "Where were you at the time Rodney was murdered?"

She flinched. Then with indignation she hastily spoke. "Right here with my boyfriend, Eric." Then she added, "He can testify to that, too!"

*   *   *

As they descended on the elevator, Tony revealed his disappointment. "Looks like another one bit the dust."

"Not at all, Tony. If she's telling the truth, I would have to agree. But, is she?"

"The boyfriend has a good thing going. Don't you think he'd lie for her? You bet he would. What we need is more information. Lots of it."

The elevator doors opened and they stepped into the lobby. Arthur was back in his usual place behind the small desk.

"Hello again, Arthur," Bo greeted him magnanimously.

"Hello to you too, Sir. Both of you."

Again a twenty-dollar bill popped into Bo's hand. Only this time he had it folded lengthwise and was wrapping it around his left index finger. "Could I ask you a couple of questions, Arthur?"

"Sure. Fire away." His eyes were fixed on the twenty.

"What is Ms. Houston's boyfriend's name? Eric something."

"Eric Willowby, Sir. From a well-known family. I have his business card." He opened one of the drawers and searched for a moment. "Ah. Here it is."

Bo looked at Tony, who was already copying down the information from the card.

"Now," Bo continued. "Do you know where they were three nights ago? Around nine-thirty."

Arthur lifted his hat and scratched his head for a moment. "I don't know about Ms. Houston, but Mr. Willowby left the day before on a business trip to L. A. He gave me ten bucks to look after Ms. Houston for him. He didn't get back until last night. And I don't remember Ms. Houston going out that night." Then glancing through the open ledger on the desk, he added, "In fact, I keep a record of the comings and goings of everyone in the building, and I don't see any entries of her leaving that night."

"Could she have gotten out some other way? A back exit or something?"

"Only the fire door for emergencies, at the bottom of the staircase, over there." He pointed to the door that led to the stairwell. "But if someone slipped out that way, that big door would close behind them, locking them out. Unless, of course, they wedged something into it to keep the door ajar."

"So it is possible that someone could have sneaked out that way?"

"Yes, but I don't think Ms. Houston would do something like that, if that's what you're suggesting. She's too much of a lady." He looked a little distressed.

"Now, I agree with you on that, Arthur. She's a fine lady. I'm sure she wouldn't do something like that."

Bo handed the doorman the twenty, and the smile returned to the doorman's face.

"Well, I appreciate your help, Arthur. Thanks."

*   *   *

Out in the car as they drove away, Tony asked, "You agree with Arthur that she's too much of a lady to sneak down the back way?"

"I said that for his benefit. He wanted the twenty, but didn't want to get into any trouble with his boss, especially if Ms. Houston complained to management about his big mouth."

"Anyway," Tony pondered, "she's still a possibility."

"Yes. And so is her boyfriend, Eric."

"But he was in Los Angeles."

"How do you know that?"

Tony shrugged.

"Maybe he never went to Los Angeles. Or maybe he left the next night after the murder. Or maybe he came back the next day and then returned to L.A. the next morning. It's something we have to check out."

"Okay. But even if he had the opportunity, why would he do it? He probably didn't even know Rodney Marquette."

"He didn't have to know him to have a good motive."

Bo pulled into the office parking lot, and shut off the engine. Suddenly, it became deathly quiet in the car. He leaned back in his seat and unconsciously wiped his face with his hand. "Let me paint you a picture, a scenario, if you please.

"Let's suppose for a minute that Barbara and Eric want to get married. They love each other or whatever. But Barbara couldn't remarry before Rodney's death, because she'd lose her alimony. Always remember, Tony. Follow the money trail.

Tony nodded his head.

"Now, I mentioned that they may love each other. But I've almost always found that the marriages, the well-to-do-ones, at least, are quite often more of a convenience than for real love. Oh, they may be drawn to each other physically, but their only real love is for themselves and their security. Try to take that respectability and security away, and they'll come out fightin'. They can get real nasty, even quite dangerous."

"Oh, come on, Bo. You can't be serious."

"But I am serious, totally. You see, she was receiving money from Rodney, and that may not be a problem. But what about respectability? May be she wants to be Mrs. Eric Willowby. This might be extremely important to her."

"And what about him? What's his motive?"

"Money! He has the name, the position in the community that commands respect. There's that word again. But the family fortune has dwindled over the years, and now he even has to work to make ends meet.

"How dreadful. But there is light at the end of the tunnel...if...if Rodney dies, somehow. Then she will inherit a large lump sum. When they marry, he will then have control of all that money, and they live happily ever after; she with the title, and he with what he wants.

"Is that motive enough?"

Bo let his breath out slowly. "You bet. Now, we have some good news for Mrs. Marquette, but it's too soon. We still need to nail it down. We have no proof. He certainly has motive, but we have to prove he also had opportunity. Maybe they planned it together and executed it, forget the pun. Or maybe they operated separately. Who knows? 'Only the Shadow knows' and we'll be that shadow. And who knows what we'll find under a rock."

"What are you talking about?"

"There used to be a radio show called, "The Shadow." They used to introduce the show with an eerie voice saying, 'Only the Shadow knows.' I collect old tapes like that. I enjoy listening to them. A hobby."

"Okay, okay. 'Nuff said," Tony replied a little irritated. "Now what do we do?"

"Now, we have to check out the rest of the suspects."

"There's a lot more to this detective business than I thought."

"That's right. That's why we're called gumshoes. We stick to the job. Never give up."

"Go on," Tony grumbled and climbed out of the car.

Bo followed, but with a smile on his face.

*   *   *

Tony and Bo were seated in front of Willowby's small desk in his equally small office. There had been no secretary or receptionist when they had walked in on him.

He was thin, of average height, with mousy blond ringlets coiling down to his ears. He was conservatively dressed in a gray, pinstripe suit, obviously custom tailored. His tie sported small yellow dots on a field of black.

"It's not much," he indicated with a wave of his hand. "But then I don't need much. Just a place to park it a few hours a week and a place to make a few phone calls."

"What kind of business do you have?" Tony asked. "There was nothing on the door, not even your name."

"Import, export. But how did you find me? I'm not listed."

"That's our business. We're always looking for someone. We have people in our office that do nothing but locate people and get information about them." Bo would never give his sources, anyway. Besides, Arthur, the doorman, may still supply more information.

"Well, I don't think I should talk to you guys after the way you deceived Barbara."

Bo shrugged. "Most people don't pay any attention when we show our badges. They just assume we're from the police. Sure helps us, though." He grinned. "You don't have to cooperate, but better here than in court." He slipped the subpoena across the desk.

Eric looked at the paper and frowned. "One thing I don't need is to get mixed up in this. How can I help?"

"Do you and Ms. Houston have any plans to marry soon?"

"No. At least we haven't talked about it."

"Is marriage something the two of you have considered?"

"Yes, but we couldn't do it, because of Barbara's agreement with her ex."

"But now he's dead and you're free to marry. Correct?"

"Wait a minute. You're not trying to pin this on Barbara, are you?"

"Or on you. If the shoe fits."

"Me? I was in L.A. on business. Left last Thursday and didn't return until yesterday."

"Any witnesses?"

"Yes. Plenty of them. I was with both of the Bentley brothers, every day. I do a lot of business with them."

"All day and all night?"

"No, of course not. Most of the evenings I spent in my room at the Downtown Marriott, working."

Tony wrote this all down.

"What about last Friday night," Bo queried, "between nine and ten?"

"Yes, I was there. In my room."

"Alone?"

"Yes. But I certainly wouldn't come back here and kill the man. I had no reason."

"But what if there was a lot of money involved, like a large lump sum Ms. Houston would receive after her ex's death, which would make her eligible for remarriage, too. Huh?"

Tony stopped writing and looked at Bo with a great deal of respect.

Bo leaned back in his chair, looking intently at Mr. Willowby, waiting for an answer.

Eric's face reddened, a picture of anger. "Look," he sputtered, "I wouldn't lower myself to that level for ten times that amount, whatever it is. Money is important, but not that important. My name and reputation is. I would never jeopardize it."

"Okay, Mr. Willowby. Just one last thing. Did anyone see you or talk to you that Friday night in Los Angeles?"

"Well, I did have room service every night. I ordered their famous stickybuns with a glass of milk. Does that help you?"

"Sure. Thanks for your cooperation."

"Do you believe him?" Tony asked as they walked out to their car.

"I think I do, but he's not totally cleared until everything is verified. We'll go ahead and add him to our list on the blackboard."

CHAPTER TWENTY

Chiseled into the gray cement cornerstone were the words Champaign County Court House, 1923, a four story building with a wide central cement staircase that led to a double-door entrance. Above the doors was decorative scalloped trim around spoked windows, the hub of which was a gold painted knob.

This place is really old, Tony noticed as he entered into the large foyer of the building. *I hope this testifying doesn't take long. Feel kind of guilty framing his girlfriend. But better her than me.*

Tony, the district attorney's prime witness, sat in the hallway, outside the courtroom when the court clerk called him.

He entered the small courtroom. It was rectangular with high, coffered ceilings. The jury box sat on a tiered platform to the right side of the courtroom.

Tony glanced at the judge, a stern looking man with white hair and a black robe. Tony opened the swinging entrance gates and stood where the court reporter indicated. "Raise your right hand," she instructed. "Do you solemnly swear that the testimony you are about to give will be the whole truth and nothing but the truth, so help you God?"

"I do," Tony answered.

"You may be seated."

Tony stepped into the witness box and sat down. He observed two long tables just in front of the railing that separated the spectators from the rest of the court. On the right side sat the attorney for the defense, Marvin Wiseman, who had a reputation of living up to his last name, and next to him, his client, Nancy Idenhauer. She was wearing a light, delicately flowered dress. Her hair was coiffured in an old-fashioned style, piled on top of her head.

To the left, sitting behind their table, sat John Farrot, the deputy district attorney, who had a reputation for being hard line and having seldom lost a case. He was typically dressed in a dark suit and tie with a white shirt. His ruddy, round face displayed a permanent scowl. He was squinting at some paperwork on the table. Next to him sat a younger man, dressed the same, but he looked tense and worried.

"Mr. Farrot?" the judge prompted.

"Yes, Your Honor. I'm ready, now."

Setting down the papers he had been perusing, he walked over to Tony. "Sir, would you state your full name and address for the record?"

"Yes, Sir," Tony answered, giving his name and address.

"Now, Sir, were you present at the time the chief of police, Roger Thornfield, was shot?"

"Yes."

"When was this? Date and time, please."

"It was on a Thursday, March twenty-third, I believe. Approximately seven fifteen in the evening."

"Would you tell the court why you were there that evening?"

" I was having a business meeting with the chief."

"Was it normal to have this type of meeting in the chief's residence?"

"No, not normally. It was because of the highly confidential nature of the business."

"And that was?"

Tony gave a quick glance at Nancy before continuing. "The chief asked me to investigate Miss Idenhauer and to put her under surveillance to find out where she went and who she saw. He wanted me to find out anything I could to help him get her off his back. Those were his words."

Tony didn't want to look at Nancy. He could imagine what kind of expression she had on her face.

Mr. Farrot went back to his table and was looking at some papers when Tony realized that he had better not avoid looking at her. *I'd better make eye contact, or someone might notice and believe her story, instead of mine*, he reasoned.

He locked eyes with her. She was looking at him, too. Her eyes were asking, "Why?" Pleading with him.

Now for a little acting, he decided, knowing how important this was for his own safety. Showing a sad expression, Tony tilted his head to one side, looking directly into her puzzled eyes, trying to look as if he felt compassion for her.

He was sure it was having its effect on the jury.

Mr. Farrot found the paper he wanted. Tony returned his gaze.

The prosecutor came back to the witness box and put his hand on its railing. "Now, Mr. Garber, why did the chief want her, and I quote, 'off his back?'"

"He told me that they had been having a relationship and he felt it was over, but she wouldn't let go. In fact, he told me she was getting mean, nasty."

"Were you in the Dutch House Restaurant the morning before the murder?"

"Yes, Sir."

"Would you tell us what happened?"

"Well, my girlfriend, Sandy Forrest, and I had just finished our breakfast, when the shouting at the next table began. Miss Idenhauer over there," Tony nodded in her direction, "was having an argument with the chief of police. I only heard the last part, where Miss Idenhauer was yelling. I remember it verbatim. She said, 'You can't do this to me. You'll regret it, if you do.' And that's when she stormed out of the place."

"Now, getting back to the night of March twenty-third at about seven fifteen. What happened? Just tell us in your own words."

"I had excused myself to go refresh my drink, just off the study. I was drying my hands with a cocktail napkin, when I heard someone come in. She must have had her own key. Anyway, she was screaming something like, 'You can't dump me. I won't let you. I'll kill you, first."

No one in the courtroom moved. No one said anything. The full impact of Tony's statement penetrated the mind of every person in the room.

"Wait a minute," Mr. Farrot said sternly. "Did you hear her say, 'I'll kill you, first?' That's what she said exactly?" He knew what Tony claimed she had said, but he wanted the point to be emphasized for the sake of the jury. He looked Tony squarely in the eyes, expectantly.

"Yes, Sir," Tony answered.

Farrot looked at the spellbound jury. He knew that he had scored points with them. "Okay," he finally said, "Let's go on."

"That's when I noticed she had a gun in her hand. I tried to stop her, but before I could get near her, she fired. Twice, I think."

"Then what happened?"

Tony took a deep breath. "I wrestled with her. She was clawing and scratching. She was a little hell cat. And..."

"Objection," Mr. Wiseman shouted, jumping to his feet.

"Sustained," growled the judge.

"Just tell us what happened and what was said, if anything."

"She was putting up such a fight, that I, without thinking, grabbed the ashtray and hit her with it. It knocked her out."

"Then what did you do?"

"I caught her as she fell and sat her down in a chair behind her, kicked the gun under the desk, tied her up with Scotch tape and dialed nine one one."

"You said you believe she shot the victim twice. Is that correct?"

"Yes."

"Was the gun fired a third time?"

"Yes, I almost forgot. When we were struggling, it went off again."

He looked at Mr. Wiseman. "Your witness, counselor."

Slowly, the attorney for the defense got to his feet and walked toward Tony. He stopped and just stared at him. "Mr. Garber," Mr. Wiseman's voice finally boomed. "You said a few minutes ago that she was screaming something like, 'You can't dump me. I won't let you. I'll kill you, first.' Before your first two sentences, you indicated, and I quote, 'Something like.' These two words preceded 'You can't dump me.' And 'I won't let you.' If you're not sure of these statements, then how can you be sure you heard her right about the, 'I'll kill you, first?' You can't have it both ways. It has to be one or the other. Now, which is it?" He leaned forward with a threatening stare.

"Objection. Badgering the witness."

"Sustained. Watch it, Mr. Wiseman." The judge looked back at Tony and nodded.

"I don't understand what you're asking. Could you repeat it?"

The normally scowling prosecutor smiled.

Mr. Wiseman backed off a little. "All right. Let me rephrase that question. How can you say with such certitude that she said, 'I will kill you, first'? Especially since you have indicated that you weren't sure of what she said prior to that."

"Because of the impact of what she said. I was shocked. I've personally never heard an adult threaten someone like that, except in the movies."

Wiseman frowned. "Let's move on, Mr. Garber." He studied his notes for a moment. "When you heard and saw the defendant in the study, how far away was she from you?"

"About twenty feet."

"And when you decided to disarm her, how long did it take to reach her?"

Tony thought for a few moments, scratching behind his ear. "About two or three seconds. I'm not sure."

"She supposedly had a gun in her hand. Couldn't she have turned and fired at you before you could reach her?"

"Maybe she could have. But I didn't think about it at the time."

"You weren't worried?"

"Naw."

"Wait a minute, Mr. Garber. I find that hard to believe."

He's trying to trap me, Tony thought. *Get me to say I'm brave, without fear. But I know and he knows that everyone's afraid of something.*

"In fact, Mr. Garber, I don't believe you. You're telling me and the jury that you weren't afraid." Smugly, Wiseman looked at the jury.

"That's not what I said, Mr. whatever-your-name-is. I reacted. I wasn't thinking when I went after her. It was only afterwards, when I had time to think, that I realized how stupid I was. I said to myself, *'You dummy. You coulda got yourself killed.'*"

The smug expression disappeared. Mr. Wiseman walked to his table, then turned back toward Tony. "Mr. Garber, I believe my client is innocent. In fact, I'm sure of it. Now if she is innocent, and if there was no one else in that room, but the two of you what would that... suggest to you?"

"Objection, Your Honor!" shouted the prosecutor, jumping to his feet. "No foundation! And Mr. Garber is not on trial here. I move that it be stricken from the record and that the jury be instructed to disregard that statement."

"Motion granted," stated the judge, pounding his gavel to restore order in the courtroom. "The court reporter will strike that last statement, and I'm instructing the jury to totally disregard that statement, also."

The judge looked harshly at Mr. Wiseman and admonished him. "And you, Counselor. I'm surprised at you. You know better than that. You will refrain from blatant assertions. Is that understood?"

"Yes, Sir. I apologize to you, Your Honor, and to the court."

"All right, Mr. Wiseman, you may continue."

"I have nothing else for this witness, Your Honor."

The judge looked at Tony and said, "Mr. Garber, you're dismissed with our thanks."

Tony and Bo headed back toward the office. "What do you think?"

"About what? Bo teased.

"You know very well. My testimony. I thought I did real well."

"Yes, you did great. You certainly nailed her."

"I hated to do that to her, but what else could I do? I had to tell the truth."

"I suppose so. What is it they say. The truth will find you out, or something like that."

Inwardly, Tony shuddered. *But not in this case,* he hopefully thought.

*   *   *

Tony switched his thinking from the murder he allegedly had witnessed to the one he and Bo were investigating. But feelings of guilt were haunting him. He knew it was wrong to kill the police chief and frame his girlfriend, but he just couldn't allow the situation to mess up his life, just when things were going his way. Tony justified his actions in his thoughts and deliberately shoved the guilt to the back of his mind.

When he walked into the conference room, Bo was seated, elbows on the long table, face in his hands, studying the blackboard that had a column of suspects: Marlene Marquette, Walter Nystrom, Brian Folleta, Barbara Houston and Eric Willowby. The second column listed each person's motive; the third column was for opportunity, and fourth was for comments.

"Any answers?" Tony asked.

"A couple of ideas, but nothing solid."

"Now, how about our problem. Give." Tony also stared at the blackboard.

"All right. But let's take 'em in order. Our client we know about. The police have a lock on her at the moment. Next we have the partner. Except for the letter he has a strong motive, but..."Bo shook his head. Now, we have Rodney's former boss, Brian Folleta. 'Hate' is a good motive, and he had plenty of it. However, I talked to the cleaning woman. She verifies his story, sort of. She wasn't too sure about the time. It's still possible that he had the opportunity, but it would have been very tight scheduling for him to get over there in the time frame."

"How so?"

"Well..." Bo started to stroke his chin. "Well, she says she saw him just before going to dinner at nine. She always stops her work at nine sharp, because she says she's usually starving at that time. She disciplines herself to wait until nine. She says she's always looking at her watch every two or three minutes, because of hunger pangs.

With a speculative expression on his face, Bo continued, "I timed it by car from Folleta's office to the Marquette residence. Every time it came out between twenty-eight to thirty-one minutes. The murder took place at nine-thirty. It's possible he could have done it, but probably not. Too many 'if's.' If he left a few minutes before nine it's possible. If he left a few minutes after nine, probably not.Then there is another aspect. If he was there on time, how did he get in and get her gun, and not leave any fingerprints on it?"

"He could have taken the gun earlier," Tony piped in.

"Yes, he could have. That would mean it was preplanned, or premeditated, and if he had planned it ahead of time, he would also have planned a solid alibi. No, it doesn't quite jibe."

"So you're erasing him as a suspect?"

"No. Not entirely. We need more info on him before we finalize our decision to nail him or exonerate him."

"Okay," Tony relinquished. "But what about his ex wife? She had the best motive: money."

"Yeah, she did. And she could have slipped down the stairwell and out the fire door. Of course, she'd have to block it from closing all the way, so she could get back in. But we'd have to have some way of putting her at the scene or at least in the vicinity. And that's a tall order."

"I suppose so. And her boyfriend, Eric. What about him?"

Bo glared at the board. "Still viable. I haven't had a chance to check him out, but He's next on my agenda. I'll call room service at the hotel where he stayed. What was its name?"

Tony looked at his notes. "The Marriott Downtown."

"Oh, yeah. And this afternoon, let's go see Mr. Mueller again."

"Why?"

"Just to pump him a little more. You never know."

Tony and Bo walked through a light rain on the way up to see Jack Mueller again. It was a long, meandering sidewalk leading between four multi-storied luxurious apartment buildings. "What did you find out about Eric Willowby? Was he in L.A. at the time?"

"Yes. He ordered his sticky-buns and milk as he said he did. That gives him a solid alibi. I even talked to the waiter who delivered it to his room. A positive I.D."

"That narrows the field," Tony grumbled as they entered the building. The foyer had highly polished marble floors interrupted by a red carpet runner leading to the elevators. Large windows positioned between tall white pillars framed the entrance.

Mr. Mueller opened his door moments after they knocked. "Come in, gentlemen. I kind of thought you might be back. They always return in the movies. But I'm afraid there isn't anything else I can tell you." He led them into the living room area and gestured toward the couch. He sat opposite them.

"I understand, Mr. Mueller. It's usually a waste of time. But if you don't mind..." Bo looked at him wistfully.

"I know." He laughed. "Just tell it from the beginning again."

"Yes, Sir. Just like in the movies." Bo smiled.

"Like I told you before, I was sitting out on the balcony when I heard them arguing. At first it was just sharp words, but it escalated into a shouting match, not for just a minute or so, but a long time. They just kept on and kept on. Then the phone rang, and I went in to answer it. I was only gone a few minutes. As I hung up, I heard the shot. I knew it was a shot from a gun. I used to do a lot of hunting and target practice with hand guns."

"Just a minute, Mr. Mueller," Bo said, realizing the phone call had not been mentioned before. "How long were you on the phone?"

"Oh, just a few minutes."

"Could you think about that for a moment. It's very important. See if you can capture that moment again. Maybe reconstruct it in your mind."

"Okay. It was Penny Nichol." He chuckled. "I always thought that was a cute name. But she is a pain. She was a close friend of my deceased wife. Lately, I think she has set her eyes on me, but I act dumb. Anyway, she told me about the theater and how much fun it could be. She was hinting. And I was trying to think of an excuse in case she asked me, and trying to find a way to get off the phone. Then it hit me. I told her someone was at the door, and I have to go. Then I hung up."

"How long did it take? Please think about it."

Mr. Mueller put his fingertips together and looked off into the distance. He started to say something, then stopped. Finally, he looked at Bo and said, "It could have been as much as five minutes, but no more. When I think about it again, I remember what a talker she is."

"Could be as much as five minutes?" Bo questioned. "A full five minutes?"

"Yep, but no more than that."

"Could you hear the arguing when you were inside on the phone?"

"No, no. Besides, the curtains block out some outside sounds."

"Thank you, Mr. Mueller. You have been a tremendous help."

Mr. Mueller looked pleased..

The rain came down harder as Tony and Bo dashed for their car under the umbrella. After they were seated, Bo turned to Tony with a satisfied grin. "That's good news. It opens the door for someone else to have been there after her."

"How do you mean?"

"If the argument ended when Mr. Mueller went to answer his phone, or even within the next few minutes, someone else would have had time to go into the apartment and commit the murder. It opens it up to anyone with motive and opportunity."

Bo looked at Tony for a response.

Tony's mind was racing, cranking it up. "Wait a minute! I remember..." his voice trailed off.

Bo could almost see Tony's wheels turning. "Correct me if I'm wrong. But it seems to me that when we talked to Marlene, she said she had left the front door open as she pushed Rodney back into the living room. Isn't that right?"

"Yes. Yes, it is. You, Sir, win the kewpie doll. I never thought of it. I should have. That gives everyone the means to get in while the couple is arguing. Also, if the murderer knew about the gun, as it seems that everyone did, he or she could have grabbed it and hidden in the hall closet or the study."

"Now," Tony said, "all we have to do is figure out who?"

"Yes," Bo agreed. "All we have to do is figure out who. Let's see. We had five suspects to begin with.

Basically, we've cleared two of them. Rodney's partner, Wally Nystrom, because of the letter that took away any motive, and Eric Willowby, his ex's boyfriend. That leaves our client, who is innocent, because we represent her." Bo chortled, then continued. "There's a slim possibility that Brian Folleta had time to do it, but I doubt it. Now, there's only one left: Barbara Houston. A good candidate, a good motive, a possible opportunity, if we can place her at or near the scene."

"And how can we do that?" Tony asked.

"With a lot of legwork. We'll have to put more men on it, scour the neighborhood, and try to find someone who saw or heard something that night."

"It's going to cost a lot of money, you know."

"Yes, I know. But we're at square one again."

CHAPTER TWENTY-ONE

Tony and Bo questioned Marlene in the same room they had used before. This time they were accompanied by Mrs. Marquette's attorney, Tom Colton. Marlene looked better than the last time; she had fixed her hair and had put on some makeup. Mr. Colton sat at the end of the table, Marlene to his right. Bo was across from her, and Tony sat next to Bo.

"Mrs. Marquette," Bo started, "the last time we were here you said that when Rodney opened the door, you pushed him back until he fell on the couch. Is that correct?"

"Yes. I think at first he was very surprised that I was there and didn't realize what I was doing, until he fell onto the couch. Then he got real angry and stood up."

"You did not close the door behind you when you entered?"

"No."

"Does the door automatically close?"

"No. In fact it was still open when I went to leave. I closed it behind me, then."

"Why did you close it on your way out and not when you came in?"

"I don't know. I guess I was too mad when I first saw him. Maybe I didn't want to lose my advantage when he was backing up, which is something he doesn't usually do. But on the way out, I suppose I closed it from habit."

Bo leaned back in his chair and began stroking his chin. "That makes sense. That gives us a five-minute open door," Bo said as he looked from the attorney to his client. "Just yesterday, we found out when we re-interviewed Mr. Mueller that he had a phone call while the arguing or fighting was going on. He went inside to answer it and heard the gunshot when he was hanging up. And finally after we pressured him to remember, he determined that it could have been as much as five minutes from the time he left the balcony and heard the shot."

Mr. Colton, excited over the news, said, "Great job. We finally have something positive. Is there anything else?"

"Well, we've narrowed the field down to his ex-wife, Barbara, but we can't put her anywhere near the scene. And without that, we're up a tree."

"What about Wally?" Marlene squawked.

Everyone stared at her for a moment. This was the first time she spoke above a whisper.

Her face turned crimson. "Well," she sputtered, "I think he's the best suspect."

"He would be," Bo answered her, "but he was cleared by that letter from Rodney."

Apparently surprised, Marlene asked, "What letter?"

Bo explained the letter to her and then added, "Now, he has no motive."

"I don't believe it!" she cried out. "Rod would never write a letter like that. It would be a sign of weakness, and to put it into writing would give proof of his weakness. He would never do that."

Tony and Bo looked at each other, then at Colton, who shrugged.

"What you're saying," Tony asserted, "is that Rodney was a very proud person and would never put anything in writing that would diminish him in the eyes of anyone else. Is that correct?"

"That's it exactly."

Tony gazed at her. "Do you know how he signed his inner office memos?"

"Yes. With a large M, flourished across the bottom."

"With a tail at the end of the M?"

"Yes."

Bo said, "Very interesting. That single letter M could be a forgery. If we can prove the letter's a fake, we got him. He has no alibi for his time. We'll need a search warrant from you, Mr. Colton."

"No problem. I'm sure I can get one from Judge Wright and a couple of police officers to go with you to serve it, and help you with the search."

Turning back to Marlene, Bo looked at her squarely. "One last thing. Was Wally at the party when Rodney embarrassed you by showing everyone your gun and where you kept it?"

"Yes."

*   *   *

With a search warrant in hand, Tony, Bo and two uniformed policemen, and their computer hack, Martin Baldwin, entered Wally Nystrom's office. "Welcome back, gentlemen," Jenny said with a spectacular smile, "but Mr. Nystrom is out of town." She was wearing a revealing tight-fitting white sweater.

She's quite a gorgeous dame, Tony thought. *But why am I looking at her this way? I love Sandy. Maybe it's because I'm hot to trot and Sandy isn't. That's got to be it. She's a puritan. But you know something, maybe that's what makes her so attractive. I immediately lost interest in all those other babes after I had them.*

"Isn't that right, Tony?"

"Huh?"

"I was just telling Jenny we don't need to see Mr. Nystrom, but that we have a search warrant." Bo handed her the paper.

She turned the paper around and glanced at it. "Well, have at it, I guess."

"Thank you, Jenny. All we're interested in is Rodney's computer."

She looked a little perplexed, but without a word, she led them into Rodney's old office and pointed to the computer behind the desk.

"Jenny," Bo spoke softly, "do you think you could find the last letter Rodney wrote to Wally?"

"Sure. I printed it out and mailed it for him."

"Did you happen to read it or pay any attention to its content?"

"No, I wouldn't do that. And even if I were that kind of secretary, it would waste an awful lot of time. I wouldn't be able to get all my work done."

"I didn't mean to sound like I was accusing you. I just had to make sure. Now if you would bring up that letter, I'd appreciate it."

Jenny sat down at the computer and flipped on the power switch. Within a few moments, she entered their word processor, scrolled down to the file she wanted and clicked on it. Seconds later, the letter appeared on the screen.

Jenny leaned back, as Tony and Bo squinted over her shoulder. "It's the same letter," Tony blurted out. "The one he showed us."

Police officer Martin, a pimply faced kid of nineteen with carrot-red hair and thick glasses, spoke up. "Excuse me, Miss, but may I try something?"

"Sure."

Martin exited the word processor program, entered into the MS-DOS directory and found the file.

"All files are dated on the day they are written," Martin said. "This one was written on March fifteenth."

"That's two days before the murder," Bo said, his spirit dampened. "Which means Mr. Nystrom still doesn't have a motive. Unless he deleted the old letter and replaced it with something he wrote, but there's no way we can see if that was done."

"Pardon me, Gentlemen," Jenny broke in, " but maybe I could help. You see, each day I backup all the files for the day. Those were Mr. Marquette's orders."

Bo's eyes brightened. "Could you go back and pull up the letter Rodney wrote that day?"

"I'll have to do it from my desk. That's where we keep the backup."

The four of them filed out of Wally's office and surrounded Jenny's desk as she proceeded to bring up the requested letter on the screen. They crowded around and began to read. "We got 'im. That's not the same letter. This one proves there was no reconciliation. Would you make a half a dozen copies of that? Then we'll need to take the computer as evidence`."

"Of course."

"And Jenny, we'll need you to testify against Mr. Nystrom. That okay with you?"

"I'd be happy to. I always liked Mr. Marquette. But I may lose my job over this."

Bo looked at her with sympathy. "However," he said, "if Mr. Nystrom is arrested and convicted of murder, you won't have a job anyway."

"True," she answered. Her expression didn't reveal what she was thinking.

*   *   *

"Mr. Nystrom, may we have a word with you?" Bo asked. He and Tony were standing in the hallway outside Nystron's apartment. "I'm sure you remember us."

"I'm rather tired. I just returned from a long trip."

"I understand, Sir. This will only take a few minutes."

"Okay. But make it short."

"We will."

Nystrom led them into a messy study. None of the furniture was in place, but rather left askew, books piled on the floor and desk. "You'll have to excuse the mess. I'm in the process of reorganizing this room." He cleared a place for them to sit on the couch. He sat across from them in an easy chair.

"Now, how can I help?"

"Have you seen this before?" Tony asked as he handed him a copy of the original letter Rodney had written to him.

As Nystrom read, his face paled. "Where did you get this? What's going on?"

"Well, while you were on your trip, we went to your office with a search warrant. We found the letter Rodney had written to you. At that time we were about to give up. We had almost accepted your account of the events. That's when Jenny told us about the backup system. She was able to produce Rodney's original letter, requesting a dissolution of the partnership because of irregularities in the books you were responsible for. I guess that's just a nice way of accusing you of being a crook."

"I'm not a crook. I will admit I wrote that letter to make sure I got the business after he was dead, but that doesn't prove I killed him."

"No, but it gives you a motive, and with no alibi, you are definitely a suspect. But when you put that along with the other evidence we have, you're going to hang, or I guess it's lethal injection, now."

"What evidence?" he asked, his voice cracked with a slight quiver.

"After obtaining the original letter, we had to figure out how you committed the murder. It really wasn't that difficult, with all the information we dug up. We just had to put it all together. This is the scenario we came up with: You went to his apartment, probably in anger, or maybe in fear that he would expose you. Whatever the reason, when you arrived, the door was open, and Rodney and his wife were involved in an argument. You probably got the idea then."

Tony continued. "Pulling out your hanky, you opened the drawer in the small table, took out Mrs. Marquette's gun, and slipped quietly into either the closet or the study. When she stormed out, closing the door behind her, you stepped into the living room and shot Rodney. You dropped the gun and sneaked out."

"This is ridiculous. A bunch of poppycock. Your conjecture is not proof. If that's all you have, you don't have a case."

"Oh, but we have more. We figured it wasn't premeditated. That's why we concluded you used something to keep your prints off the gun. We got another search warrant and went to your apartment. Your residence manager let us in. Fortunately for us you haven't done your laundry for a while. We found a number of dirty hankies in your clothes hamper. We took them to the police lab, and they found gunpowder residue on one of them. The nose discharge blown into that hanky, the one with the powder residue, is being analyzed. It's only a matter of time before we get the DNA proof. That's why I said it's a lock. And it really is just that."

Wally's face flushed. He jumped up, grabbed a pair of scissors from atop a pile of papers and waved them at Tony and Bo. "Don't come near me. I'm getting out of here."

Bo stood up slowly and remained calm. "I'm sorry, Mr. Nystrom, but you're not going anywhere. The police are already outside your door."

"I don't believe you. You're trying to trick me."

"No, Mr. Nystrom," Bo said as he moved a little closer, "It's the truth."

Wally spoke through gritted teeth, "Don't come any closer. I don't want to use this, but I will."

Bo stuck his right hand up and at the same time took one more step with his right foot, then his left came up swiftly. The toe of his shoe struck Wally's wrist with such force that the scissors flew up and over the couch. Bo grabbed Wally's arm and twisted it behind his back, pushing Wally toward the front door. With his free hand, Bo opened the door to allow a policeman to enter.

"This is your suspect, Danny Boy," Bo said, releasing Wally's arm. "You can take him down and book 'im."

"Look, I've got fifteen grand in my safe. That's five thousand for each of you, if you let me go. Just give me twenty minutes, that's all."

Danny gave a hard twist to the handcuffs on Nystrom's wrist.

Wally squealed in pain.

"Now, we add bribery to the charge of murder," Danny sneered.

"Look, I didn't mean to kill him. I was just going to threaten him. Honest."

"I don't think you should say any more, Mr. Nystrom, Until I've read you your rights. You have the right to remain silent...."

*   *   *

Marlene Marquette stepped into the conference room where Tom Colton, Tony, and Bo were waiting. She was still wearing the drab, gray, prison dress, but now it was even more wrinkled. Her face, chalky white, had an expectant look, not knowing if it was good news or bad.

Colton took Marlene's shoulders in his large hands and looked squarely into her eyes with a wide grin. "You're free, Marlene. You can go home, now."

Her face went blank. "You mean... you mean the judge is going to release me on bail?"

"No. All murder charges against you have been dropped. Tony and Bo here found the real culprit and got the evidence that will probably convict him. You're free to go home and to stay there, if you wish."

Marlene's eyes filled with tears. She looked at Tony and Bo. "Thank you. I can never thank you enough." Then she stepped forward and gave each of them a warm hug.

"We're just delighted we could be of service," Bo said, softly.

Glancing back at her attorney, she asked, "Who was it?"

"Wally Nystrom. Just like you suspected."

"When you were so adamant about Rodney never writing a letter like that, we started to zero in on it," Tony said. "And it was the key to solving the whole thing and putting the blame on the right person."

"Thank you again," Marlene said, wiping away the tears. "In fact, there will be a nice bonus in the mail for a job well done."

"Come," Tom said, taking her elbow, "We'll get your personal belongings and check you out."

She patted her hair as they left, saying, "The first thing I'm going to do is get my hair fixed and buy some new clothes."

"Typical," Tony said to Bo, laughing.

CHAPTER TWENTY-TWO

Tony was working at his desk, which was strewn with papers and books. It was late afternoon and the sun was painting the city below his window with sharp shadows. He was about to pick up the phone when it rang. He grabbed it before the first ring ended. "Yes?"

"Sandy Forrest on line three, Mr. Garber," his receptionist informed him.

Punching the blinking line three, he gleefully said, "Hi. What's up?"

"Well, I have some good news and some bad news. Which first?"

A little apprehensive, he said, "Either way."

"Well, the bad news is I can't be there for dinner tonight. I have to go up to Chicago to handle a deposition, and I won't be back until tomorrow. The good news is that Dad still wants you to come. He has some business he wants to go over with you. And Matty will make you a special dinner for my not being there. Sound good?"

"Yeah, but why do you have to go, especially overnight?"

"It's an accident case. The man I have to question is in the hospital. He's not able to come down here. We're doing it in the evening because his lawyer is booked solid during the day."

"Well, I don't like it."

"It's only for one night. And I'll make it up to you when I get back."

"Promise you'll do anything to make it up?" His voice rose in expectation.

"I didn't say anything, you rascal. But I will take you out on the town, my treat. You'd better grab it, Tony; it's the only offer I'm going to make."

"All right, you win. Bye," he said hanging up the phone, then wishfully continuing, "but one of these days..."

*   *   *

Matty outdid herself. First, she served hors d'oeuvres of tiny rolled ham with cheddar cheese in the center and large prawns hooked on the edge of a bowl containing cocktail sauce, this followed by a light salad with a touch of honey-mustard dressing. The main course included beef medallions, asparagus tips in Hollandaise sauce and au gratin potatoes.

"Mr. G," Tony said as Matty served the cherries jubilee, "did you know that at one time I asked Matty to marry me, and she turned me down?"

"Really? Is that true, Matty?"

"Yes, it's true. You ask me now, young fella, and I say yes."

Tony's grin was contagious as he glanced at Mr. G then back at Matty. "Why have you changed your mind?" he asked her.

"I find out you're rich. We get married, and I no have to work anymore. We hire help."

"You'd better be careful what you say around here, Tony," Mr G admonished him, chuckling.

When both men had finished their dessert, Mr. G suggested, "Let's have our coffee in the library. Then we can talk." Mr. G poked his head into the kitchen. "Matty," he said, "we'll have our coffee in the library."

Moments later, they were seated in overstuffed mahogany chairs. On the coffee table between them sat an ornate letter opener. Tony picked it up and admired it as Matty poured their coffee.

"A gift given to me by Sandy for Father's Day," Mr. G said proudly. "I don't know how it got here on the coffee table. I always keep it on my desk."

"It's beautiful. Sandy has good taste," Tony said as he stood up, walked over and set it on Mr. G's desk.

"Yes, she does. Were you including yourself in that 'good taste' she has?"

Tony blushed. "No. I didn't mean it that way."

Mr. G said, "Changing the subject, I have more good news from our friend in Chi. Your investment of a hundred twenty-five grand has increased to over a half a mil, a three-hundred-percent profit. Not bad, huh?"

"Has any of that been deposited into my bank account?"

"No, because he's getting ready for a big kill. It's coming up in the next couple of days. He says we should double our money, at least. Then he'll deposit most of it in our accounts."

"Sounds good." His voice sounded a little tentative.

Mr. G looked sharply at Tony. "Are you sure it sounds good to you? Your voice lacks enthusiasm. If you want out, that's okay with me, and I'm sure it won't make any difference with my friend up in Chi."

Now it's 'his' friend up in Chi, Tony thought.

"No, no," Tony answered, "I want to stay in. Honest. It's just that I've been a little worried. As you know, if the big boss up in Chi finds out, we're history. That's my only problem."

"I can understand that, but not to worry. There's no way he can find out, because there is no paper trail. Before the Internet bank, people were always caught by their paper trails. But no one knows about our transactions except you, our friend, and me."

At least we're back to 'our' friend up in Chi.

"I feel a lot better now, Mr. G., really."

"Good!"

I know one thing. When I leave here, I'm checking my account to make sure the money's in the net.

Tony set his cup down on the coffee table. "Can I use your little room over there?" He nodded his head in the direction of the bathroom.

"Sure. Go ahead." Mr. G picked up his coffee cup and sipped.

When Tony had finished and was drying his hands on the towel, he heard Mr. G say, "Hi, Karla. What a pleasant surprise. What brings you down here?"

Tony poked his head out the door to see Mr. G standing up, arms outstretched to receive her. Then looking at the woman, Tony noted that she was probably in her late twenties, had charcoal black hair, and wore a black, leather mini-skirt and vest with a white blouse underneath.

There was a noise from the kitchen at the back of the house. Karla stopped momentarily just inside the door, her gloved hand in her purse. She glanced at the desk. A weapon of convenience, a fancy letter opener sat on his desk. She took her hand out of her purse and picked up the letter opener as she passed the desk. Smiling at him, she said, "Hi, Sam. I'm sorry about this, but it's orders." Then she plunged the letter opener into his chest.

Mr. G's eyes widened in surprise and shock.

As he slumped to the floor, she pulled the opener out and was about to drive it in again, when Tony, taking three quick steps, hurtled himself over the stuffed chair with a flying leap and hit the woman in the middle of her back. Her head snapped back, then forward, striking the corner of the desk with force, causing instant death.

Tony's momentum slammed him into the side of the desk. Gingerly, he rose to his feet, rubbing the right shoulder that took the brunt of his collision with the desk. He looked down at Karla. He instinctively knew she was dead.

He stepped over her and checked Mr. G.

Dead.

Turning back to the woman, he stared at her for a moment. Something was wrong. Then he noticed something. She's wearing gloves, but why? When he glanced at the letter opener on the floor next to her body, it struck him. My fingerprints, not hers, are all over it. Swiftly, he bent down, removed the gloves, and stuffed them into his pocket.

Matty came into the room. "Oh, my God. What's happened here?" she wailed.

Tony stood up quickly. "She's murdered Mr. G, Matty. Call the police. Hurry."

Matty moved toward the desk phone.

"No," Tony hollered. "Fingerprints. Use the phone in the hall."

Matty hurriedly left the room. Tony took out a kleenex from a box setting on a table behind him and wiped off the handle of the letter opener. He pressed it into the dead girl's hand, squeezing her fingers around it as he heard Matty hang up the phone. She reentered the room just as Tony stood up.

"I checked them, and both are dead," he said.

Matty stared at Mr. G and said, sadly, "My Sandy is going to take this very hard."

*   *   *

"Déjà vu," Lt. Daniel Moynahan muttered as he walked into the library. Mr. G and the woman were still lying on the floor next to the desk.

Tony and Patrolman Karl Lugerman were staring at the bodies. "What?" Tony asked, turning to the Lieutenant.

"Déjà vu. It's the feeling of having been here before."

"Oh." On reflection he added, "It's not exactly the same."

"No, not exactly the same, but enough to look awfully suspicious."

Insulted, Tony said, "Don't look at me when you say that."

"That's just the way my mind works, until I have all the facts," the lieutenant added.

Tony sat down heavily on one of the overstuffed chairs. "I suppose you want me to go over it in detail for you again."

"No, not again for me, but the first time for me. And you'll probably have to tell the story a number of times, again and again."

"Okay. Okay. Mr. G and I were talking business..."

"Just like you and the chief were?" the lieutenant interrupted.

Tony didn't like the direction this was going. "Yes," he answered sharply.

"What business?"

Tony was about to say private business, but remembered what happened the last time. Instead he continued with "Investments. We were thinking of joining together in some tips he had on certain stocks."

"What stocks?"

He knew he had to be very careful with what he said to this detective. "I don't know. Mr. G hadn't mentioned them by name, yet."

"All right. Go ahead."

"We were sitting just like we are, except on opposite sides. You here, me there," he said pointing. "Then I excused myself to go over to that bathroom."

"Like you excused yourself with the chief to refresh your drink?"

"Are you accusing me of something? I don't understand this line of questioning, the way you're doing this."

"What way is that?"

"The way you keep going back to the murder of the Chief. I didn't have anything to do with that."

"But don't you see the similarity, the way they are parallel?"

"Of course there's some similarity, but that is where it stops."

"Let's see. First, two prominent men from our community are murdered. Second, they are murdered in their homes in their libraries. Third, they are supposed to have been murdered by their lovers, because of rejection. Fourth, you are the only witness to the murder. That's too many similarities, as far as I'm concerned."

"So what are you going to do about it?"

"I'm going to ask you to finish your story."

Tony fidgeted, looking at his feet. *I don't get it,* he thought. *When I'm totally innocent, he's suspicious. Go figure. I don't understand.*

Finally he looked back at the detective and said, "Now, where was I when you so rudely took off on a tangent?"

"You were going to the bathroom."

"Oh, yeah. I was drying my hands when I heard someone come into the room." He thought the detective would say something like, just like when you saw the chief's girlfriend come into his room, but the detective did not say anything, although Tony was sure the detective was thinking it. "I poked my head out the door," Tony continued. "Mr. G said something like, 'Hi, Karla. What're you doing here? He stood up, spread his arms to give her a big hug, and she stabs him in the chest with the letter opener she had picked up as she walked past his desk."

Tony took a deep breath before he proceeded, "I saw she was going to do it again, and I leaped across the chair there," he was pointing, "and I crashed into her. But I had no idea what was going to happen."

"What did happen?"

Frustrated, he said, "You can see for yourself. Her head must have hit the corner of the desk. Take a look for yourself."

Lt. Moynahan glanced at the bodies, then back at Tony and said, "We found her purse, but no identification. And her car is stolen. Do you happen to know the woman, or at least her name?"

"No. I've never seen her before. But I'm pretty sure Mr. G called her Karla."

"All right, Mr. Garber, you can go. But as they say in the movies, don't leave town."

On the way home Tony threw the woman's gloves into a garbage bin behind a supermarket.

CHAPTER TWENTY-THREE

Tony stared out the window as Dr. Seigelwitz talked on the phone. Outside, the rain fell from the low, dark clouds that hung in the sky. The dreary weather didn't help Tony's feeling of depression. He knew he was in trouble with the police, or at the very least they were very suspicious. No matter how much he tried to explain to them, the deeper he dug the hole.

His mind was in a state of confusion when Dr. Seigelwitz finished her call. "Sorry about the delay, Tony. Some people are very impatient. Please have a seat, and we'll get started."

Tony flopped into the easy chair opposite Dr. Seigelwitz. Despondent, he uttered, "This is not a good day for me, Doc. I can't seem to get a grip on things."

"Like what?"

"Did you read in the morning paper about the murder of Samuel G. Forrest?"

"Yes, as a matter of fact, I gave Sandy a sedative last night. She was really quite shaken up about her dad. They were very close. The healing process is going to take time."

"I wasn't there when she got home. The police had taken me in for questioning. Later, when I called, Matty said Sandy had taken something and was already asleep. But when I did see her this morning after the police had talked to her, she looked at me like she was wondering if I might have killed her father. She didn't say it, but she was distant and reserved, not as friendly as usual."

"You think the police suspect you and may have convinced Sandy to think it, too?"

"I guess."

"Did you do it?"

"No!" Tony said. "I was just a witness. I saw the lady do it. The police keep saying it's very unlikely that two prominent men could have been murdered with the same witness, under the same circumstances. I can't seem to convince them otherwise. More importantly I have to convince Sandy. I love her and I think she loves me. But if she believes that I killed her dad, I'm finished with her forever. And I wouldn't blame her. But I'm innocent. Could you intercede for me?"

"It wouldn't do any good. It needs to come from you. You would need something that would convince her, something startling and very convincing."

Tony wiped his face in frustration. "I gotta go," he muttered. "I gotta think."

"That's a good idea. In the meantime, I'll mull it over myself."

"Okay. Will you be seeing Sandy later today?"

"Yes. In fact, I'll be heading over to her house in about an hour."

"Would you give her message for me?"

"Sure. What is it?"

"Well, first, tell her how sorry I am about her losing her father. Then tell her that I love her and I did not do it. Her father and I were partners in some futures investments, and we've been making a lot of money together and would have continued to prosper. It would be stupid to kill the goose that lays the golden egg. Tell her the proof of what I've just said is in a ledger he keeps in the locked drawer of his desk. In fact, it may have contained his number for his Internet Bank account and the password to get into it. There should be a lot of money in it. Now it belongs to her. It was going to facilitate his retirement. Would you tell her all that, Doc? Especially that I love her."

"You bet, Tony. But I can't guarantee how she'll receive it."

"I know. Just do the best you can."

*   *   *

After Dr. Seigelwitz gave Sandy another tranquilizer and Tony's message, she left.

Finally when Sandy was alone, she wandered into her father's library. In the middle of his desk, in a brown paper envelope, were his personal affects that Lt. Moynahan had given her.

She sat down in his swivel chair and dumped the contents on his desk. For a moment, she just stared at the items; a wallet, a neatly folded hanky, pocket comb, some change and his key chain. Picking up the latter, she inserted the short, fat, round key into the desk drawer lock and opened it. The ledger was underneath an eight-by-eleven-and-a-half sheet of paper. She picked up both items, placed them on the desk and slid the top sheet to the side. She tried to study the ledger, but the medication interfered. She couldn't concentrate. *I'll look at it later*, she thought. *Maybe tomorrow.*

Placing the ledger back in the drawer, she picked up the single sheet of paper and was about to put it back in the drawer also, but her father's handwriting at the top of the page caught her attention. *"Tony Garber, AKA Burton Alexander Helmsley."* *What does it mean?* she asked herself. But when she read the entire rap sheet, she knew what it was. With reluctance she dialed the police station and asked for Lt. Moynahan.

*   *   *

The next morning as Tony headed for his office, fearful thoughts whirled in his anxious mind. His mind filled with negative thoughts. *I can't believe what's happening. The police think these murders are not a coincidence. 'Déjà vu,' Lt. Moynahan called it. I can see his point, but...* Tony shook his head. He wiped his sweaty palms on his pants. *Timing. That was the problem. Why did Karla have to choose that moment to kill Mr. G? At any other time, I wouldn't have been involved.* Tony cursed. *Why? Why? Why?* rattled around in his brain.

Tony crossed the busy boulevard, oblivious to the traffic and noises of the city. He entered the bank building and walked unenthusiastically toward the elevator. As Tony emerged from the elevator and walked toward his office, a feeling of dread steadily grew within him. When he opened the door, he spotted Lieutenant Moynahan, accompanied by a uniformed police officer, talking to Bo. His insides filled with fear.

"Mr. Garber," the lieutenant said as Tony entered. "I'm placing you under arrest for the murder of Mr. Samuel G. Forrest."

Tony looked at Bo questioningly. Bo just shrugged and shook his head as the lieutenant continued. "You have the right to remain silent ..."

In the middle of Moynahan's reading of Tony's rights, Tony said to Bo, "Call my lawyers for me. Tell them what's happening and ask them to have someone meet me at the police station."

Bo nodded and left the room.

Turning back to the lieutenant, Tony asked, "How do you figure I did it? I told you the whole story last night."

"That was before we found out that the fingerprints were in a position on the letter opener that would have made it impossible for the dead woman to have committed the murder."

"What're you talking about?"

"It seems that her right thumbprint was next to the blade, and her pinky was at the base of the handle. That means she could not have stabbed him. The entry wound was at a forty-five degree angle coming down. Her fingerprints were at the wrong ends. You had to have put the letter opener in her hand, but in your haste, you placed it in the opposite position.

"Secondly, Miss Forrest found your rap sheet in a locked drawer of Mr. G's desk. That's a strong motive. Put it all together, and we have a very solid case against you. Murder One and, with the woman you admitted killing, maybe two murders along with armed robbery up in Chicago. You're going away for a long time and maybe.. . Well, that's up to the D.A."

As they handcuffed Tony, all he could think about was that Sandy had found the rap sheet. *Now, she'll be certain that I killed her father*, he thought. *I'll never be able to convince her otherwise.* He wasn't even aware of the stares from his employees as the police led him through the outer office.

*   *   *

Tony was booked and fingerprinted. *I can't believe I got nailed for something I didn't do,* Tony thought. His world was crashing down around him.

It was almost two hours later before Craig Colton arrived. He had been in court on another case.

"Mr. Garber, your lawyer's here," the guard said.

In the conference room, Craig Colton shook hands with Tony and said, "I'll be working with my father on your case. He's tied up on another case. But don't worry, he'll be doing all the arguing for you in court. I'll assist him. Is that okay with you?"

"Sure."

"Detective Moynahan briefed me on the evidence. I think they're going for Murder One. They feel they have a strong enough case. Give it to me from your side. Start at the beginning."

"First, I want you to know that I didn't do it. I know how it looks and all that, but I'm innocent."

After Tony had concluded his story in detail, he finished with, "And that's when the police arrived and took me downtown for questioning."

"Why did you take the gloves off the woman?"

"I told you. Because my fingerprints were all over that letter opener. She stabbed him, not me, and I had to get my fingerprints off and put hers on it."

"What did you do with the gloves?"

"I threw them in a dumpster behind the market on Main near First."

"I'll tell Lt. Moynahan and have him send someone over to see if they can find those gloves. They're important to our case. And I'll have to put you on the stand to introduce them. But the problem is that the D.A. is going to try to rip you up one side and down the other. It isn't going to be easy. Think you can handle it?"

"Yeah. No problem."

"The main thing is to remain calm. He's going to try to get you angry, hoping you'll blurt something out that will incriminate you."

"I understand."

"I'm going to talk to Matty and see what she remembers."

"Would you do me a favor and call Dr. Seigelwitz and ask her to come and see me?"

"Sure. And I'll probably see you again tomorrow afternoon."

*   *   *

It was late afternoon before Dr. Seigelwitz could get away from her office to visit Tony. The rain had just stopped. He was staring out through the barred window of the conference room, looking through the occasional drops of water dripping from the eaves of the courthouse. Wet leaves cluttered the lawns. Tires swished on a wet road. But Tony was unaware. His mind was plagued with anxiety and fears.

"I gave Sandy your message. However, right now she's in a state of confusion."

"Anyone would be, I guess."

"How are you doing, Tony? Any problems with your cell or the guards?"

"No, thank goodness. They put me in a cell that's next to the hallway light that falls directly across the foot of my bed. If, and I don't believe they will, but if they do put me in prison, I want to ask you if you would act as my doctor and tell the authorities that I have to have a night light. I know it sounds childish, but you're the only one I've ever admitted this to. Would you do that? Darkness is the only thing that frightens me, and that fear has been growing through the years. I know if I'd had the time to work with you more, you could have helped. But now..." Tony shuddered.

"I'll do that, Tony. I'll make sure it's done. It'll be a prescription that the prison doctor will put into practice."

"Thank you, Dr. Seigelwitz. But what am I going to do, now?" he asked the doctor. "My lawyer tells me they have a very good case."

"Well, I can't help you there, Tony. But have you come up with any ideas on how to clear yourself with Sandy? She may be confused now, but when she comes out of it, she's going to look at the evidence against you and then be convinced you are guilty."

"I understand. But I only have one idea that might help. However, it could be dangerous. But before I tell you about it I have to find out something. Am I correct when I say that everything I tell you is in strict confidence?"

"Yes, that is correct. Why?"

"Because what I'm about to tell you is incriminating...that is incriminating against me. So I have to be sure you can't tell the police or anyone else, except to tell Sandy."

"You can rest assured about that. I can never reveal to anyone the matters you disclose to me."

"Okay. First, I want to say again that I did not kill Mr. G." Tony hesitated and took a deep breath. "But I did kill the chief of police a few weeks ago." Tony paused to see her reaction.

She seemed stunned, but said nothing.

"Now, would this be startling enough to convince Sandy that I didn't kill her father?"

"Probably. That's certainly startling enough to get a reaction. I'm inclined to believe she will accept your explanation. In fact, I will let her know that I believe you're telling the truth. This should help."

"How can I protect myself in case she doesn't believe me?"

"I'm no lawyer, but if you hire her to assist Craig Colton and his father, you will be protected under the lawyer-client relationship."

"That's right. You're one smart cookie, Doc. Now, do you think you can convince her to come and see me?"

"I don't think that it will be a problem. I'll go talk to her. Just one thing. If she comes, and I'm sure she will, don't try to give her a hug, kiss, or any sort of affection. She may not be ready for it. Let her do the leading. Okay?"

Tony nodded.

*   *   *

It was very hard for Tony to keep his hands to himself when Sandy, rather shyly, entered the conference room. She looked pale. Her luscious violet blue eyes were red rimmed and her hair did not seem to have its usual bounce. She was wearing a black business suit with a white frilly blouse and flat shoes.

"Hi, Sandy. Thanks for coming."

Tony indicated a chair across from him, then sat down himself.

"Dr. Seigelwitz said you had something important to tell me. Is that right?"

"Yes, but first, how are you?"

"Okay, considering things." Her eyes began to fill with tears.

Hurriedly, Tony continued, trying to avoid any real rush of emotions. "I want you to know first and foremost that I did not kill your father. We had become friends and did business together. I would never do something like that, especially because of my respect and love for you."

"I can understand that. But the evidence is overwhelming. I found the police report about your activities up in Chicago. At first I couldn't believe it. But when I gave it to the police, they were excited, because they said it gave you a strong motive to kill my father."

"I know it sounds bad, but that was before I met you. Now things are different. Even your dad saw that in me. He didn't turn me in to the police."

"I wonder why."

"I hate to say it, but your dad saw an opportunity. He knew that in a few years he would be retiring, and he had no nest egg. He said that he could put my ill-gotten gains into the Internet Bank, which he did for a ten percent fee. He put his share in the Internet Bank also. There is no way the IRS or anyone else can find out about it. I was happy to give him his ten percent."

"That's called laundering money. It's illegal. For a long time I've suspected he wasn't totally on the up and up, but I always suppressed it. I guess I didn't want to know."

"I'm really sorry, Sandy, but his concern for his retirement was paramount, and I don't blame him..

"The laundering worked just like he said it would. The police are asking me where I hid it. But I'm keeping my mouth shut."

"But I'm an officer of the court. I'll have to reveal this. It's the law."

"Well, one of the things I wanted to ask you is to become an associate of Craig's and help him represent me. That way everything I've told you is privileged and you won't have to tell anybody anything. Right?"

"Wrong. Everything you've confessed to me was told to me before I became your attorney. I'm obligated by law to inform the police."

"Okay. Tell them. I don't care. The information I gave you is meaningless against me under the circumstances. They have me under very serious charges. They're not going to bother with these others. Besides, if you do tell the police, you will be debasing your father's reputation. I don't think you want to do that. Do you?"

"No," Sandy said thoughtfully. "Like you said, it really would be meaningless."

"That's exactly right. Now to the other part. Will you help Craig represent me?"

"Yes, but only if you can convince me that you didn't...do that to Daddy."

"Fair enough. But I want your word that everything I tell you now will come under the lawyer-client privilege."

"I agree. But after that, if you haven't convinced me, I'll drop you as a client. But for now, you are covered. Say what you want."

Tony ran his fingers through his hair before he began. "Again, I want to say that I did not kill your father..."

"Then tell me what happened."

He stood up and began to pace the floor as he told her his story in detail. When he had finished he said, "And that's the God's honest truth, so help me."

"And you threw the gloves away. They could have helped, if you still had them. But not much."

"I know."

"But all this proves nothing."

"I know, but now for the kicker. Just remember you can't tell anyone what I'm about to tell you, right?"

"That's right, Tony."

"Okay. I didn't kill your father, but I did kill the chief of police."

"You what?"

"I killed the chief, but not your father."

"I can't believe this," Sandy said. "But how?"

Tony sat down again and explained what happened with the police chief. The chief had tried to blackmail him. So he lost control and shot him. "I really didn't know what I was doing. It was over before I realized what had happened."

"My God," Sandy said. "That poor innocent woman and what you have put her through! How could you do that, Tony? How could you do such an awful thing?"

"I didn't have a choice. It was either me or her."

"I'm totally shocked, Tony. And I thought I knew you, but I most certainly did not."

"But now the big question is whether you believe I'm innocent when it comes to your dad."

Sandy stared in amazement. "I guess I do. Although it certainly is the most bizarre thing I've ever heard."

"It is. And even if I'd had a reason to do both murders, and I didn't, I certainly wouldn't plan and commit murders that are almost identical. That would be stupid, and that I'm not."

"I see your point. One thing for sure is we can't let that poor woman suffer any longer."

"But what do we do?"

"Let me talk it over with Craig, and I'll get back to you."

*　　*　　*

An hour later, Sandy was in her office working at her computer when Craig stepped into the room. "What're you doing?" he asked.

"Trying to get this computer to do what it's supposed to. The macro just isn't working. I don't know what's wrong with it."

"Let me see what I can do," he said, pulling up a chair next to hers. He put his right arm across the back of her chair and leaned forward. With his left index finger he tapped two function keys. Craig punched the return key and said, "There. That's got it."

"Thank you, Craig," she said, turning to give him a kiss on the cheek.

He turned toward her to say, You're welcome, but the words stuck in his throat.

Their lips met, and both drew back slightly, hesitated, then resumed.

Sandy pulled away, trembling. "We shouldn't have done that."

"Why? Was it that bad?"

"Well, no, but..."

"No buts about it," he interrupted, with a smile. "It may have been accidental, but it was inevitable. You know how I feel about you, and I hope you feel the same about me."

"Hold it, young man. You're moving much too fast for me." *Seems to me I've said this before,* Sandy thought, *but to Tony.*

"That's fine, as long as we're both moving in the same direction."

"We'll see. But right now I have to talk to you about the Tony Garber case."

"What about it?"

"He retained my services to work with you and your father."

"But why?"

"Because he wanted attorney-client privileges before he confessed something. And now I think we need to discuss what he told me."

CHAPTER TWENTY-FOUR

It had been raining most of the night, but as Sandy and Craig Colton approached the court house in late morning, the dark clouds had started to break up. Brilliant sunshine streaked through the openings in the clouds and down through crisp, clean air, causing shadows to follow them up the steps, ending as they entered the courthouse.

Tony was pacing nervously in his cell when the guard came to get him. "Come along, Garber, your lawyers are here." He was a muscular six footer. Tony followed him down the long hallway, looking at the back of the guard's peppery gray hair that was pulled into a pony tail. He couldn't remember what the man's face looked like, but then decided he didn't care as he reached the conference room.

The guard opened the door and Tony entered. Sandy and Craig were already seated on the other side of the table. Without any greeting he sat down heavily and asked, "Did you come up with anything?"

"Yes," Craig said. "We just came from the DA's office. I think we have a deal. They said that if you give them a written confession for the murder of the chief, they in return would drop the charges for the murder of Mr. Forrest."

Tony quickly glanced at Sandy with the mention of her father's murder. She didn't appear to react, but her pale face and tense demeanor betrayed her inner feelings. "Why a written confession? Why not just verbal?"

"They wouldn't go for that," Craig said. "We asked, but they feel you could back out. With it in writing, it would give them a stronger case. And Sandy and I recommend that you agree. This would be a good move for you, Tony. You're charged with premeditated murder for Mr. G. But, the chief's murder was not premeditated, because you did it in a fit of anger. Plus, we would let the jury know that you are completely exonerating Nancy, the woman who was charged with the Chief's murder. They may agree to a term in prison, rather than the death sentence."

Those last three words hit Tony hard. The death sentence, he repeated in his mind. He definitely didn't like that. He rubbed his finger in a scar on the table. The scenarios that flooded his mind were more than he could bear. He groaned and tried to get a hold of himself. Finally, nodding his head, he grudgingly said, "Okay. I'll go along with that."

But flashes of those memories were still echoing through his head when Craig said, "We'll let them know. Someone will come for you probably later today."

"Come for me?"

"Yes. They will book you again on the new charges. The former charges will be dropped, once you sign your confession."

*   *   *

It was almost two hours later before a young, uniformed police officer came for Tony. He had been staring at the cell walls, going over everything that had happened, trying to figure out what went wrong. He still had lots of questions, but no answers, at least not ones he liked.

"Mr. Garber," the young officer said. "My name is Donald Delaney. I need to take you up for your new booking."

He held the door for Tony who grumbled, "Okay."

"So you're the owner of the Holmes Detective Agency?" the police officer asked as he escorted Tony down the long hallway.

"Yes. Why?"

"I've heard a lot about the kind of work you guys do. Sounds great."

"Thanks." He didn't feel thankful, but he said it automatically.

"I've only been a cop for a little over a month. My partner is supposed to be with me, but his wife is having her third baby. He's over at the hospital helping her to breathe right. Anyway, the sergeant had a splitting headache and said I should take care of this. I've done it before, but then my partner was hanging over me to make sure I did it right. And I always did."

They reached a heavy door. "Here we are," the young officer said.

Tony followed the young man into the booking room. He already knew the routine. He stepped up to the red line in front of the white wall and faced the strobe lights set for portraiture.

"Good," Delaney said as he positioned himself behind the camera. "Move a little to your right, so I can get your height in the frame."

When Officer Delaney was finished, he opened a door off the booking room and ushered Tony inside. It was a small room containing a desk with a computer, printer, and three upright chairs. A young police woman sat on the middle chair. Her large rump covered the seat and then some. Her belt was almost invisible in the folds of her blouse. On her right side was an empty holster. Her dark hair was pulled into a French roll. When she turned toward Tony, he saw a pretty, but plump face.

"Sit over here," she said. "Next to the desk. My name is Margaret Buckler. I'm going to type your confession on this computer. You'll be able to see what I'm typing at the top of the screen."

She moved the monitor at a forty-five degree angle so they both could see it. "We'll start with today's date. And then I'll need your name and address."

Tony, in a monotone, gave his name, address, and all the details of what had happened when he shot the chief of police, including the date and time of the incident.

Delaney slipped out of the room and returned with Lt. Moynahan.

When Buckler concluded, she clicked on print. The printer hummed until finished.

Lt. Moynahan pulled the sheet of paper from the printer and placed it on the desk in front of Tony. "Sign right there," he indicated.

Tony read it over carefully, not because he didn't know what it said, but because of his reluctance to sign his death warrant.

As soon as Tony's signature was on the confession, Lt. Moynahan snatched it up and handed it to officer Delaney and said to him, "Take this up to the commander. I'll take Mr. Garber back to his cell."

Tony didn't speak until he was back in his cell. "What's going to happen now?"

"In a couple of days, you'll go up for your preliminary hearing."

"Then what?"

"Don't worry about it. It's a long process. If you want to know more, ask your lawyers, that's their job."

Lt. Moynahan started to walk away, then stopped and returned to the front of the cell. "By the way, Mr. Garber, I should tell you that just this morning we received word from a very reliable informant that the Outfit up in Chicago had put out a contract on Mr. Forrest. The woman you killed at his house was assigned the hit. Her name was Angie Montello, AKA Karla Zambini. And, lucky for you, we also found the woman's gloves just where you said they'd be. We were just about to drop all charges on you for the murder of Mr. Forrest, when you and your attorneys made this wonderful offer of a confession. At least we have you for the murder of the chief."

Tony's vision blurred. His hands began to shake in anger. He swore profusely, then yelled, "Timing! I can't believe the timing that has gone against me!"

Lt. Moynahan was smiling. "That's true. A couple of hours later, and you would have been a free man, except for the armed robbery. Of course, that would have given you a sentence almost as good...twenty to life."

The maddening anger that was exploding in Tony's mind was almost more than he could contain. He wanted to scream curses and destroy something or someone. He directed his fury to his cell wall, slamming both fists into it, then turned and gripped the bars, and stared at the lieutenant with loathing. "You knew all this when you had them take my confession?"

"Of course."

Tony's grip tightened as he tried parting the unyielding bars. His face flushed a bright red. He became apoplectic. In a state of shock, he slipped to the floor, his body jerking convulsively.

The lieutenant showed concern on his face. "Are you all right?" he asked Tony. When there was no response, Lt. Moynahan hurried down the hall, entered a small office and called for a doctor.

*   *   *

Sandy received word that Tony had been taken to ICU at Memorial Hospital after his collapse in his cell. She rushed over to be with him.

A young police officer was sitting in a chair next to the door of ICU. He held up his hand as Sandy approached. "This is a restricted area, Ma'am."

"I know, Officer..." She had looked at his name tag and continued, "Officer Price, I'm Mr. Garber's lawyer." She handed him her business card.

"Okay, Ma'am, but you'd better check with his nurse or doctor."

"I'll do that," Sandy said as she entered the Intensive Care Unit.

The nurse, sitting behind the counter, was monitoring six screens for the patients in the unit. Pulling out another business card, Sandy said, "Good morning. I'm Mr. Garber's lawyer and friend. May I see him?"

"He's unconscious right now, but I'm sure he'd appreciate seeing a friendly face when he wakes up. He's in room two-twenty-two. Over there." She pointed.

Sandy quietly stepped into the room and focused on Tony's bed. He was all wired up for monitoring and had an oxygen mask over his mouth. He looked deathly pale with eyes closed and hands folded across his chest.

She moved in and sat in a chair next to the bed, her eyes never leaving his face. *And this is the man I was getting very serious about,* she thought. *I even identified myself to the nurse as his friend. But knowing what he has done has changed all that. I may be his lawyer, but I can never be serious about him again. He's a confessed thief and killer. I've been fooled. But how could I have known? He seemed so nice. Now that he has this problem, I'll have to be gentle when I break up with him. We absolutely cannot continue as we were before. But that can wait awhile.*

Tony began to stir. "Nurse, I think he's coming to." Sandy said.

The nurse, wearing a white, starched uniform called back, "I'll get the doctor." As she hurried away, her long brown pony tail swished back and forth.

Dr. Harvey Lindstrom quietly walked into the room and up to Tony's bedside. He was a tall, lanky man with a narrow nose on a thin face. His gray hair fringed the sides of his head with just a wisp on top. "I see you're finally waking up," the doctor said. "How do you feel?"

Tony slowly looked up at the doctor. "I don't know. I guess I feel all right," he mumbled through the oxygen mask.

"Well, we believe you had a heart attack. Because of the emotional stress you have been under, and especially just before you collapsed, the heart was working overtime, demanding more blood than the arteries could produce. From now on, young man, you must be very careful. Any stress could cause a repeat attack, and if severe enough, even death. However, if you moderate your emotions, you'll be all right. Do you understand?"

"But I'm so young."

"That's true. And it is also true that older men usually have this problem, but it can occur at any age, if the weakness is there and the stress is great enough."

"You're saying I have a weakness?"

"Evidently. Do you know of anyone in your family who has or had a heart problem?"

"No."

"Well, the fact is that you have this problem and it is imperative for your own good to get control over these emotions. Right now I want you to just rest and not let yourself get excited about anything. Do you understand?"

"Yes, Sir," Tony answered with a slight frown on his face.

"I'll check back later," the doctor said and left the room.

The nurse stepped up to Tony's bed. She leaned over and tucked Tony in. "My name is Mary. If you need me, just press the button over your head." She turned and headed for the ICU desk.

He turned his head and then spotted her. "Sandy," he whispered, feasting his eyes on her.

"You're still the most gorgeous woman I've ever known."

"You're still a charmer, I see."

"What happened to me?" Tony asked, changing the subject. "I don't remember much of anything."

"From what I've been told, you got extremely upset when you were informed about the woman who murdered my father. And that you would have been released, had you not signed the confession for the murder of the chief of police."

The memory flooded back. His face began to contort in anger and redden again.

"Stop it, Tony! Remember what the doctor said. You've got to remain calm. Let it go. It's not worth it."

As her words sank in, he began to relax again, his anger slowly draining. "It's just that it's so ironic to think how close I came to being free."

"You still would have the charge of armed robbery. That would have put you away for a long time."

"Yeah, but I wouldn't have to face the death sentence."

"You're jumping to conclusions, Tony. You haven't been tried and convicted, yet. There is much that we probably can do."

"Like what?"

"Well for starters, we might be able to make a better deal for you, if you were to give the money back."

"Give it back?" Tony's mind raced. *I could give it back, if it would help. I've made enough in the futures market to do it. It would wipe out my internet bank account, but I would still have the Holmes Detective Agency, if and when I get out of jail.*

"Yes. I'm not sure we can get a reduced charge, but it's sure worth a try."

"Okay, I agree, but only if it's a good deal."

"Craig and I will see what we can do," she said standing. "It depends on the D.A., of course. I"ll talk to you later."

Tony watched as she headed toward the door. "I love the way you walk," he sighed under his breath.

*   *   *

Two days later, Craig went alone to see Tony. It was a cold blustery day, indicated by the ruddy complexion on Craig's face.

"Where's Sandy?' Tony asked.

"Tied up on another case."

"I'd rather look at her than you," he said smiling.

"I don't doubt that for a minute. But today, you'll just have to suffer with me." He was smiling, too. "By the way, Lt. Moynahan called and said they have finished their investigation. They're ready for the prelim. Now that's fast."

"So?"

"I guess they want a speedy trial. It's been that way from the beginning, since your new arrest: the reading of your rights, booking and then taking your confession..."

"Wait a minute, Craig. They didn't read me my rights. At least not on the second charge."

"Let me get this straight. When you were first arrested, they read you your rights, but when they charged you with the murder of the chief, they did not read you your rights. Is that correct?"

"Yes. Everything was left up to that new patrolman. His partner was with his wife at the hospital, having a baby."

"That young cop screwed up in spades. We can have your confession and all the evidence they have gathered since then thrown out of court. They won't have a case."

Tony's eyes were sparkling with anticipation. "Do you mean I'll be free, and they can't touch me?"

"That's exactly what I mean. You're going to be a free man, as soon as I move for dismissal. The judge and the cops are not going to be very happy, because they know you're guilty and that you're going to be freed on a technicality. Whoa, wait a minute. Except you'll still be facing charges for the robbery up North."

Slowly the joy left Tony's face. He still had one problem.

CHAPTER TWENTY-FIVE

Sandy wrapped her coat around her tightly. She waited for Tony in front of the closed recreation center in the park. It was a cold, clear day. Old man winter was trying to come early, blowing a brisk breeze through almost barren trees. A few leaves hung tenaciously to their branches, twisting and turning in the wind.

She finally spotted Tony trudging through ankle-deep leaves in all the fall colors. They danced around his legs as he kicked at them playfully. He seemed to be in high spirits. *He should be*, Sandy thought. *He's free on a technicality, when he should be on trial for murder. I know it's not right for him to get away with it, but it's the law, and I have to respect it.*

"Hi, Sandy," Tony said cheerfully, swinging his arms back and forth to warm up his chilled body. "You look like you're freezing."

"I am. Why did you want to meet here?"

"Because I love walking through the leaves, but I didn't expect the wind to come up. When it's calm, it really is nice. We could go to the little coffee shop at the other end of the park. And I'll keep you warm in the meantime," he added as he put his arm around her.

Sandy didn't object. She just snuggled in. They did not speak again until they were in the coffee shop. "Two coffees," Tony ordered. Then to Sandy, he asked, "Would you care for anything else. Sweet roll, doughnuts, or breakfast?"

She shook her head as she sat down in a booth, pulling her coat tightly around her, trying to ward off the chill that still permeated her body.

As soon as the coffee was served, Sandy rubbed her hands together, picked up the cup and began sipping the steaming brew.

Tony on the other hand sipped and looked over the cup, staring at her. Finally putting his cup down, he looked at her intently and said, "I want to take this opportunity to thank you for what you and Craig have done for me. I've already thanked Craig."

"You don't have to thank me. I was just doing my job, even though I have mixed feelings about it. On the one hand, knowing you're guilty and getting away with it bugs me, but on the other hand, I'm happy for you. Except, of course, you'll be gone a long time on the armed robbery charges."

"No, no. I'll probably only be gone for three to five years."

"How?"

"I just talked to Craig this morning. He's trying to get a reduced charge of attempted robbery, if I give all the money back. He said I had a good chance. The people I robbed will do anything to get their money back. However, I know the D.A. will have to agree."

"Oh. I didn't know Craig was going to do that."

"He just told me about it after getting me released on bail this morning.

"Do you still have the money?"

"Sure. But giving it back is going to wipe me out, except for my business, the Holmes Detective Agency. I'll get to keep that."

"Will Bo run it for you while you're gone?"

"I think so. He's been very good about taking care of it since I've been in the joint."

"I hate to hear you talk that way. It sounds so... so..."

"Crude? Like gangster talk?"

"Yes."

"But that's what I'll be when I'm in the uh... prison. And by the way, will you wait for me when I'm gone?"

"Wait for you? I, well, three to five is a long time to wait."

"But I'm worth it," he said nervously.

Sandy hesitated just a moment before answering. "Tony, I really can't say. I've lost a lot of respect for you, and five years is long time. Many things can happen between now and then. You might change your mind, too."

"No. I'll never change my feelings for you. I'll always love you."

"Well, you know I never have made any commitments to you. I've always been sitting on the fence. But at least I've always been upfront with you. Haven't I?"

"Yes. But I was just hoping that you'd be willing to wait for me."

"I can't promise you anything. But I will say this, that I have no other plans for now, anyway."

"Great. Will you also visit me?"

"Tony! That's asking a lot. Oh, maybe I will, once in a while. But don't expect it to be too often. I won't have a lot of time, because of my job. It's very demanding."

"Okay, but come as often as you can." Sticking out his hand, Tony said, "Come on. I'll walk you to your office."

*   *   *

Tony spent an uncomfortable day in the office. He felt eyes on him, even if he didn't see them. Everyone was nice, but he was sensing a lot of mixed feelings from his employees. He felt he could just be imagining it. But that still didn't relieve him of the feelings.

When everyone else had left for the day, he hung around. He had nothing to look forward to at home. On the other hand, he didn't have anything to do at the office, either. Finally he picked up his newspaper and walked out to his car. The parking lot was empty, except for a black sedan parked next to his car.

As he was unlocking the car door, a voice spoke to him. "Mr. Garber."

Tony turned. "Yes?" Then he saw a gun sticking out the back window of the black sedan.

"Would you get in the front seat? And please don't try anything funny. You'll only get yourself killed. There is someone who wants to talk to you. Now get in!" The voice was commanding and self assured.

Reluctantly, Tony obeyed. After closing the car door, Tony glanced at the driver. *It's one of Sal Fratenello's boys,* he said to himself. *Oh, my God. What do they want? What am I going to do?*

"Don't worry, Tony. The boss ain't gonna knock you off. If that's what he wanted, you'd be dead already. He just wants to talk, so settle back and enjoy the ride. It may be your last." With that the two men in the back and the driver all laughed heartily. "Just kidding, Tony," the driver chuckled.

Tony wasn't laughing.

*   *   *

The tall wrought iron gates opened slowly. They drove past the spacious lawn. Tony noticed that the lawns were clean and free of leaves. *Must have a big gardening crew*, he thought. *But then, with his dough, he can have whatever he wants, and lots of it.*

Tony was ushered into an entertainment room. In the center of the room there was a projection booth with a wide screen for movies and on the left side a large projection TV. On the right was a bank of computer monitors with a complete sound system.

Sal Fratenello sat in front of one of the computers. "I'll be with you in a minute, Tony. Sit down and relax."

True to his word, when he was finished at the computer, Sal walked over to Tony. He stuck his thick-fingered hand out and shook hands. "Just finishing up a little business. I hope you had a good ride up here. No problems, were there?"

"Naw," Tony said, a little more composed, his fears allayed.

"Good. I told my boys no rough stuff, because if there's going to be any rough stuff, I want to do it."

Tony looked Sal square in the eyes to see if he was kidding. There was no answer there. "Did I do something wrong, Mr. Fratenello?"

"Well, yes and no. You see, Karla Zambini worked for me. So, yes, you did something wrong. And for that I have to do something to you, like maybe break your leg or..." he shrugged. "On the other hand, Karla was giving me some trouble, so you saved me the trouble of getting rid of her. That's why I'm not having you killed. I have too much on my mind tonight to decide. You stay the night, and tomorrow I'll make up my mind. Boys, take him to our special suite for the night."

The two men led Tony down steep steps into the basement. One of the "Boys" pointed to a corner, and said, "This room is sound proofed to protect Sal's family from the sounds that sometimes come from it."

"What do you mean a special suite?"

"It's for friends like you," the one guard said as he pushed Tony inside and firmly closed the door.

The total darkness took Tony by surprise. "Wait!" he screeched. "Wait! It's dark in here!" He reached for the doorknob only to find none. No light switch, either. With the realization that they couldn't hear him, coupled with the absolute darkness, he succumbed to complete terror. As total fear gripped him, he let out a blood-curdling scream that continued until a chest-wrenching pain filled him, causing him to gasp for air. My heart, my heart, his mind shrieked as he clutched his chest, trying to stop the excruciating pain. It was exploding in him, causing red flashes inside his eyes. Terror overwhelmed him. He wanted to scream again, but the intense severity of his fear caused only a gurgle to escape. Finally, he slipped to the floor and curled up in a fetal position, his mouth open and his eyes filled with horror. With his last breath, he whispered, "Mama." Then death engulfed him as he slipped into total, absolute, eternal darkness.

Epilogue

Sandy was the only one in Champaign who believed Tony was dead. It had been a full year since his disappearance. In her heart she knew he would not leave without saying something to her. Or at least, he would have called from some other place in the world to let her know he was safe. He would have tried to convince her to join him, to travel the world.

"If he's dead," Craig Colton said to Sandy, "where is his body? No. I think he's alive somewhere, living it up on those millions in the Internet Bank he almost gave back. And everyone I've talked to agrees. The police have APB's out on him, even with Interpol, but I don't think they'll ever catch him."

*   *   *

Craig invited Sandy to a picnic in the woods, and they decided to take a hike first, before eating. They were crossing a creek by way of a fallen log, when Craig stopped, turned around and gently took Sandy by the shoulders.

"What're you doing?" she asked nervously as she looked at the shallow, swirling water below.

"Proposing. What else?"

"You're crazy."

"Yes, crazy about you. Now the question is: Are you going to marry me, or do you want to get wet?" He nodded toward the water.

"You wouldn't dare," she said smiling.

"You bet I would," he grinned mischievously.

"I'm beginning to believe you would. In that case, I accept."

Craig was so surprised that he just looked at her. "I'm serious. Do you really mean it?"

The expression on her face gave him the answer he wanted. Happily, he stepped closer to embrace her. He stubbed his foot on a knot in the log, though, and lost his balance. Instinctively he hung on to Sandy, and they both tumbled into the water.

Sitting up, drenched, Craig looked at Sandy, her beautiful hair plastered to her head, her gorgeous violet blue eyes wide open. Their laughter echoed through the woods.

"You sure fell for me," she giggled.

"And when I fall, I really fall."

"Yes, you do. But this water is cold." She shivered.

"I'll take care of that," he said as he took her in his arms, looked down into her luscious eyes and kissed her passionately as the water eddied around them.